A Book of Short Stories 2

PERSPECTIVES IN LITERATURE

SECOND EDITION

A Book of Short Stories 1
A Book of Poetry 1
A Book of Drama 1
A Book of Nonfiction 1

A Book of Short Stories 2
A Book of Poetry 2
A Book of Drama 2
A Book of Nonfiction 2

SECOND EDITION

A BOOK OF SHORT STORIES 2

Secondary English Editorial Staff
Harcourt Brace Jovanovich, Publishers

HARCOURT BRACE JOVANOVICH, PUBLISHERS
New York Chicago San Francisco Atlanta Dallas *and* London

Printed in the United States of America.
ISBN 0-15-336781-4

For permission to reprint copyrighted material, grateful acknowledgment is made to the following sources:

Arthur C. Clarke and Scott Meredith Literary Agency, Inc., 845 Third Avenue, New York, New York 10022: "History Lesson" by Arthur C. Clarke.

Joan Daves and Alfred A. Knopf, Inc.: "My Oedipus Complex" from *Collected Stories* by Frank O'Connor. Copyright 1950 by Frank O'Connor.

Delacorte Press/Seymour Lawrence: "Tom Edison's Shaggy Dog" excerpted from the book *Welcome to the Monkey House* by Kurt Vonnegut Jr. Copyright © 1953 by Kurt Vonnegut Jr. Originally published in *Collier's*.

Doubleday & Company, Inc.: "A Visit to Grandmother" from *Dancers on the Shore* by William Melvin Kelley. Copyright © 1964 by William Melvin Kelley.

Farrar, Straus & Giroux, Inc.: "Trial by Combat" from *The Lottery* by Shirley Jackson. Copyright 1944 by Shirley Jackson. Copyright renewed © 1972 by Laurence Hyman, Barry Hyman, Mrs. Sarah Webster, and Mrs. Joanne Schnurer. This story first appeared in *The New Yorker*.

Harcourt Brace Jovanovich, Inc.: "The Pacing Goose" by Jessamyn West reprinted from her volume *The Friendly Persuasion*. Copyright 1945, 1973 by Jessamyn West. "Why I Live at the PO" by Eudora Welty reprinted from her volume *A Curtain of Green and Other Stories*. Copyright 1941, 1969 by Eudora Welty.

Johnson Publishing Company and Eugenia Collier: "Marigolds" by Eugenia Collier. Copyright © November, 1969 by Johnson Publishing Company, Inc.

Alfred A. Knopf, Inc.: "The Lucid Eye in Silver Town" from *Assorted Prose*, by John Updike. Copyright 1950 by John Updike.

Harold Matson Company, Inc.: "Footfalls" by Wilbur Daniel Steele. Copyright © 1921, 1949 by Wilbur Daniel Steele.

Harold Ober Associates Incorporated: "The Twins" in *The Go-Away Bird and Other Stories* by Muriel Spark. Copyright © 1958 by Muriel Spark.

The Pirandello Estate and Toby Cole, agent: "War" in *The Medals and Other Stories* by Luigi Pirandello. © E. P. Dutton & Co., 1939, 1967.

Laurence Pollinger Limited and Viking Penguin Inc.: "Across the Bridge" in *Collected Stories* by Graham Greene. Copyright 1947, © renewed 1975 by Graham Greene. Published by The Bodley Head and William Heinemann.

Critical reader: L. Harlan Ford, Ed.D.
President of American Technological University, Killeen, Texas
Former Deputy Commissioner of Education for the State of Texas

Cover photo: © H. Abernathy/H. Armstrong Roberts

Production: LMD Service for Publishers

CONTENTS

INTRODUCTION

As a literary form, the modern short story may be considered America's contribution to literature. Ever since people first began gathering around campfires for companionship as well as warmth, there have been stories—fables, myths, legends, tales—but the short story as we know it today really began in the mid-nineteenth century with Edgar Allan Poe.

As a critic of descriptive "sketches" and imaginative "tales" written in his time, Poe stated that a short story should be unified around a single effect, and that every word of the story should contribute to this effect. Poe's ideas influenced European writers before they were accepted in this country. Over the past one hundred years, French, English, Russian, and Italian, as well as American authors have made contributions to the short story.

You can, of course, enjoy a short story for its own sake, but your appreciation of it will be heightened by a knowledge of the form and the techniques used by a writer to achieve the effects he or she wants. There is great variety in short story form today, but many stories contain such elements as conflict, plot, tone, setting, character, and theme. To develop these, the writer may use such devices as foreshadowing, flashbacks, symbols, methods of characterization, and a particular point of view. (Explanations and examples of all these terms are found in the Glossary, beginning on page 281.)

Conflict in a short story is the basic struggle or problem faced by the hero or heroine. The conflict may be that of (1) person against person, (2) one person or several people against nature, (3) a person or group against society, or (4) an internal conflict, a person struggling against his or her own feelings or values.

The *plot* is the sequence of events in a story, the plan of what happens. Because these events happen to people, at specific times and places, every short story has one or more *characters* and a *setting*.

The *tone* of a short story results from a writer's attitude toward the subject and characters he or she has chosen to write about. And the *theme* of a story is simply the comment about life, or the evaluation of an aspect of life, that the author conveys to the reader through the story. Some stories have conventional themes—themes that conform to approved and traditional practices and beliefs. These stories are usually written only to entertain; their appeal to a large number of readers may make them commercially successful, although few are good literature. In contrast, the well written short story often refutes themes that are popular. Rather, the "quality" short story gives insight that may be hard to accept, but that reflects a truth about life realistically.

In many short stories, the theme serves as a unifying element, and conflict, plot, setting, and character all relate to the comment about life that the author is trying to convey to the reader. But not all stories have such controlling ideas. Many adventure and detective stories seek merely to entertain the reader with a suspenseful plot. In some twentieth-century stories, plot and theme may be quite unimportant. Instead, a recurring detail or symbol may dominate a work and give it focus.

The majority of short stories offer more than just diversion. The reader who appreciates good literature and the vision of life it offers will never be satisfied with merely a "What happens next?" approach. Nor is such a reader satisfied with an analysis of technique. It is the realization of the total effect of the story—the idea that underlies and unifies all its elements—that gives a discriminating reader the greatest satisfaction. An understanding of *form* as well as *content* provides lasting enjoyment.

MAURICE WALSH
(1879–1964)

Ireland and Scotland provide the setting for the short stories and novels of Maurice Walsh. His fiction is characterized by romantic conflicts, heroic characters, picturesque settings, dialect, humor, and, in many instances, first-rate fights.

Mr. Walsh was born in Kerry, Ireland, and attended St. Michael's College in Listowel, Kerry. He said he did not see the "walls of a city" until he was in his twenties, when he went to Dublin to take the examination for the British Civil Service. He became a customs officer and traveled throughout Ireland, Scotland, Wales, and England. After he married a Scottish woman, he lived in Scotland until the 1920s, when Ireland became a self-governing dominion within the British Empire. Returning to Ireland, Mr. Walsh worked for the Irish government until 1934, when he resigned to devote more time to his writing career.

Ireland in the opening days of the fighting between the I.R.A. and the Black and Tans* is the scene of *Green Rushes* (1935), a collection of five short stories, one of which is "The Quiet Man." In 1952, "The Quiet Man" was made into a film, and it still appears often on television.

THE QUIET MAN

Shawn Kelvin, a blithe[1] young lad of twenty, went to the States to seek his fortune. And fifteen years thereafter he returned to his native Kerry, his blitheness sobered and his youth dried to the core, and whether he had made his fortune or whether

Introduction of main character.

Setting.

* **I.R.A. . . . Black and Tans:** From 1919 to 1921, there were many violent conflicts between the Irish Republican Army and the Black and Tans. The I.R.A. is a nationalist organization originally formed to obtain Irish independence from British rule. The troops recruited by England to put down the rebellion were popularly called the Black and Tans because they wore black and tan uniforms.

1. blithe (blīth): lighthearted, gay.

Mystery about Shawn suggested.

Note the repetition of the word quiet.

Physical description.

Partial exposition of Shawn's past; mystery about it sustained.

he had not, no one could be knowing for certain. For he was a quiet man, not given to talking about himself and the things he had done. A quiet man, under middle size, with strong shoulders and deep-set blue eyes below brows darker than his dark hair—that was Shawn Kelvin. One shoulder had a trick of hunching slightly higher than the other, and some folks said that came from a habit he had of shielding his eyes in the glare of an open-hearth furnace[2] in a place called Pittsburgh, while others said it used to be a way he had of guarding his chin that time he was a sort of sparring-partner punching bag at a boxing camp.

Introduction of another character.

Hint given of future conflict.

The word quietly is repeated to stress this characteristic.

Shawn Kelvin came home and found that he was the last of the Kelvins, and that the farm of his forefathers had added its few acres to the ranch of Big Liam O'Grady, of Moyvalla. Shawn took no action to recover his land, though O'Grady had got it meanly. He had had enough of fighting, and all he wanted now was peace. He quietly went among the old and kindly friends and quietly looked about him for the place and peace he wanted; and when the time came, quietly produced the money for a neat, handy, small farm on the first warm shoulder of Knockanore Hill below the rolling curves of heather. It was not a big place but it was in good heart, and it got all the sun that was going; and best of all, it suited Shawn to the tiptop notch of contentment for it held the peace that tuned to his quietness, and it commanded the widest view in all Ireland—vale and mountain and the lifting green plain of the Atlantic Sea.

Foreshadowing of future complications.

There, in a four-roomed, lime-washed, thatched cottage, Shawn made his life, and though his friends hinted his needs and obligations, no thought came to him of bringing a wife into the place. Yet Fate had the thought and the dream in

2. open-hearth furnace: a type of furnace used in making steel. Its open construction requires workers to withstand great heat.

her loom for him.[3] One middling imitation of a man he had to do chores for him, an ex-navy pensioner handy enough about the house and byre,[4] but with no relish for the sustained work of the field—and indeed, as long as he kept house and byre shipshape, he found Shawn an easy master.

Shawn himself was no drudge toiler. He knew all about drudgery and the way it wears out a man's soul. He plowed a little and sowed a little, and at the end of the furrow he would lean on the handles of the cultivator, wipe his brow, if it needed wiping, and lose himself for whole minutes in the great green curve of the sea out there beyond the high black portals of Shannon mouth.[5] And sometimes of an evening he would see, under the glory of the sky, the faint smoke smudge of an American liner. Then he would smile to himself—a pitying smile—thinking of the poor devils, with dreams of fortune luring them, going out to sweat in Ironville, or to bootleg bad whisky down the hidden way, or to stand in a bread line. All these things were behind Shawn forever.

Shawn's character revealed through author's direct analysis and description of his surroundings and behavior.

Market days he would go down and across to Listowel town, seven miles, to do his bartering; and in the long evenings, slowly slipping into the endless summer gloaming,[6] his friends used to climb the winding lane to see him. Only the real friends came that long road, and they were welcome—fighting men who had been out in the "Sixteen":[7] Matt Tobin the thresher, the school-

Introduction of other characters.

3. Yet Fate . . . for him: The personification of Fate at a loom is the author's variation of the Greek myth of the three goddesses of destiny; Clotho, Lachesis, and Atropos. Clotho spun the thread of life, Lachesis decided its length, and Atropos cut it off.

4. byre (bīr): a cow barn.

5. Shannon mouth: where the Shannon River empties into the Atlantic Ocean.

6. gloaming: dusk, twilight.

7. the "Sixteen": a reference to the Easter Rebellion of 1916 in which Irish rebels unsuccessfully attempted to seize Dublin by force and declare Ireland free from English rule.

master, the young curate[8]—men like that. A stone jar of malt whisky would appear on the table, and there would be a haze of smoke and a maze of warm, friendly disagreements.

Second reference to Shawn's need for a wife.

"Shawn, old son," one of them might hint, "aren't you sometimes terrible lonely?"

"Like hell I am!" might retort Shawn derisively. "Why?"

"Nothing but the daylight and the wind and the sun setting with the wrath o' God."

"Just that! Well?"

"But after the stirring times beyond in the States—"

"Ay! Tell me, fine men, have you ever seen a furnace in full blast?"

"A great sight."

Confirmation of Shawn's experience as an ironworker.

"Great surely! But if I could jump you into a steel foundry this minute, you would be sure that God had judged you faithfully into the very hob[9] of hell."

And then they would laugh and have another small one from the stone jar.

Narrator's comment advances plot and foreshadows complications.

And on Sundays Shawn used to go to church, three miles down to the gray chapel above the black cliffs of Doon Bay. There Fate laid her lure for him.

Sitting quietly on his wooden bench or kneeling on the dusty footboard, he would fix his steadfast, deep-set eyes on the vestmented celebrant and say his prayers slowly, or go into that strange trance, beyond dreams and visions, where the soul is almost at one with the unknowable.

But after a time, Shawn's eyes no longer fixed themselves on the celebrant. They went no farther than two seats ahead. A girl sat there, Sunday after Sunday she sat in front of him, and Sunday after Sunday his first casual admiration grew warmer.

8. curate (kyo͝or′ĭt) : a priest who assists the pastor of a parish.
9. hob: in an open fireplace, a hob is a shelf at the back or side on which something is placed to be kept warm.

She had a white nape to her neck and short red hair above it, and Shawn liked the color and wave of that flame. And he liked the set of her shoulders and the way the white neck had of leaning a little forward and she at her prayers—or her dreams. And the service over, Shawn used to stay in his seat so that he might get one quick but sure look at her face as she passed out. And he liked her face, too—the wide-set gray eyes, cheekbones firmly curved, clean-molded lips, austere yet sensitive. And he smiled pityingly at himself that one of her name should make his pulses stir—for she was an O'Grady.

Description of the girl in the story.

Romantic complication linked to conflict; girl identified as an O'Grady.

One person, only, in the crowded chapel noted Shawn's look and the thought behind the look. Not the girl. Her brother, Big Liam O'Grady of Moyvalla, the very man who as good as stole the Kelvin acres. And that man smiled to himself, too—the ugly, contemptuous smile that was his by nature—and, after another habit he had, he tucked away his bit of knowledge in his mind corner against a day when it might come in useful for his own purposes.

Characterization of Liam.

The girl's name was Ellen—Ellen O'Grady. But in truth she was no longer a girl. She was past her first youth into that second one that has no definite ending. She might be thirty—she was no less—but there was not a lad in the countryside would say she was past her prime. The poise of her and the firm set of her bones below clean skin saved her from the fading of mere prettiness. Though she had been sought in marriage more than once, she had accepted no one, or rather, had not been allowed to encourage anyone. Her brother saw to that.

Additional description and background of Ellen.

Big Liam O'Grady was a great raw-boned, sandy-haired man, with the strength of an ox and a heart no bigger than a sour apple. An overbearing man given to berserk rages. Though he was a churchgoer by habit, the true god of that man was Money—red gold, shining silver, dull copper—the

Description of Liam.

Liam's values.

First mention of Liam's attitude toward money.

trinity that he worshipped in degree. He and his sister Ellen lived on the big ranch farm of Moyvalla, and Ellen was his housekeeper and maid of all work. She was a careful housekeeper, a good cook, a notable baker, and she demanded no wage. All that suited Big Liam splendidly, and so she remained single—a wasted woman.

First reference to dowry.

Big Liam himself was not a marrying man. There were not many spinsters with a dowry[10] big enough to tempt him, and the few there were had acquired expensive tastes—a convent education, the deplorable art of hitting jazz out of a piano, the damnable vice of cigarette smoking, the purse-emptying craze for motor cars—such things.

But in due time, the dowry and the place—with a woman tied to them—came under his nose, and Big Liam was no longer tardy. His neighbor, James Carey, died in March and left his fine farm and all on it to his widow, a youngish woman without children, a woman with a hard name for saving pennies. Big Liam looked once at Kathy Carey and looked many times at her broad acres. Both pleased him. He took the steps required by tradition. In the very first week of the following Shrovetide,[11] he sent an accredited emissary to open formal negotiations, and that emissary came back within the hour.

"My soul," said he, "but she is the quick one! I hadn't ten words out of me when she was down my throat. 'I am in no hurry,' says she, 'to come to a house with another woman at the fire corner. When Ellen is in a place of her own, I will listen to what Liam O'Grady has to say.' "

"She will, I say!" Big Liam stopped him. "She will so."

10. dowry (dour′ē): the money or property a woman brings to her husband at marriage.

11. Shrovetide (shrōv′tīd′): *shrove* is the past tense of the verb *shrive,* which means to make or hear confession. Shrovetide was formerly a time particularly set aside for going to confession just before and during the forty-day Lenten season.

There, now, was the right time to recall Shawn Kelvin and the look in his eyes. Big Liam's mind corner promptly delivered up its memory. He smiled knowingly and contemptuously. Shawn Kelvin daring to cast sheep's eyes at an O'Grady! The undersized chicken heart, who took the loss of the Kelvin acres lying down! The little Yankee runt hidden away on the shelf of Knockanore! But what of it? The required dowry would be conveniently small, and the girl would never go hungry, anyway. There was Big Liam O'Grady, far descended from many chieftains.

Conflict between Shawn and Liam developed.

The very next market day at Listowel he sought out Shawn and placed a huge, sandy-haired hand on the shoulder that hunched to meet it.

"Shawn Kelvin, a word with you! Come and have a drink."

Shawn hesitated. "Very well," he said then. He did not care for O'Grady, but he would hurt no man's feelings.

They went across to Sullivan's bar and had a drink, and Shawn paid for it. And Big Liam came directly to his subject—almost patronizingly, as if he were conferring a favor.

"I want to see Ellen settled in a place of her own," said he.

Shawn's heart lifted into his throat and stayed there. But that steadfast face with the steadfast eyes gave no sign, and moreover, he could not say a word with his heart where it was.

"Your place is small," went on the big man, "but it is handy, and no load of debt on it, as I hear. Not much of a dowry ever came to Knockanore, and not much of a dowry can I be giving with Ellen. Say two hundred pounds [12] at the end of harvest, if prices improve. What do you say, Shawn Kelvin?"

First mention of a dowry for Ellen.

12. pounds: the standard monetary unit of the United Kingdom. In American money, a pound is presently worth about $2.00.

Ellen's characterization developed.

Shawn swallowed his heart, and his voice came slow and cool: "What does Ellen say?"

"I haven't asked her," said Big Liam. "But what would she say, blast it?"

"Whatever she says, she will say it herself, not you, Big Liam."

But what could Ellen say? She looked within her own heart and found it empty; she looked at the granite crag[13] of her brother's face and contemplated herself a slowly withering spinster at his fire corner; she looked up at the swell of Knockanore Hill and saw the white cottage among the green small fields below the warm brown of the heather. Oh, but the sun would shine up there in the lengthening spring day and pleasant breezes blow in sultry summer; and finally she looked at Shawn Kelvin, that firmly built, small man with the clean face and the lustrous eyes below steadfast brow. She said a prayer to her God and sank head and shoulders in a resignation more pitiful than tears, more proud than the pride of chieftains. Romance? Welladay!

Shawn was far from satisfied with that resigned acceptance, but then was not the time to press for a warmer one. He knew the brother's wizened[14] soul, guessed at the girl's clean one, and saw that she was doomed beyond hope to a fireside sordidly bought for her. Let it be his own fireside then. There were many worse ones—and God was good.

Ellen O'Grady married Shawn Kelvin. One small statement; and it holds the risk of tragedy, the chance of happiness, the probability of mere endurance—choices wide as the world.

But Big Liam O'Grady, for all his resolute promptness, did not win Kathy Carey to wife. She, foolishly enough, took to husband her own cat-

13. crag (krăg): steep cliff or rock; here, a figurative way of describing Liam's hard, unkindly face.

14. wizened (wĭz′ənd): shriveled, dried up.

tleman, a gay night rambler, who gave her the devil's own time and a share of happiness in the bygoing. For the first time, Big Liam discovered how mordant[15] the wit of his neighbors could be, and to contempt for Shawn Kelvin he now added an unreasoning dislike.

Conflict between Shawn and Liam heightened.

Shawn Kelvin had got his precious, red-haired woman under his own roof now. He had no illusions about her feelings for him. On himself, and on himself only, lay the task of molding her into a wife and lover. Darkly, deeply, subtly, away out of sight, with gentleness, with restraint, with a consideration beyond kenning,[16] that molding must be done, and she that was being molded must never know. He hardly knew, himself.

First he turned his attention to material things. He hired a small servant maid to help her with the housework. Then he acquired a rubber-tired tub cart and a half-bred gelding with a reaching knee action. And on market days husband and wife used to bowl down to Listowel, do their selling and their buying, and bowl smoothly home again, their groceries in the well of the cart and a bundle of second-hand American magazines on the seat at Ellen's side. And in the nights, before the year turned, with the wind from the plains of the Atlantic keening[17] above the chimney, they would sit at either side of the flaming peat fire, and he would read aloud strange and almost unbelievable things out of the high-colored magazines. Stories, sometimes, wholly unbelievable.

Ellen would sit and listen and smile, and go on with her knitting or her sewing; and after a time it was sewing she was at mostly—small things. And when the reading was done, they would sit

Characterization of Shawn and Ellen through description of activities.

15. mordant (môr′dənt)**:** biting, sarcastic.
16. beyond kenning: beyond one's knowledge (ken) or range of sight.
17. keening (kēn′ing)**:** wailing; moaning. A *keen* is a lamentation for the dead. It may be a wordless cry or, sometimes, a rhythmic recounting of the life and character of the dead person.

Another reference to Shawn's past—and to his experiences in the boxing ring.

and talk quietly in their own quiet way. For they were both quiet. Woman though she was, she got Shawn to do most of the talking. It could be that she, too, was probing and seeking, unwrapping the man's soul to feel the texture thereof, surveying the marvel of his life as he spread it diffidently[18] before her. He had a patient, slow, vivid way of picturing for her the things he had seen and felt. He made her see the glare of molten metal, lambent yet searing,[19] made her feel the sucking heat, made her hear the clang; she could see the roped square under the dazzle of the hooded arcs with the curling smoke layer above it, understand the explosive restraint of the game, thrill when he showed her how to stiffen wrist for the final devastating right hook. And often enough the stories were humorous, and Ellen would chuckle, or stare, or throw back her red, lovely curls in laughter. It was grand to make her laugh.

Shawn's friends, in some hesitation at first, came in ones and twos up the slope to see them. But Ellen welcomed them with her smile that was shy and at the same time frank, and her table was loaded for them with scones and crumpets[20] and cream cakes and heather honey; and at the right time it was herself that brought forth the decanter of whisky—no longer the half-empty stone jar—and the polished glasses. Shawn was proud as sin of her. She would sit then and listen to their discussions and be forever surprised at the knowledgeable man her husband was—the way he could discuss war and politics and the making of songs, the turn of speech that summed up a man or a situation. And sometimes she would put in a word or two and be listened to, and they would look to see if her smile commended them, and be a little

18. diffidently (dĭf′ə•dənt•lē)**:** unassertively, shyly.
19. lambent (lăm′bənt) **yet searing:** softly bright and flickering yet burning.
20. scones and crumpets: Scones are a type of tea cake, and crumpets are thin flat cakes cooked on a griddle.

chastened by the wisdom of that smile—the age-old smile of the matriarch from whom they were all descended. In no time at all, Matt Tobin the thresher, who used to think, "Poor old Shawn! Lucky she was to get him," would whisper to the schoolmaster: "Herrin's alive! That fellow's luck would astonish nations."

Women, in the outside world, begin by loving their husbands; and then, if Fate is kind, they grow to admire them; and if Fate is not unkind, may descend no lower than liking and enduring. And there is the end of lawful romance. Look now at Ellen O'Grady. She came up to the shelf of Knockanore and in her heart was only a nucleus of fear in a great emptiness, and that nucleus might grow into horror and disgust. But, glory of God, she, for reason piled on reason, presently found herself admiring Shawn Kelvin; and with or without reason, a quiet liking came to her for this quiet man who was so gentle and considerate; and then, one great heart-stirring dark o'night, she found herself fallen head and heels in love with her own husband. There is the sort of love that endures, but the road to it is a mighty chancy one.

A woman, loving her husband, may or may not be proud of him, but she will fight like a tiger if anyone, barring herself, belittles him. And there was one man that belittled Shawn Kelvin. Her brother, Big Liam O'Grady. At fair or market or chapel that dour[21] giant deigned not to hide his contempt and dislike. Ellen knew why. He had lost a wife and farm; he had lost in herself a frugally cheap housekeeper; he had been made the butt of a sly humor; and for these mishaps, in some twisted way, he blamed Shawn. But—and there came in the contempt—the little Yankee runt, who dared say nothing about the lost Kelvin acres, would not now have the gall or guts to demand the dowry that was due. Lucky the hound to steal

Heightening of conflict.

21. **dour** (do͝or, dour): sullen, surly.

an O'Grady to hungry Knockanore! Let him be satisfied with that luck!

Reference to dowry.

One evening before a market day, Ellen spoke to her husband: "Has Big Liam paid you my dowry yet, Shawn?"

"Sure there's no hurry, girl," said Shawn.

"Have you ever asked him?"

"I have not. I am not looking for your dowry, Ellen."

Ellen's request adds to complication.

"And Big Liam could never understand that." Her voice firmed. "You will ask him tomorrow."

"Very well so, *agrah*,"[22] agreed Shawn easily.

And the next day, in that quiet, diffident way of his, he asked Big Liam. But Big Liam was brusque and blunt. He had no loose money and Kelvin would have to wait until he had. "Ask me again, Shawneen,"[23] he finished, his face in a mocking smile, and turning on his heel, he plowed his great shoulders through the crowded market.

His voice had been carelessly loud and people had heard. They laughed and talked amongst themselves. "Begogs! The devil's own boy, Big Liam! What a pup to sell! Stealing the land and keeping a grip on the fortune! Ay, and a dangerous fellow, mind you, the same Big Liam! He would smash little Shawn at the wind of a word. And devil the bit his Yankee sparring tricks would help him!"

A friend of Shawn's, Matt Tobin the thresher, heard that and lifted his voice: "I would like to be there the day Shawn Kelvin loses his temper."

"A bad day for poor Shawn!"

"It might then," said Matt Tobin, "but I would come from the other end of Kerry to see the badness that would be in it for someone."

22. **agrah** (ȧ•grŏ'): *Gaelic,* my love.
23. **Shawneen:** The suffix *-een* when added to nouns means small; when used in addressing an adult, it means that the person is insignificant or unworthy of consideration.

Shawn had moved away with his wife, not heeding or not hearing.

"You see, Ellen?" he said in some discomfort. "The times are hard on ranchers, and we don't need the money, anyway."

"Do you think Big Liam does?" Her voice had a cut in it. "He could buy you and all Knockanore and be only on the fringe of his hoard. You will ask him again."

First reference to conflict between Shawn and Ellen.

"But, girl dear, I never wanted a dowry with you."

She liked him to say that, but far better would she like to win for him the respect and admiration that was his due. She must do that now at all costs. Shawn, drawing back now, would be the butt of his fellowmen.

"You foolish lad! Big Liam would never understand your feelings, with money at stake." She smiled and a pang went through Shawn's breast. For the smile was the smile of an O'Grady, and he could not be sure whether the contempt in it was for himself or for her brother.

Shawn asked Big Liam again, unhappy in his asking, but also dimly comprehending his woman's object. And Shawn asked again a third time. The issue was become a famous one now. Men talked about it, and women too. Bets were made on it. At fair or market, if Shawn was seen approaching Big Liam, men edged closer and women edged away. Some day the big fellow would grow tired of being asked, and in one of his terrible rages half kill the little lad as he had half killed other men. A great shame! Here and there, a man advised Shawn to give up asking and put the matter in a lawyer's hands. "I couldn't do that," was Shawn's only answer. Strangely enough, none of these prudent advisers were among Shawn's close friends. His friends frowned and said little, but they were always about, and always among them was Matt Tobin.

The day at last came when Big Liam grew

tired of being asked. That was the big October cattle fair at Listowel, and he had sold twenty head of fat, polled Angus beeves at a good price. He was a hard dealer and it was late in the day before he settled at his own figure, so that the banks were closed and he was not able to make a lodgment.[24] He had, then, a great roll of bills in an inner vest pocket when he saw Shawn and Ellen coming across to where he was bargaining with Matt Tobin for a week's threshing. Besides, the day being dank, he had had a drink or two more than was good for him and the whisky had loosened his tongue and whatever he had of discretion. By the powers!–it was time and past time to deal once and for all with this little gadfly[25] of a fellow, to show him up before the whole market. He strode to meet Shawn, and people got out of his savage way and edged in behind to lose nothing of this dangerous game.

He caught Shawn by the hunched shoulder–a rending grip–and bent down to grin in his face.

"What is it, little fellow? Don't be ashamed to ask!"

Another hint that Shawn knows something about fighting. Foreshadowing of outcome of conflict.

Matt Tobin was probably the only one there to notice the ease with which Shawn wrenched his shoulder free, and Matt Tobin's eyes brightened. But Shawn did nothing further and said no word. His deep-set eyes gazed steadily at the big man.

The big man showed his teeth mockingly. "Go on, you whelp![26] What do you want?"

"You know, O'Grady."

"I do. Listen, Shawneen!" Again he brought his hand clap on the little man's shoulder. "Listen, Shawneen! If I had a dowry to give my sister, 'tis not a little shrimp like you would get her. Go to hell out o'that!"

24. lodgment: deposit.
25. gadfly: a fly that bites cattle; by extension, the word means a person who irritates or persistently bothers another.
26. whelp (hwĕlp)**:** cub or puppy; a contemptuous term.

His great hand gripped and he flung Shawn backward as if he were only the image of a man filled with chaff.[27]

Shawn went backward, but he did not fall. He gathered himself like a spring, feet under him, arms half-raised, head forward into hunched shoulder. But as quickly as the spring coiled, as quickly it slackened, and he turned away to his wife. She was there facing him, tense and keen, her face pale and set, and a gleam of the race in her eyes.

Another example of foreshadowing of outcome of conflict.

"Woman, woman!" he said in his deep voice. "Why would you and I shame ourselves like this?"

"Shame!" she cried. "Will you let him shame you now?"

"But your own brother, Ellen—before them all?"

"And he cheating you—"

"Glory of God!" His voice was distressed. "What is his dirty money to me? Are you an O'Grady, after all?"

That stung her and she stung back in one final effort. She placed a hand across her breast and looked *close* into his face. Her voice was low and bitter, and only he heard: "I am an O'Grady. It is a great pity that the father of this my son is a Kelvin and a coward."

The bosses[28] of Shawn Kelvin's cheekbones were like hard marble, but his voice was as soft as a dove's.

"Is that the way of it? Let us be going home then, in the name of God!"

He took her arm, but she shook his hand off; nevertheless, she walked at his side, head up, through the people that made way for them. Her brother mocked them with his great, laughing bellow.

Another reference to Shawn-Ellen conflict.

"That fixes the pair of them!" he cried,

27. chaff (chăf): finely cut straw or hay.
28. bosses: the raised, prominent parts of the cheekbones.

brushed a man who laughed out of his way, and strode off through the fair.

There was talk then—plenty of it. "Murder, but Shawn had a narrow squeak that time! Did you see the way he flung him? I wager he'll give Big Liam a wide road after this. And he by the way of being a boxer! That's a pound you owe me, Matt Tobin."

"I'll pay it," said Matt Tobin, and that is all he said. He stood wide-legged, looking at the ground, his hand ruefully rubbing the back of his head and dismay and gloom on his face. His friend had failed him in the face of the people.

Shawn and Ellen went home in their tub cart and had not a single word or glance for each other on the road. And all that evening, at table or fireside, a heart-sickening silence held them in its grip. And all that night they lay side by side, still and mute. There was only one subject that possessed them and on that they dared speak no longer. They slept little. Ellen, her heart desolate, lay on her side staring into the dark, grieving for what she had said and unable to unsay it. Shawn, on his back, contemplated things with a cold clarity. He realized that he was at the fork of life and that a finger pointed unmistakably. He must risk the very shattering of all happiness, he must do a thing so final and decisive that, once done, it could never again be questioned. Before morning, he came to his decision, and it was bitter as gall. He cursed himself. "Oh, you fool! You might have known that you should never have taken an O'Grady without breaking the O'Gradys."

He got up early in the morning at his usual hour and went out as usual to do his morning chores—rebedding and foddering[29] the cattle, rubbing down the half-bred, helping the servant maid with the milk in the creaming pans—and as usual, he came in to his breakfast and ate it unhungrily

29. foddering (fŏd′ər·ĭng): feeding with fodder, a food for domestic animals.

and silently, which was not usual. But thereafter he again went out to the stable, harnessed his gelding and hitched him to the tub cart. Then he returned to the kitchen and spoke for the first time.

"Ellen, will you come with me down to see your brother?"

Rising action.

She hesitated, her hands thrown wide in a helpless, hopeless gesture. "Little use you going to see my brother, Shawn. 'Tis I should go and—not come back."

"Don't blame me now or later, Ellen. It has been put on me and the thing I am going to do is the only thing to be done. Will you come?"

"Very well," she said tonelessly. "I will be ready in a minute."

And they went the four miles down into the vale to the big farmhouse of Moyvalla. They drove into the great square of cobbled yard and found it empty.

On one side of the square was the long, low, lime-washed dwelling house; on the other, fifty yards away, the two-storied line of steadings[30] with a wide arch in the middle; and through the arch came the purr and zoom of a threshing machine. Shawn tied the half-bred to the wheel of a farm cart and, with Ellen, approached the house.

A slattern[31] servant girl leaned over the half-door and pointed through the arch. The master was out beyond in the haggard[32]—the rickyard[33]—and would she run across for him?

"Never mind, *achara*,"[34] said Shawn, "I'll get him. . . . Ellen, will you go in and wait?"

"No," said Ellen, "I'll come with you." She knew her brother.

30. steadings: *British dialect,* farm buildings.
31. slattern (slăt′ərn)**:** untidy; slovenly. From the German word *schlottern* meaning to hang loosely, stouch; used as both a noun and an adjective.
32. haggard (hăg′ərd)**:** a yard for stacking hay.
33. rickyard: on a farm stacks of hay, called ricks, are kept in the open air.
34. achara (ă•kăr′ă)**:** *Gaelic,* dear friend.

Description of noise and activities contrasts with Shawn's quiet determination and heightens the tension at a critical moment.

As they went through the arch, the purr and zoom grew louder, and turning the corner, they walked into the midst of activity. A long double row of cone-pointed cornstacks stretched across the yard and, between them, Matt Tobin's portable threshing machine was busy. The smooth-flying, eight-foot driving wheel made a sleepy purr and the black driving belt ran with a sag and heave to the red-painted thresher. Up there on the platform, barearmed men were feeding the flying drum with loosened sheaves, their hands moving in a rhythmic sway. As the toothed drum bit at the corn sheaves, it made an angry snarl that changed and slowed into a satisfied zoom. The wide conveying belt was carrying the golden straw up a steep incline to where other men were building a long rick; still more men were attending to the corn shoots, shoulders bending under the weight of the sacks as they ambled across to the granary. Matt Tobin himself bent at the face of his machine, feeding the firebox with sods of hard black peat. There were not less than two score of men about the place, for, as was the custom, all Big Liam's friends and neighbors were giving him a hand with the threshing—"the day in harvest."

Big Liam came around the flank of the engine and swore. He was in his shirt sleeves, and his great forearms were covered with sandy hair.

"Hell and damnation! Look who's here!"

He was in the worst of tempers this morning. The stale dregs of yesterday's whisky were still with him, and he was in the humor that, as they say, would make a dog bite its father. He took two slow strides and halted, feet apart and head truculently[35] forward.

"What is it this time?" he shouted. That was the un-Irish welcome he gave his sister and her husband.

35. truculently (trŭk′yə•lənt•lē): meanly; savagely.

Shawn and Ellen came forward steadily, and as they came, Matt Tobin slowly throttled down his engine. Big Liam heard the change of pitch and looked angrily over his shoulder.

Focus narrows to Shawn and Liam with the silencing of the engine.

"What the hell do you mean, Tobin? Get on with the work!"

"To hell with yourself, Big Liam! This is my engine, and if you don't like it, you can leave it!" And at that he drove the throttle shut and the purr of the flywheel slowly sank.

"We will see in a minute," threatened Big Liam, and turned to the two now near at hand. "What is it?" he growled.

"A private word with you. I won't keep you long." Shawn was calm and cold.

"You will not—on a busy morning," sneered the big man. "There is no need for private words between me and Shawn Kelvin."

"There is need," urged Shawn. "It will be best for us all if you hear what I have to say in your own house."

"Or here on my own land. Out with it! I don't care who hears!"

Shawn looked around him. Up on the thresher, up on the straw rick, men leaned idle on fork handles and looked down at him; from here and there about the stackyard, men moved in to see, as it might be, what had caused the stoppage, but only really interested in the two brothers-in-law. He was in the midst of Clan O'Grady, for they were mostly O'Grady men—big, strong, blond men, rough, confident, proud of their breed. Matt Tobin was the only man he could call a friend. Many of the others were not unfriendly, but all had contempt in their eyes, or, what was worse, pity. Very well! Since he had to prove himself, it was fitting that he do it here amongst the O'Grady men.

Shawn brought his eyes back to Big Liam—deep, steadfast eyes that did not waver.

Simple statement of the main conflict of the story.

"O'Grady," said he—and he no longer hid his contempt—"you set a great store by money."

"No harm in that. You do it yourself, Shawneen."

"Take it so! I will play that game with you, till hell freezes. You would bargain your sister and cheat; I will sell my soul. Listen, you big brute! You owe me two hundred pounds. Will you pay it?" There was an iron quality in his voice that was somehow awesome. The big man, about to start forward overbearingly, restrained himself to a brutal playfulness.

"I will pay it when I'm ready."

"Today."

"No, nor tomorrow."

"Right. If you break your bargain, I break mine."

"What's that?" shouted Big Liam.

"If you keep your two hundred pounds, you keep your sister."

"What is it?" shouted Big Liam again, his voice breaking in astonishment. "What is that you say?"

"You heard me. Here is your sister Ellen! Keep her!"

"Fires o'hell!" He was completely astounded out of his truculence. "You can't do that!"

"It is done," said Shawn.

Ellen O'Grady had been quiet as a statue at Shawn's side, but now, slow like doom, she faced him. She leaned forward and looked into his eyes and saw the pain behind the strength.

"To the mother of your son, Shawn Kelvin?" she whispered that gently to him.

His voice came cold as a stone out of a stone face: "In the face of God. Let him judge me."

"I know—I know!" That was all she said, and walked quietly across to where Matt Tobin stood at the face of his engine.

Matt Tobin placed a hand on her arm. "Give

him time, *acolleen,*"[36] he whispered urgently. "Give him his own time. He's slow but he's deadly as a tiger when he moves."

Big Liam was no fool. He knew exactly how far he could go. There was no use, at this juncture, in crushing the runt under a great fist. There was some force in the little fellow that defied dragooning.[37] Whatever people might think of Kelvin, public opinion would be dead against himself. Worse, his inward vision saw eyes leering in derision, mouths open in laughter. The scandal on his name would not be bounded by the four seas of Erin. He must change his stance while he had time. These thoughts passed through his mind while he thudded the ground three times with iron-shod heel. Now he threw up his head and bellowed his laugh.

Characterization by revealing character's thoughts.

"You fool! I was only making fun of you. What are your dirty few pounds to the likes of me? Stay where you are."

He turned, strode furiously away, and disappeared through the arch.

Shawn Kelvin was left alone in that wide ring of men. The hands had come down off the ricks and thresher to see closer. Now they moved back and aside, looked at one another, lifted eyebrows, looked at Shawn Kelvin, frowned and shook their heads. They knew Big Liam. They knew that, yielding up the money, his savagery would break out into something little short of killing. They waited, most of them, to prevent that savagery going too far.

Shawn Kelvin did not look at anyone. He stood still as a rock, his hands deep in his pockets, one shoulder hunched forward, his eyes on the ground and his face strangely calm. He seemed the least perturbed man there. Matt Tobin held Ellen's

36. acolleen (ä•kōl′lēn): *Gaelic,* dear girl.
37. dragooning (drə•go͞on′ing): being forced into submission by violence.

arm in a steadying grip and whispered in her ear: "God is good, I tell you."

Big Liam was back in two minutes. He strode straight to Shawn and halted within a pace of him.

"Look, Shawneen!" In his raised hands was a crumpled bundle of greasy bank notes. "Here is your money. Take it, and then see what will happen to you. Take it!" He thrust it into Shawn's hands. "Count it. Make sure you have it all—and then I will kick you out of this haggard—and look"—he thrust forward a hairy fist—"if I ever see your face again, I will drive that through it. Count it, you spawn!"[38]

Climax.

Shawn did not count it. Instead he crumpled it into a ball in his strong fingers. Then he turned on his heel and walked, with surprising slowness, to the face of the engine. He gestured with one hand to Matt Tobin, but it was Ellen, quick as a flash, who obeyed the gesture. Though the hot bar scorched her hand, she jerked open the door of the firebox and the leaping peat flames whispered out at her. And forthwith, Shawn Kelvin, with one easy sweep, threw the crumpled ball of notes into the heart of the flame. The whisper lifted one tone and one scrap of burned paper floated out of the funnel top. That was all the fuss the fire made of its work.

But there was fuss enough outside.

Big Liam O'Grady gave one mighty shout. No, it was more anguished scream than a shout:

"My money! My good money!"

He gave two furious bounds forward, his great arms raised to crush and kill. But his hands never touched the small man.

"You dumb ox!" said Shawn Kelvin between his teeth. That strong, hunched shoulder moved a little, but no one there could follow the terrific

38. **spawn** (spôn): young produced in great quantity; a contemptuous term.

drive of that hooked right arm. The smack of bone on bone was sharp as whip crack, and Big Liam stopped dead, went back on his heel, swayed a moment, and staggered back three paces.

"Now and forever! Man of Kelvins!" roared Matt Tobin.

But Big Liam was a man of iron. That blow should have laid him on his back—blows like it had tied men to the ground for the full count. But Big Liam only shook his head, grunted like a boar, and drove in at the little man. And the little man, instead of circling away, drove in at him, compact of power.

The men of the O'Gradys saw then an exhibition that they had not knowledge enough to appreciate fully. Thousands had paid as much as ten dollars each to see the great Tiger Kelvin in action, his footwork, his timing, his hitting; and never was his action more devastating than now. He was a thunderbolt on two feet and the big man a glutton.

Big Liam never touched Shawn with clenched fist. He did not know how. Shawn, actually forty pounds lighter, drove him by sheer hitting power across the yard.

Men for the first time saw a two-hundred pound man knocked clean off his feet by a body blow. They saw for the first time the deadly restraint and explosion of skill.

Turning point.

Shawn set out to demolish his enemy in the briefest space of time, and it took him five minutes to do it. Five, six, eight times he knocked the big man down, and the big man came again, staggering, slavering, raving, vainly trying to rend and smash. But at last he stood swaying and clawing helplessly, and Shawn finished him with his terrible double hit—left below the breastbone and right under the jaw.

Big Liam lifted on his toes and fell flat on his back. He did not even kick as he lay.

Shawn did not waste a glance at the fallen giant. He swung full circle on the O'Grady men and his voice of iron challenged them:

"I am Shawn Kelvin, of Knockanore Hill. Is there an O'Grady amongst you thinks himself a better man? Come then."

His face was deep-carved stone, his great chest lifted, the air whistled through his nostrils; his deep-set flashing eyes dared them.

No man came.

He swung around then and walked straight to his wife. He halted before her.

His face was still of stone, but his voice quivered and had in it all the dramatic force of the Celt:[39]

"Mother of my son, will you come home with me?"

She lifted to the appeal, voice and eye:

"Is it so you ask me, Shawn Kelvin?"

Dénouement

His face of stone quivered at last. "As my wife only—Ellen Kelvin!"

"Very well, heart's treasure." She caught his arm in both of hers. "Let us be going home."

"In the name of God," he finished for her.

And she went with him, proud as the morning, out of that place. But a woman, she would have the last word.

"Mother of God!" she cried. "The trouble I had to make a man of him!"

"God Almighty did that for him before you were born," said Matt Tobin softly.

39. Celt (sĕlt, kĕlt): an individual of any of various Celtic-speaking peoples, of whom the ancient Gauls and Britons and the modern Irish, Scots, Welsh, and Bretons are the best known.

Meaning

1. On his return to his native Kerry, how do Shawn Kelvin's actions show the quiet side of his personality? How does the author hint that Kelvin is not as meek as he seems?
2. After several months of marriage, how have Ellen's feelings about her husband changed? How does the change come about?
3. *Conflict,* the struggle between opposing forces, may be external or internal. The fist fight that takes place between Shawn and Liam is an example of *external* or *physical conflict.*

   Inner conflict is the struggle within the mind and heart of a character. Identify three of the inner conflicts in the story.
4. The *climax* is the high point of a story, the moment of greatest interest and intensity. It usually occurs near a narrative's major *turning point,* the moment when the fortunes of the main character turn from bad to good or from good to bad, and a probable solution to his or her problem is seen.

   At the climax of this story, how does Ellen's decision to open the firebox point the way to a happy solution to the conflict that has developed between her and Shawn? What does her action reveal about her attitude toward money?

   What do Shawn's actions at the turning point of this story prove to the O'Grady men?

Method

1. *Suspense* or uncertainty about the outcome of the plot is basic to every good story. It is created **a.** when an author withholds information that would satisfy our curiosity about a character and **b.** when we anxiously await the outcome of a conflict, especially if the person in conflict is someone with whom we sympathize or identify. Illustrate each of these methods of creating suspense with an example from the story.
2. The various *methods of characterization* that an author may use to make an invented character appear lifelike include:

   a. describing appearance.

   b. showing the character in action, especially at key moments in the story.

   c. revealing thoughts and feelings.

   d. presenting conversations.

e. showing the reactions of others to the character's behavior and in some cases giving their remarks about the character.

f. contrasting attitudes and values with those of another character in the story.

How does Maurice Walsh use these methods to develop the personality of Shawn Kelvin? Choose two of the methods and illustrate them with an example from the text.

3. This story is told in the third person, from the *point of view* of an *omniscient author.* This means that the author is able to enter the minds of all the characters and reveal to us what they are thinking. Why is it essential for the reader to know what all the characters in this story are thinking?

Language: Denotation and Connotation

As Shawn works on his farm on Knockanore Hill, he thinks of his life in America and "of the poor devils, with dreams of fortune luring them, going out to sweat in Ironville, or to bootleg bad whisky down the hidden way, or to stand in a bread line." The *connotation* of a word refers to the associations that a word has in addition to its explicit literal meaning. The connotations or implications of words such as *bootleg* and *bread line* suggest that Shawn was in the United States during the Depression of the 1930s.

The *denotation* of a word is its exact, dictionary meaning. For example, the denotation of the word *bread line* is "a line of persons waiting to be given bread or other food as charity." However, to those familiar with the Depression, which began with the stock market crash in 1929, a bread line *connotes* widespread unemployment, low wages, and bank failures.

The verb *bootleg,* which is derived from the smuggler's habit of hiding a liquor bottle in the top of his boot, means "to make or sell liquor illegally." The term is usually associated with Prohibition, which lasted from 1920 until 1933, when the Eighteenth Amendment, which forbade the sale of liquor, was repealed. *Bootleg* connotes such things as speakeasies, racketeers, and bribery. Sometimes words have pleasant or unpleasant connotations because of personal experience or associations connected with them.

After each of the following words, write one or two adjectives or nouns that tell what the word connotes to you.

1. athlete	**5.** cigarettes	**9.** winter
2. intellectual	**6.** whale	**10.** textbook
3. spinster	**7.** litter	**11.** drugs
4. husband	**8.** spider	**12.** housewife

Discussion and Composition

1. Discuss Maurice Walsh's ideas of love and marriage as revealed in this story. Tell why you agree or disagree with him.

2. Write a narrative about a personal decision you or someone you know (or have read about) had to make to preserve a value or an ideal that would "risk the very shattering of all happiness." Describe the situation, the inner conflict, and the final result.

3. The author's love for Ireland is apparent. Does he make Ireland sound like the kind of country you would want to visit or live in for several months? In a paragraph, identify the country you would most like to visit or live in (other than your own country). Tell why.

ARTHUR CONAN DOYLE
(1859–1930)

Sherlock Holmes, one of the most famous characters in fiction, was the creation of Sir Arthur Conan Doyle, a surgeon who began writing to supplement the income from his medical practice. Doyle was born in Edinburgh, Scotland, and attended schools in Scotland and Germany before studying medicine at the University of Edinburgh. He was a ship's surgeon on a voyage to the Arctic and to Africa before he married and practiced medicine in Portsmouth, England.

Doyle decided that he would try to invent a new kind of story that he hoped would capture a mass readership. He modeled the character of Sherlock Holmes on a medical school instructor whose deductive powers had amazed everyone.

The first Sherlock Holmes story, "A Study in Scarlet" (1887), received little attention when it was published after many rejections. About a year later, an American magazine editor called Doyle and asked Doyle to write another Sherlock Holmes story. That story, "The Sign of Four," launched Doyle's career as a master writer of detective stories. The public demanded and received so many stories about Sherlock Holmes that Doyle became bored with the character he had created. In "The Final Problem" (1893), he had Holmes killed by his arch enemy. Public protest was so great that Doyle had to bring Holmes back to life in the next story he wrote.

Doyle wrote fifty-six stories based on the character of Sherlock Holmes. He also wrote historical novels and nonfiction books. He was knighted in 1902 for his history of the South African (Boer) War, and for his work in a field hospital in South Africa.

THE MUSGRAVE RITUAL

An anomaly[1] which often struck me in the character of my friend Sherlock Holmes was that, although in his methods of thought he was the neatest and most methodical of mankind, and although also he affected a certain quiet primness of dress, he was none the less in his personal habits one of the most untidy men that ever drove a fellow-lodger to distraction. Not that I am in the least conventional in that respect myself. The rough-and-tumble work in Afghanistan, coming on the top of natural Bohemianism[2] of disposition, has made me rather more lax than befits a medical man. But with me there is a limit, and when I find a man who keeps his cigars in the coal-scuttle, his tobacco in the toe end of a persian slipper, and his unanswered correspondence transfixed by a jack-knife into the very centre of his wooden mantelpiece, then I begin to give myself virtuous airs. I have always held, too, that pistol practice should be distinctly an open-air pastime; and when Holmes, in one of his queer humours,[3] would sit in an armchair with his hair-trigger[4] and a hundred Boxer cartridges and proceed to adorn the opposite wall with a patriotic V. R.[5] done in bullet-pocks, I felt strongly that neither the atmosphere nor the appearance of our room was improved by it.

Our chambers were always full of chemicals and of criminal relics which had a way of wandering into unlikely positions, and of turning up in the butter-dish or in even less desirable places. But his papers were my great crux.[6] He had a horror of destroying documents, especially those which were connected with his past cases, and yet it was only once in every year or two that he would

1. anomaly (a•nŏm′ə•lē): irregularity.

2. Bohemianism: unconventionalism. Because gypsies traveled through Bohemia the adjective *Bohemian* came to be associated with those who like the gypsies chose to live outside the usual life style of those around them.

3. humours: British spelling of *humors,* moods. Humors were thought to be body fluids that determine an individual's health and mood. The four humors were black bile (sadness), yellow bile (anger), phlegm (calmness or stolidity), and blood (cheerfulness).

4. hair-trigger: gun with a trigger that operates with very slight pressure.

5. V. R.: Victoria Regina (1819–1901) queen of Britain. *Regina* is Latin for queen.

6. crux (krŭks): cross; here, most difficult habit.

muster energy to docket[7] and arrange them; for, as I have mentioned somewhere in these incoherent memoirs, the outbursts of passionate energy when he performed the remarkable feats with which his name is associated were followed by reactions of lethargy during which he would lie about with his violin and his books, hardly moving save from the sofa to the table. Thus month after month his papers accumulated until every corner of the room was stacked with bundles of manuscript which were on no account to be burned, and which could not be put away save by their owner. One winter's night, as we sat together by the fire, I ventured to suggest to him that, as he had finished pasting extracts into his commonplace[8] book, he might employ the next two hours in making our room a little more habitable. He could not deny the justice of my request, so with a rather rueful face he went off to his bedroom, from which he returned presently pulling a large tin box behind him. This he placed in the middle of the floor, and, squatting down upon a stool in front of it, he threw back the lid. I could see that it was already a third full of bundles of paper tied up with red tape into separate packages.

"There are cases enough here, Watson," said he, looking at me with mischievous eyes. "I think that if you knew all that I had in this box you would ask me to pull some out instead of putting others in."

"These are the records of your early work, then?" I asked. "I have often wished that I had notes of those cases."

"Yes, my boy, these were all done prematurely before my biographer had come to glorify me." He lifted bundle after bundle in a tender caressing sort of way. "They are not all successes, Watson," said he. "But there are some pretty little problems among them. Here's the record of the Tarleton murders, and the case of Vamberry, the wine merchant, and the adventure of the old Russian woman, and the singular affair of the aluminum crutch, as well as a full account of Ricoletti of the club-foot, and his abominable wife. And here—ah, now, this really is something a little *recherché*."[9]

He dived his arm down to the bottom of the chest and

7. docket: label.
8. commonplace: reference; here, a book used for reference.
9. recherché (rə•shār′shā or rə•shār′•shā): French for rare or unusual.

brought up a small wooden box with a sliding lid such as children's toys are kept in. From within he produced a crumpled piece of paper, an old-fashioned brass key, a peg of wood with a ball of string attached to it, and three rusty old discs of metal.

"Well, my boy, what do you make of this lot?" he asked, smiling at my expression.

"It is a curious collection."

"Very curious, and the story that hangs round it will strike you as being more curious still."

"These relics have a history, then?"

"So much so that they *are* history."

"What do you mean by that?"

Sherlock Holmes picked them up one by one and laid them along the edge of the table. Then he reseated himself in his chair and looked them over with a gleam of satisfaction in his eyes.

"These," said he, "are all that I have left to remind me of the adventure of the Musgrave Ritual."

"I had heard him mention the case more than once, though I had never been able to gather the details. "I should be so glad," said I, "if you would give me an account of it."

"And leave the litter as it is?" he cried mischievously. "Your tidiness won't bear much strain, after all, Watson. But I should be glad that you should add this case to your annals, for there are points in it which make it quite unique in the criminal records of this or, I believe, of any other country. A collection of my trifling achievements would certainly be incomplete which contained no account of this very singular business.

"You may remember how the affair of the *Gloria Scott,* and my conversation with the unhappy man whose fate I told you of, first turned my attention in the direction of the profession which has become my life's work. You see me now when my name has become known far and wide, and when I am generally recognized both by the public and by the official force as being a final court of appeal in doubtful cases. Even when you knew me first, at the time of the affair which you have commemorated in 'A Study in Scarlet,' I had already established a considerable, though not a very lucrative, connection. You can hardly realize, then, how difficult I found it at first, and how long I had to wait before I succeeded in making any headway.

"When I first came up to London I had rooms in Montague

Street, just around the corner from the British Museum, and there I waited, filling in my too abundant leisure time by studying all those branches of science which might make me more efficient. Now and again cases came in my way, principally through the introduction of old fellow-students, for during my last years at the university there was a good deal of talk there about myself and my methods. The third of these cases was that of the Musgrave Ritual, and it is to the interest which was aroused by that singular chain of events, and the large issues which proved to be at stake, that I trace my first stride towards the position which I now hold.

"Reginald Musgrave had been in the same college as myself, and I had some slight acquaintance with him. He was not generally popular among the undergraduates, though it always seemed to me that what was set down as pride was really an attempt to cover extreme natural diffidence. In appearance he was a man of an exceedingly aristocratic type, thin, high-nosed, and large-eyed, with languid and yet courtly manners. He was indeed a scion[10] of one of the very oldest families in the kingdom, though his branch was a cadet[11] one which had separated from the northern Musgraves some time in the sixteenth century and had established itself in western Sussex, where the Manor House of Hurlstone is perhaps the oldest inhabited building in the county. Something of his birth-place seemed to cling to the man, and I never looked at his pale, keen face or the poise of his head without associating him with gray archways and mullioned[12] windows and all the venerable wreckage of a feudal keep.[13] Once or twice we drifted into talk, and I can remember that more than once he expressed a keen interest in my methods of observation and inference.

"For four years I had seen nothing of him until one morning he walked into my room in Montague Street. He had changed little, was dressed like a young man of fashion—he was always a bit of a dandy—and preserved the same quiet, suave manner which had formerly distinguished him.

"'How has all gone with you, Musgrave?' I asked after we had cordially shaken hands.

"'You probably heard of my poor father's death,' said he; 'he

10. scion (sī′ən)**:** descendant.
11. cadet (kə•dĕt′)**:** younger son.
12. mullioned (mŭl′yənd)**:** vertically barred panels between panes of glass.
13. keep: fortress.

was carried off about two years ago. Since then I have of course had the Hurlstone estate to manage, and as I am member[14] for my district as well, my life has been a busy one. But I understand, Holmes, that you are turning to practical ends those powers with which you used to amaze us?'

"'Yes,' said I, 'I have taken to living by my wits.'

"'I am delighted to hear it, for your advice at present would be exceedingly valuable to me. We have had some very strange doings at Hurlstone, and the police have been able to throw no light upon the matter. It is really the most extraordinary and inexplicable business.'

"You can imagine with what eagerness I listened to him, Watson, for the very chance for which I had been panting during all those months of inaction seemed to have come within my reach. In my inmost heart I believed that I could succeed where others failed, and now I had the opportunity to test myself.

"'Pray let me have the details,' I cried.

"Reginald Musgrave sat down opposite to me and lit the cigarette which I had pushed towards him.

"'You must know,' said he, 'that though I am a bachelor, I have to keep up a considerable staff of servants at Hurlstone, for it is a rambling old place and takes a good deal of looking after. I preserve,[15] too, and in the pheasant months I usually have a house-party, so that it would not do to be short-handed. Altogether there are eight maids, the cook, the butler, two footmen, and a boy. The garden and the stables of course have a separate staff.

"'Of these servants the one who had been longest in our service was Brunton, the butler. He was a young schoolmaster out of place when he was first taken up by my father, but he was a man of great energy and character, and he soon became quite invaluable in the household. He was a well-grown, handsome man, with a splendid forehead, and though he has been with us for twenty years he cannot be more than forty now. With his personal advantages and his extraordinary gifts—for he can speak several languages and play nearly every musical instrument—it is wonderful that he should have been satisfied so long in such a position, but I suppose that he was comfortable and lacked energy to make

14. member: member of Parliament.
15. preserve: to protect and maintain game for shooting.

any change. The butler of Hurlstone is always a thing that is remembered by all who visit us.

"'But this paragon has one fault. He is a bit of a Don Juan,[16] and you can imagine that for a man like him it is not a very difficult part to play in a quiet country district. When he was married it was all right, but since he has been a widower we have had no end of trouble with him. A few months ago we were in hopes that he was about to settle down again, for he became engaged to Rachel Howells, our second housemaid; but he has thrown her over since then and taken up with Janet Tregellis, the daughter of the head game-keeper. Rachel—who is a very good girl, but of an excitable Welsh temperament—had a sharp touch of brain-fever and goes about the house now—or did until yesterday—like a black-eyed shadow of her former self. That was our first drama at Hurlstone; but a second one came to drive it from our minds, and it was prefaced by the disgrace and dismissal of butler Brunton.

"'This was how it came about. I have said that the man was intelligent, and this very intelligence had caused his ruin, for it seems to have led to an insatiable curiosity about things which did not in the least concern him. I had no idea of the lengths to which this would carry him until the merest accident opened my eyes to it.

"'I have said that the house is a rambling one. One day last week—on Thursday night, to be more exact—I found that I could not sleep, having foolishly taken a cup of strong *café noir*[17] after my dinner. After struggling against it until two in the morning, I felt that it was quite hopeless, so I rose and lit the candle with the intention of continuing a novel which I was reading. The book, however, had been left in the billiard-room,[18] so I pulled on my dressing-gown and started off to get it.

"'In order to reach the billiard-room I had to descend a flight of stairs and then to cross the head of a passage which led to the library and the gun-room. You can imagine my surprise when, as I looked down this corridor, I saw a glimmer of light coming from

16. Don Juan (dŏn′wän′): lover; Don Juan was a legendary Spanish nobleman who was the hero-villain of countless novels, plays, and poems. Mozart's opera *Don Giovanni* (1787) is based on the Don Juan legend.

17. café noir (kä fā nwär): French for black coffee (without cream or milk).

18. billiard (bĭl′yərd): table game played with balls and a long stick. The game of pool is one kind of billiard game.

the open door of the library. I had myself extinguished the lamp and closed the door before coming to bed. Naturally my first thought was of burglars. The corridors at Hurlstone have their walls largely decorated with trophies of old weapons. From one of these I picked a battle-axe, and then, leaving my candle behind me, I crept on tiptoe down the passage and peeped in at the open door.

"'Brunton, the butler, was in the library. He was sitting, fully dressed, in an easy-chair, with a slip of paper which looked like a map upon his knee, and his forehead sunk forward upon his hand in deep thought. I stood dumb with astonishment, watching him from the darkness. A small taper[19] on the edge of the table shed a feeble light which sufficed to show me that he was fully dressed. Suddenly, as I looked, he rose from his chair, and, walking over to a bureau at the side, he unlocked it and drew out one of the drawers. From this he took a paper, and, returning to his seat, he flattened it out beside the taper on the edge of the table and began to study it with minute attention. My indignation at this calm examination of our family documents overcame me so far that I took a step forward, and Brunton, looking up, saw me standing in the doorway. He sprang to his feet, his face turned livid with fear, and he thrust into his breast the chart-like paper which he had been originally studying.

"'"So!" said I. "This is how you repay the trust which we have reposed in you. You will leave my service to-morrow."

"'He bowed with the look of a man who is utterly crushed and slunk past me without a word. The taper was still on the table, and by its light I glanced to see what the paper was which Brunton had taken from the bureau. To my surprise it was nothing of any importance at all, but simply a copy of the questions and answers in the singular old observance called the Musgrave Ritual. It is a sort of ceremony peculiar to our family, which each Musgrave for centuries past has gone through on his coming of age—a thing of private interest, and perhaps of some little importance to the archaeologist, like our own blazonings, and charges,[20] but of no practical use whatever.'

19. taper: a slender candle.
20. blazonings, and charges: shields and bearings (symbols of the shield); refers to hereditary coats-of-arms used to distinguish families and individuals. In the West, hereditary symbols (called *heraldry*) were first used on armor and on seals.

"'We had better come back to the paper afterwards,' said I.

"'If you think it really necessary,' he answered with some hesitation. 'To continue my statement, however: I relocked the bureau, using the key which Brunton had left, and I had turned to go when I was surprised to find that the butler had returned, and was standing before me.

"'"Mr. Musgrave, sir," he cried in a voice which was hoarse with emotion. "I can't bear disgrace, sir. I've always been proud above my station in life, and disgrace would kill me. My blood will be on your head, sir—it will, indeed—if you drive me to despair. If you cannot keep me after what has passed, then for God's sake let me give you notice and leave in a month, as if on my own free will. I could stand that, Mr. Musgrave, but not to be cast out before all the folk that I know so well."

"'"You don't deserve much consideration, Brunton," I answered. "Your conduct has been most infamous. However, as you have been a long time in the family, I have no wish to bring public disgrace upon you. A month, however, is too long. Take yourself away in a week, and give what reason you like for going."

"'"Only a week, sir?" he cried in a despairing voice. "A fortnight[21]—say at least a fortnight!"

"'"A week," I repeated, "and you may consider yourself to have been very leniently dealt with."

"'He crept away, his face sunk upon his breast, like a broken man, while I put out the light and returned to my room.

"'For two days after this Brunton was most assiduous in his attention to his duties. I made no allusion to what had passed and waited with some curiosity to see how he would cover his disgrace. On the third morning, however, he did not appear, as was his custom, after breakfast to receive my instructions for the day. As I left the dining-room I happened to meet Rachel Howells, the maid. I have told you that she had only recently recovered from an illness and was looking so wretchedly pale and wan that I remonstrated with her for being at work.

"'"You should be in bed," I said. "Come back to your duties when you are stronger."

"'She looked at me with so strange an expression that I began to suspect that her brain was affected.

21. **fortnight:** two weeks.

"'"I am strong enough, Mr. Musgrave," said she.

"'"We will see what the doctor says," I answered. "You must stop work now, and when you go downstairs just say that I wish to see Brunton."

"'"The butler is gone," said she.

"'"Gone! Gone where?"

"'"He is gone. No one has seen him. He is not in his room. Oh, yes, he is gone, he is gone!" She fell back against the wall with shriek after shriek of laughter, while I, horrified at this sudden hysterical attack, rushed to the bell to summon help. The girl was taken to her room, still screaming and sobbing, while I made inquiries about Brunton. There was no doubt about it that he had disappeared. His bed had not been slept in, he had been seen by no one since he had retired to his room the night before, and yet it was difficult to see how he could have left the house, as both windows and doors were found to be fastened in the morning. His clothes, his watch, and even his money were in his room, but the black suit which he usually wore was missing. His slippers, too, were gone, but his boots were left behind. Where then could butler Brunton have gone in the night, and what could have become of him now?

"'Of course we searched the house from cellar to garret,[22] but there was no trace of him. It is, as I have said, a labyrinth[23] of an old house, especially the original wing, which is now practically uninhabited; but we ransacked every room and cellar without discovering the least sign of the missing man. It was incredible to me that he could have gone away leaving all his property behind him, and yet where could he be? I called in the local police, but without success. Rain had fallen on the night before, and we examined the lawn and the paths all round the house, but in vain. Matters were in this state, when a new development quite drew our attention away from the original mystery.

"'For two days Rachel Howells had been so ill, sometimes delirious, sometimes hysterical, that a nurse had been employed to sit up with her at night. On the third night after Brunton's disap-

22. garret (găr′ĭt): attic.
23. labyrinth (lăb′ə•rĭnth′): a confusing and difficult place to find one's way. In Greek legend, Daedalus built a labyrinth, or maze, for King Minos of Crete. At the center of the maze was the Minotaur, a monster half-bull, half-man.

pearance, the nurse, finding her patient sleeping nicely, had dropped into a nap in the armchair, when she woke in the early morning to find the bed empty, the window open, and no signs of the invalid. I was instantly aroused, and, with the two footmen, started off at once in search of the missing girl. It was not difficult to tell the direction which she had taken, for, starting from under her window, we could follow her footmarks easily across the lawn to the edge of the mere,[24] where they vanished close to the gravel path which leads out of the grounds. The lake there is eight feet deep, and you can imagine our feelings when we saw that the trail of the poor demented girl came to an end at the edge of it.

"'Of course, we had the drags[25] at once and set to work to recover the remains, but no trace of the body could we find. On the other hand, we brought to the surface an object of a most unexpected kind. It was a linen bag which contained within it a mass of old rusted and discoloured metal and several dull-coloured pieces of pebble or glass. This strange find was all that we could get from the mere, and, although we made every possible search and inquiry yesterday, we know nothing of the fate either of Rachel Howells or of Richard Brunton. The county police are at their wit's end, and I have come up to you as a last resource.'

"You can imagine, Watson, with what eagerness I listened to this extraordinary sequence of events, and endeavoured to piece them together, and to devise some common thread upon which they might all hang. The butler was gone. The maid was gone. The maid had loved the butler, but had afterwards had cause to hate him. She was of Welsh blood, fiery and passionate. She had been terribly excited immediately after his disappearance. She had flung into the lake a bag containing some curious contents. These were all factors which had to be taken into consideration, and yet none of them got quite to the heart of the matter. What was the starting-point of this chain of events? There lay the end of this tangled line.

"'I must see that paper, Musgrave,' said I, 'which this butler of yours thought it worth his while to consult, even at the risk of the loss of his place.'

"'It is rather an absurd business, this ritual of ours,' he an-

24. mere (mîr)**:** small lake.
25. drags: hooks and nets used to search for a drowned person's body.

swered. 'But it has at least the saving grace of antiquity to excuse it. I have a copy of the questions and answers here if you care to run your eye over them.'

"He handed me the very paper which I have here, Watson, and this is the strange catechism[26] to which each Musgrave had to submit when he came to man's estate. I will read you the questions and answers as they stand.

"'Whose was it?'

"'His who is gone.'

"'Who shall have it?'

"'He who will come.'

"'Where was the sun?'

"'Over the oak.'

"'Where was the shadow?'

"'Under the elm.'

"'How was it stepped?'

"'North by ten and by ten, east by five and by five, south by two and by two, west by one and by one, and so under.'

"'What shall we give for it?'

"'All that is ours.'

"'Why should we give it?'

"'For the sake of the trust.'

"'The original has no date, but is in the spelling of the middle of the seventeenth century,' remarked Musgrave. 'I am afraid, however, that it can be of little help to you in solving this mystery.'

"'At least,' said I, 'it gives us another mystery, and one which is even more interesting than the first. It may be that the solution of the one may prove to be the solution of the other. You will excuse me, Musgrave, if I say that your butler appears to me to have been a very clever man, and to have had a clearer insight than ten generations of his masters.'

"'I hardly follow you,' said Musgrave. 'The paper seems to me to be of no practical importance.'

"'But to me it seems immensely practical, and I fancy that Brunton took the same view. He had probably seen it before that night on which you caught him.'

"'It is very possible. We took no pains to hide it.'

26. catechism (kăt′ə•kĭz′•əm): series of questions and answers.

"'He simply wished, I should imagine, to refresh his memory upon that last occasion. He had, as I understand, some sort of map or chart which he was comparing with the manuscript, and which he thrust into his pocket when you appeared.'

"'That is true. But what could he have to do with this old family custom of ours, and what does this rigmarole mean?'

"'I don't think that we should have much difficulty in determining that,' said I; 'with your permission we will take the first train down to Sussex and go a little more deeply into the matter upon the spot.'

"The same afternoon saw us both at Hurlstone. Possibly you have seen pictures and read descriptions of the famous old building, so I will confine my account of it to saying that it is built in the shape of an L, the long arm being the more modern portion, and the shorter the ancient nucleus from which the other has developed. Over the low, heavy-lintelled[27] door, in the centre of this old part, is chiselled the date, 1607, but experts are agreed that the beams and stonework are really much older than this. The enormously thick walls and tiny windows of this part had in the last century driven the family into building the new wing, and the old one was used now as a storehouse and a cellar, when it was used at all. A splendid park with fine old timber surrounds the house, and the lake, to which my client had referred, lay close to the avenue, about two hundred yards from the building.

"I was already firmly convinced, Watson, that there were not three separate mysteries here, but one only, and that if I could read the Musgrave Ritual aright I should hold in my hand the clue which would lead me to the truth concerning both the butler Brunton and the maid Howells. To that then I turned all my energies. Why should this servant be so anxious to master this old formula? Evidently because he saw something in it which had escaped all those generations of country squires, and from which he expected some personal advantage. What was it then, and how had it affected his fate?

"It was perfectly obvious to me, on reading the Ritual, that the measurements must refer to some spot to which the rest of the document alluded, and that if we could find that spot we should

27. heavy-lintelled: heavy-beamed. A lintel is a stone or wooden beam over a window or door.

be in a fair way towards finding what the secret was which the old Musgraves had thought it necessary to embalm[28] in so curious a fashion. There were two guides given us to start with, an oak and an elm. As to the oak there could be no question at all. Right in front of the house, upon the left-hand side of the drive, there stood a patriarch among oaks, one of the most magnificent trees that I have ever seen.

"'That was there when your Ritual was drawn up,' said I as we drove past it.

"'It was there at the Norman Conquest[29] in all probability,' he answered. 'It has a girth of twenty-three feet.'

"Here was one of my fixed points secured.

"'Have you any old elms?' I asked.

"'There used to be a very old one over yonder, but it was struck by lightning ten years ago, and we cut down the stump.'

"'You can see where it used to be?'

"'Oh, yes.'

"'There are no other elms?'

"'No old ones, but plenty of beeches.'

"'I should like to see where it grew.'

"We had driven up in a dog-cart, and my client led me away at once, without our entering the house, to the scar on the lawn where the elm had stood. It was nearly midway between the oak and the house. My investigation seemed to be progressing.

"'I suppose it is impossible to find out how high the elm was?' I asked.

"'I can give you it at once. It was sixty-four feet.'

"'How do you come to know it?' I asked in surprise.

"'When my old tutor used to give me an exercise in trigonometry, it always took the shape of measuring heights. When I was a lad I worked out every tree and building in the estate.'

"This was an unexpected piece of luck. My data were coming more quickly than I could have reasonably hoped.

"'Tell me,' I asked, 'did your butler ever ask you such a question?'

28. embalm (ĕm•bäm′)**:** preserve.
29. Norman Conquest: Normans, under the leadership of William the Conqueror, conquered England in 1066. Normandy is an area in Northwestern France.

"Reginald Musgrave looked at me in astonishment. 'Now that you call it to my mind,' he answered, 'Brunton *did* ask me about the height of the tree some months ago in connection with some little argument with the groom.'

"This was excellent news, Watson, for it showed me that I was on the right road. I looked up at the sun. It was low in the heavens, and I calculated that in less than an hour it would lie just above the topmost branches of the old oak. One condition mentioned in the Ritual would then be fulfilled. And the shadow of the elm must mean the farther end of the shadow, otherwise the trunk would have been chosen as the guide. I had, then, to find where the far end of the shadow would fall when the sun was just clear of the oak."

"That must have been difficult, Holmes, when the elm was no longer there."

"Well, at least I knew that if Brunton could do it, I could also. Besides, there was no real difficulty. I went with Musgrave to his study and whittled myself this peg, to which I tied this long string with a knot at each yard. Then I took two lengths of a fishing-rod, which came to just six feet, and I went back with my client to where the elm had been. The sun was just grazing the top of the oak. I fastened the rod on end, marked out the direction of the shadow, and measured it. It was nine feet in length.

"Of course the calculation now was a simple one. If a rod of six feet threw a shadow of nine, a tree of sixty-four feet would throw one of ninety-six, and the line of the one would of course be the line of the other. I measured out the distance, which brought me almost to the wall of the house, and I thrust a peg into the spot. You can imagine my exultation, Watson, when within two inches of my peg I saw a conical depression in the ground. I knew that it was the mark made by Brunton in his measurements, and that I was still upon his trail.

"From this starting-point I proceeded to step, having first taken the cardinal[30] points by my pocket-compass. Ten steps with each foot took me along parallel with the wall of the house, and again I marked my spot with a peg. Then I carefully paced off five to the east and two to the south. It brought me to the very threshold of the old door. Two steps to the west meant now that I was to

30. cardinal: main or primary. The cardinal points of the compass are north, south, east, and west.

go two paces down the stone-flagged passage, and this was the place indicated by the Ritual.

"Never have I felt such a cold chill of disappointment, Watson. For a moment it seemed to me that there must be some radical mistake in my calculations. The setting sun shone full upon the passage floor, and I could see that the old, foot-worn gray stones with which it was paved were firmly cemented together, and had certainly not been moved for many a long year. Brunton had not been at work here. I tapped upon the floor, but it sounded the same all over, and there was no sign of any crack or crevice. But, fortunately, Musgrave, who had begun to appreciate the meaning of my proceedings, and who was now as excited as myself, took out his manuscript to check my calculations.

"'And under,' he cried. 'You have omitted the "and under."'

"I had thought that it meant that we were to dig, but now, of course I saw at once that I was wrong. 'There is a cellar under this then?' I cried.

"'Yes, and as old as the house. Down here, through this door.'

"We went down a winding stone stair, and my companion, striking a match, lit a large lantern which stood on a barrel in the corner. In an instant it was obvious that we had at last come upon the true place, and that we had not been the only people to visit the spot recently.

"It had been used for the storage of wood, but the billets,[31] which had evidently been littered over the floor, were now piled at the sides, so as to leave a clear space in the middle. In this space lay a large and heavy flagstone with a rusted iron ring in the centre to which a thick shepherd's-check muffler[32] was attached.

"'By Jove!' cried my client. 'That's Brunton's muffler. I have seen it on him and could swear to it. What has the villain been doing here?'

"At my suggestion a couple of the county police were summoned to be present, and I then endeavoured to raise the stone by pulling on the cravat.[33] I could only move it slightly, and it was with the aid of one of the constables that I succeeded at last in

31. billets (bĭl′ĭts): thick wooden sticks.
32. muffler: scarf.
33. cravat (krə•vat′): scarf.

carrying it to one side. A black hole yawned beneath into which we all peered, while Musgrave, kneeling at the side, pushed down the lantern.

"A small chamber about seven feet deep and four feet square lay open to us. At one side of this was a squat, brass-bound wooden box, the lid of which was hinged upward, with this curious old-fashioned key projecting from the lock. It was furred outside by a thick layer of dust, and damp and worms had eaten through the wood, so that a crop of livid fungi was growing on the inside of it. Several discs of metal, old coins apparently, such as I hold here, were scattered over the bottom of the box, but it contained nothing else.

"At the moment, however, we had no thought for the old chest, for our eyes were riveted upon that which crouched beside it. It was the figure of a man, clad in a suit of black, who squatted down upon his hams with his forehead sunk upon the edge of the box and his two arms thrown out on each side of it. The attitude had drawn all the stagnant blood to the face, and no man could have recognized that distorted liver-coloured countenance; but his height, his dress, and his hair were all sufficient to show my client, when we had drawn the body up, that it was indeed his missing butler. He had been dead some days, but there was no wound or bruise upon his person to show how he had met his dreadful end. When his body had been carried from the cellar we found ourselves still confronted with a problem which was almost as formidable as that with which we had started.

"I confess that so far, Watson, I had been disappointed in my investigation. I had reckoned upon solving the matter when once I had found the place referred to in the Ritual; but now I was there, and was apparently as far as ever from knowing what it was which the family had concealed with such elaborate precautions. It is true that I had thrown a light upon the fate of Brunton, but now I had to ascertain how that fate had come upon him, and what part had been played in the matter by the woman who had disappeared. I sat down upon a keg in the corner and thought the whole matter carefully over.

"You know my methods in such cases, Watson. I put myself in the man's place, and, having first gauged his intelligence, I try to imagine how I should myself have proceeded under the same circumstances. In this case the matter was simplified by Brunton's intelligence being quite first-rate, so that it was unnecessary to make any allowance for the personal equation, as the astronomers have dubbed it. He knew that something valuable was concealed. He had spotted the place. He found that the stone which covered it was just too heavy for a man to move unaided. What would he do next? He could not get help from outside, even if he had someone whom he could trust, without the unbarring of doors and considerable risk of detection. It was better, if he could, to have his helpmate inside the house. But whom could he ask? This girl had been devoted to him. A man always finds it hard to realize that he may have finally lost a woman's love, however badly he may have treated her. He would try by a few attentions to make his peace with the girl Howells, and then would engage her as his accomplice. Together they would come at night to the cellar, and their united force would suffice to raise the stone. So far I could follow their actions as if I had actually seen them.

"But for two of them, and one a woman, it must have been heavy work, the raising of that stone. A burly Sussex policeman and I had found it no light job. What would they do to assist them? Probably what I should have done myself. I rose and examined carefully the different billets of wood which were scattered round the floor. Almost at once I came upon what I expected. One piece, about three feet in length, had a very marked indentation at one end, while several were flattened at the sides as if they had been compressed by some considerable weight. Evidently, as they had dragged the stone up, they had thrust the chunks of wood into the chink until at last when the opening was large enough to crawl through, they would hold it open by a billet placed lengthwise, which might very well become indented at the lower end, since the whole weight of the stone would press it down on to the edge of this other slab. So far I was still on safe ground.

"And now how was I to proceed to reconstruct this midnight drama? Clearly, only one could fit into the hole, and that one was Brunton. The girl must have waited above. Brunton then unlocked the box, handed up the contents presumably—since they were not to be found—and then—and then what happened?

"What smouldering fire of vengeance had suddenly sprung into flame in this passionate Celtic woman's soul when she saw the man who had wronged her—wronged her, perhaps, far more than we suspected—in her power? Was it a chance that the wood had slipped and that the stone had shut Brunton into what had become his sepulchre?[34] Had she only been guilty of silence as to his fate? Or had some sudden blow from her hand dashed the support away and sent the slab crashing down into its place? Be that as it might, I seemed to see that woman's figure still clutching at her treasure trove and flying wildly up the winding stair, with her ears ringing perhaps with the muffled screams from behind her and with the drumming of frenzied hands against the slab of stone which was choking her faithless lover's life out.

"Here was the secret of her blanched face, her shaken nerves, her peals of hysterical laughter on the next morning. But what had been in the box? What had she done with that? Of course, it must have been the old metal and pebbles which my client had dragged from the mere. She had thrown them in there at the first opportunity to remove the last trace of her crime.

"For twenty minutes I had sat motionless, thinking the matter out. Musgrave still stood with a very pale face, swinging his lantern and peering down into the hole.

"'These are coins of Charles the First,'[35] said he, holding out the few which had been in the box; you see we were right in fixing our date for the Ritual.'

"'We may find something else of Charles the First,' I cried, as the probable meaning of the first two questions of the Ritual broke suddenly upon me. 'Let me see the contents of the bag which you fished from the mere.'

"We ascended to his study, and he laid the débris before me. I could understand his regarding it as of small importance when I looked at it, for the metal was almost black and the stones lustreless and dull. I rubbed one of them on my sleeve, however, and it glowed afterwards like a spark in the dark hollow of my hand. The metal work was in the form of a double ring, but it had been bent and twisted out of its original shape.

"'You must bear in mind,' said I, 'that the royal party made head in England even after the death of the king, and that when they at last fled they probably left many of their most precious

34. sepulchre (sĕp′əl•kər): burial place.
35. Charles the First: Charles Stuart (1609–1649), an authoritarian British king who dissolved Parliament in 1629 and ruled without a legislative body. After eleven years, he was forced to call Parliament again because he needed money for his war against the Scots. After surrendering to the Scots in 1646, he was convicted of treason and beheaded by Parliamentarian forces.

possessions buried behind them, with the intention of returning for them in more peaceful times.'

"'My ancestor, Sir Ralph Musgrave, was a prominent cavalier and the righthand man of Charles the Second[36] in his wanderings,' said my friend.

"'Ah, indeed!' I answered. 'Well now, I think that really should give us the last link that we wanted. I must congratulate you on coming into the possession, though in rather a tragic manner, of a relic which is of great intrinsic value, but of even greater importance as a historical curiosity.'

"'What is it, then?' he gasped in astonishment.

"'It is nothing less than the ancient crown of the kings of England.'

"'The crown!'

"'Precisely. Consider what the Ritual says. How does it run? "Whose was it?" "His who is gone." That was after the execution of Charles. Then, "Who shall have it?" "He who will come." That was Charles the Second, whose advent was already foreseen. There can, I think, be no doubt that this battered and shapeless diadem once encircled the brows of the royal Stuarts.'[37]

"'And how came it in the pond?'

"'Ah, that is a question that will take some time to answer.' And with that I sketched out to him the whole long surmise and of proof which I had constructed. The twilight had closed in and the moon was shining brightly in the sky before my narrative was finished.

"'And how was it then that Charles did not get his crown when he returned?' asked Musgrave, pushing back the relic into its linen bag.

"'Ah, there you lay your finger upon the one point which we shall probably never be able to clear up. It is likely that the Musgrave who held the secret died in the interval, and by some oversight left this guide to his descendant without explaining the meaning of it. From that day to this it has been handed down from father to son, until at last it came within reach of a man who tore its secret out of it and lost his life in the venture.'

36. Charles the Second: British king, son of Charles the First. Charles the Second (1630–1685) was proclaimed king by the Scots and was restored to the throne in 1660.

37. Stuarts: surname of Scottish family that ruled Scotland, England, and Ireland through most of the seventeenth and eighteenth centuries.

"And that's the story of the Musgrave Ritual, Watson. They have the crown down at Hurlstone—though they had some legal bother and a considerable sum to pay before they were allowed to retain it. I am sure that if you mentioned my name they would be happy to show it to you. Of the woman nothing was ever heard, and the probability is that she got away out of England and carried herself and the memory of her crime to some land beyond the seas."

Meaning

1. At what point in Sherlock Holmes' career did the Musgrave Ritual case take place? Why did Holmes consider this case important?
2. Holmes pulled the following "relics" from a wooden box: a crumpled piece of paper, a brass key, a peg of wood with a ball of string attached to it, and three rusty old discs of metal. Where does each of these items fit into the story?
3. Holmes said that his methods were observation and inference. What are some examples of his use of these methods in the story?
4. What had the maid thrown into the lake?

Method

1. Who is the primary narrator of the story? Who tells the story within the story? At what point is there even a third narrator? Is this method of telling the story confusing, or interesting and important to the plot? Why do you think so?
2. Describe the character of Sherlock Holmes. Do you find him a likeable personality? Why or why not?
3. What questions keep the readers in suspense as the case unfolds?
4. Which element is most important to this story: character, plot, theme, setting, or tone?
5. Describe the style (choice of words, length of sentences, description, dialogue, etc.) of "The Musgrave Ritual." Why is this style appropriate for the subject and narrator?

Language: Differences in British and American Words, Spelling, and Pronounciations

British and Americans sometimes use different words to mean the same thing. In this story, Brunton begs to be allowed to stay on as butler for a fortnight. The American equivalent for *fortnight* is two weeks. Rachel Howells' footprints end at the edge of the *mere*—a word that the British use poetically to mean *lake.*

There are also some differences in British and American spellings. Some words that end in *-er* in this country end in *-re* in England. In this story, for example, *center* is spelled *centre; sepulcher* becomes *sepulchre; lusterless* becomes *lustreless.* In America, words that contain *-or* may be spelled *-our* in England. Instead of *discolored,* the British write *discoloured;* instead of *endeavored,* they write *endeavoured;* instead of *humors,* they spell it *humours.*

Sometimes, even when the spelling is the same, the pronunciation is different. For example, the British pronunciation of *tomato* is tə•mä′tō with a broad *a,* and the words *laboratory* and *schedule* are pronounced lə•bŏr′ə•trē and schĕd′yo͞ol.

See if you can find out the American equivalents of the following British expressions:

1. telly
2. bobby
3. cinema
4. underground
5. lift
6. diversion (a road sign)

Discussion and Composition

1. Decide what you think might have become of Rachel Howells. Use the information about her in the story as your starting point. Reveal her fate in a newspaper story. You may write an obituary, a feature story, or a news report.

2. Write a critical review of a movie or television murder mystery story you have watched. Consider the detective's personality and method. How realistic or contrived is the mystery and its solution?

WILLIAM MELVIN KELLEY
(born 1937)

Born in New York City, William Melvin Kelley chose writing as a career while he was a student at Harvard University. The success of *A Different Drummer,* published when he was twenty-five, proved that he made the right decision. On the dedication page of *Dancers on the Shore* (1964), the short story collection that includes "A Visit to Grandmother," Kelley explains that the person who listened to him and encouraged his ambition to write rather than choosing "a more secure and respectable occupation" was his grandmother, Jessie Garcia, "who was the only family I had."

Kelley has received several literary awards for his novels and short stories, which have been widely praised. His stories and articles appear in popular magazines such as *Esquire, Mademoiselle, The Negro Digest,* and *The Saturday Evening Post.*

In recent years, Kelley has been author-in-residence at the State University of New York in Geneseo.

A VISIT TO GRANDMOTHER

Chig knew something was wrong the instant his father kissed her. He had always known his father to be the warmest of men, a man so kind that when people ventured timidly into his office, it took only a few words from him to make them relax, and even laugh. Doctor Charles Dunford cared about people.

But when he had bent to kiss the old lady's black face, something new and almost ugly had come into his eyes: fear, uncertainty, sadness, and perhaps even hatred.

Ten days before in New York, Chig's father had decided suddenly he wanted to go to Nashville to attend his college class reunion, twenty years out. Both Chig's brother and sister, Peter and Connie, were packing for camp and besides were too young for such an affair. But Chig was seventeen, had nothing to do that summer, and his father asked if he would like to go along. His father had given him additional reasons: "All my running buddies got their diplomas and were snapped up by them crafty young gals, and had kids within a year—now all those kids, some of them gals, are your age."

The reunion had lasted a week. As they packed for home, his father, in a far too offhand way, had suggested they visit Chig's grandmother. "We this close. We might as well drop in on her and my brothers."

So instead of going north, they had gone farther south, had just entered her house. And Chig had a suspicion now that the reunion had been only an excuse to drive south, that his father had been heading to this house all the time.

His father had never talked much about his family, with the exception of his brother, GL, who seemed part con man, part practical joker, and part Don Juan; he had spoken of GL with the kind of indulgence he would have shown a cute but ill-behaved and potentially dangerous five-year-old.

Chig's father had left home when he was fifteen. When asked why, he would answer: "I wanted to go to school. They didn't have a Negro high school at home, so I went up to Knoxville and lived with a cousin and went to school."

They had been met at the door by Aunt Rose, GL's wife, and ushered into the living room. The old lady had looked up from her seat by the window. Aunt Rose stood between the visitors.

The old lady eyed his father. "Rose, who that? Rose?" She squinted. She looked like a doll made of black straw, the wrinkles in her face running in one direction like the head of a broom. Her hair was white and coarse and grew out straight from her head. Her eyes were brown—the whites, too, seemed light brown—and were hidden behind thick glasses, which remained somehow on a tiny nose. "That Hiram? That was another of his father's brothers. "No, it ain't Hiram; too big for Hiram." She turned then to Chig. "Now that man, he look like Eleanor, Charles's wife, but Charles wouldn't never send my grandson to see me. I never even hear from Charles." She stopped again.

"It Charles, Mama. That who it is." Aunt Rose, between them, led them closer. "It Charles come all the way from New York to see you, and brung little Charles with him."

The old lady stared up at them. "Charles? Rose, that really Charles?" She turned away, and reached for a handkerchief in the pocket of her clean, ironed, flowered housecoat, and wiped her eyes. "God have mercy. Charles." She spread her arms up to him, and he bent down and kissed her cheek. That was when Chig saw his face, grimacing. She hugged him; Chig watched the muscles in her arms as they tightened around his father's neck. She half rose out of her chair. "How are you, son?"

Chig could not hear his father's answer.

She let him go, and fell back into her chair, grabbing the arms. Her hands were as dark as the wood, and seemed to become part of it. "Now, who that standing there? Who that man?"

"That's one of your grandsons, Mama." His father's voice cracked. "Charles Dunford, junior. You saw him once, when he was a baby, in Chicago. He's grown now."

"I can see that, boy!" She looked at Chig squarely. "Come here, son, and kiss me once." He did. "What they call you? Charles too?"

"No, ma'am, they call me Chig."

She smiled. She had all her teeth, but they were too perfect to be her own. "That's good. Can't have two boys answering to Charles in the same house. Won't nobody at all come. So you that little boy. You don't remember me, do you? I used to take you to church in Chicago, and you'd get up and hop in time to the music. You studying to be a preacher?"

"No, ma'am. I don't think so. I might be a lawyer."

"You'll be an honest one, won't you?"

"I'll try."

"Trying ain't enough! You be honest, you hear? Promise me. You be honest like your daddy."

"All right. I promise."

"Good. Rose, where's GL at? Where's that thief? He gone again?"

"I don't know, Mama." Aunt Rose looked embarrassed. "He say he was going by his liquor store. He'll be back."

"Well, then where's Hiram? You call up those boys, and get them over here—now! You got enough to eat? Let me go see." She started to get up. Chig reached out his hand. She shook him off. "What they tell you about me, Chig? They tell you I'm all laid up? Don't believe it. They don't know nothing about old ladies. When I want help, I'll let you know. Only time I'll need help getting anywheres is when I dies and they lift me into the ground."

She was standing now, her back and shoulders straight. She came only to Chig's chest. She squinted up at him. "You eat much? Your daddy ate like two men."

"Yes, ma'am."

"That's good. That means you ain't nervous. Your mama, she

ain't nervous. I remember that. In Chicago, she'd sit down by a window all afternoon and never say nothing, just knit." She smiled. "Let me see what we got to eat."

"I'll do that, Mama." Aunt Rose spoke softly. "You haven't seen Charles in a long time. You sit and talk."

The old lady squinted at her. "You can do the cooking if you promise it ain't because you think I can't."

Aunt Rose chuckled. "I know you can do it, Mama."

"All right. I'll just sit and talk a spell." She sat again and arranged her skirt around her short legs.

Chig did most of the talking, told all about himself before she asked. His father only spoke when he was spoken to, and then only one word at a time, as if by coming back home he had become a small boy again, sitting in the parlor while his mother spoke with her guests.

When Uncle Hiram and Mae, his wife, came, they sat down to eat. Chig did not have to ask about Uncle GL's absence; Aunt Rose volunteered an explanation: "Can't never tell where the man is at. One Thursday morning he left here and next thing we knew, he was calling from Chicago, saying he went up to see Joe Louis fight. He'll be here though; he ain't as young and footloose as he used to be." Chig's father had mentioned driving down that GL was about five years older than he was, nearly fifty.

Uncle Hiram was somewhat smaller than Chig's father; his short-cropped kinky hair was half gray, half black. One spot, just off his forehead, was totally white. Later, Chig found out it had been that way since he was twenty. Mae (Chig could not bring himself to call her Aunt) was a good deal younger than Hiram, pretty enough so that Chig would have looked at her twice on the street. She was a honey-colored woman, with long eyelashes. She was wearing a white sheath.

At dinner, Chig and his father sat on one side, opposite Uncle Hiram and Mae; his grandmother and Aunt Rose sat at the ends. The food was good; there was a lot and Chig ate a lot. All through the meal, they talked about the family as it had been thirty years before, and particularly about the young GL. Mae and Chig asked questions; the old lady answered; Aunt Rose directed the discussion, steering the old lady onto the best stories; Chig's father laughed from time to time; Uncle Hiram ate.

"Why don't you tell them about the horse, Mama?" Aunt Rose,

over Chig's weak protest, was spooning mashed potatoes onto his plate. "There now, Chig."

"I'm trying to think." The old lady was holding her fork halfway to her mouth, looking at them over her glasses. "Oh, you talking about that crazy horse GL brung home that time."

"That's right, Mama." Aunt Rose nodded and slid another slice of white meat onto Chig's plate.

Mae started to giggle. "Oh, I've heard this. This is funny, Chig."

The old lady put down her fork and began: Well, GL went out of the house one day with an old, no-good chair I wanted him to take over to the church for a bazaar, and he met up with this man who'd just brung in some horses from out West. Now, I reckon you can expect one swindler to be in every town, but you don't rightly think there'll be two, and God forbid they should ever meet—but they did, GL and his chair, this man and his horses. Well, I wish I'd-a been there; there must-a been some mighty high-powered talking going on. That man with his horses, he told GL them horses was half-Arab, half-Indian, and GL told that man the chair was an antique he'd stole from some rich white folks. So they swapped. Well, I was a-looking out the window and seen GL dragging this animal to the house. It looked pretty gentle and its eyes was most closed and its feet was shuffling.

"GL, where'd you get that thing?" I says.

"I swapped him for that old chair, Mama," he says. "And made myself a bargain. This is even better than Papa's horse."

Well, I'm a-looking at this horse and noticing how he be looking more and more wide awake every minute, sort of warming up like a teakettle until, I swears to you, that horse is blowing steam out its nose.

"Come on, Mama," GL says, "come on and I'll take you for a ride." Now George, my husband, God rest his tired soul, he'd brung home this white folks' buggy which had a busted wheel and fixed it and was to take it back that day and GL says: "Come on, Mama, we'll use this fine buggy and take us a ride."

"GL," I says, "no, we ain't. Them white folks'll burn us alive if we use their buggy. You just take that horse right on back." You see, I was sure that boy'd come by that animal ungainly.

"Mama, I can't take him back," GL says.

"Why not?" I says.

"Because I don't rightly know where that man is at," GL says.

"Oh," I says. "Well, then I reckon we stuck with it." And I turned around to go back into the house because it was getting late, near dinner time, and I was cooking for ten.

"Mama," GL says to my back. "Mama, ain't you coming for a ride with me?"

"Go on, boy. You ain't getting me inside kicking range of that animal." I was eying that beast and it was boiling hotter all the time. I reckon maybe that man had drugged it. "That horse is wild, GL," I says.

"No, he ain't. He ain't. That man say he is buggy and saddle broke and as sweet as the inside of a apple."

My oldest girl, Essie, had-a come out on the porch and she says: "Go on, Mama. I'll cook. You ain't been out the house in weeks."

"Sure, come on, Mama," GL says. "There ain't nothing to be fidgety about. This horse is gentle as a rose petal." And just then that animal snorts so hard it sets up a little dust storm around its feet.

"Yes, Mama," Essie says, "you can see he gentle." Well, I looked at Essie and then at that horse because I didn't think we could be looking at the same animal. I should-a figured how Essie's eyes ain't never been so good.

"Come on, Mama," GL says.

"All right," I says. So I stood on the porch and watched GL hitching that horse up to the white folks' buggy. For a while there, the animal was pretty quiet, pawing a little, but not much. And I was feeling a little better about riding with GL behind that crazy-looking horse. I could see how GL was happy I was going with him. He was scurrying around that animal buckling buckles and strapping straps, all the time smiling, and that made me feel good.

Then he was finished, and I must say, that horse looked mighty fine hitched to that buggy and I knew anybody what climbed up there would look pretty good too. GL came around and stood at the bottom of the steps, and took off his hat and bowed and said: "Madam," and reached out his hand to me and I was feeling real elegant like a fine lady. He helped me up to the seat and then got up beside me and we moved out down our alley. And I remember how colored folks come out on their porches and shook their heads, saying: "Lord now, will you look at Eva Dunford, the fine lady! Don't she look good sitting up there!" And I pretended not to hear and sat up straight and proud.

We rode on through the center of town, up Market Street, and all the way out where Hiram is living now, which in them days was all woods, there not being even a farm in sight, and that's when that horse must-a first realized he weren't at all broke or tame, or maybe thought he was back out West again, and started to gallop.

"GL," I says, "now you ain't joking with your mama, is you? Because if you is, I'll strap you purple if I live through this."

Well, GL was pulling on the reins with all his meager strength, and yelling, "Whoa, you. Say now, whoa!" He turned to me just long enough to say, "I ain't fooling with you, Mama. Honest!"

I reckon that animal weren't too satisfied with the road, because it made a sharp right turn just then, down into a gulley, and struck out across a hilly meadow. "Mama," GL yells. "Mama, do something!"

I didn't know what to do but I figured I had to do something, so I stood up, hopped down onto the horse's back and pulled it to a stop. Don't ask me how I did that; I reckon it was that I was a mother and my baby asked me to do something, is all.

"Well, we walked that animal all the way home; sometimes I had to club it over the nose with my fist to make it come, but we made it, GL and me. You remember how tired we was, Charles?"

"I wasn't here at the time." Chig turned to his father and found his face completely blank, without even a trace of a smile or a laugh.

"Well, of course you was, son. That happened in . . . in . . . it was a hot summer that year and—"

"I left here in June of that year. You wrote me about it."

The old lady stared past Chig at him. They all turned to him; Uncle Hiram looked up from his plate.

"Then you don't remember how we all laughed?"

"No, I don't, Mama. And I probably wouldn't have laughed. I don't think it was funny." They were staring into each other's eyes.

"Why not, Charles?"

"Because in the first place, the horse was gained by fraud. And in the second place, both of you might have been seriously injured or even killed." He broke off their stare and spoke to himself more than to any of them: "And if I'd done it, you would've beaten me good for it."

"Pardon?" The old lady had not heard him; only Chig had heard.

Chig's father sat up straight as if preparing to debate. "I said that if I had done it, if I had done just exactly what GL did, you would have beaten me good for it, Mama." He was looking at her again.

"Why you say that, son?" She was leaning toward him.

"Don't you know? Tell the truth. It can't hurt me now." His voice cracked, but only once. "If GL and I did something wrong, you'd beat me first and then be too damn tired to beat him. At dinner, he'd always get seconds and I wouldn't. You'd do things with him, like ride in that buggy, but if I wanted you to do something with me, you were always too busy." He paused and considered whether to say what he finally did say: "I cried when I left here. Nobody loved me, Mama. I cried all the way up to Knoxville. That was the last time I ever cried in my life."

"Oh, Charles." She started to get up, to come around the table to him.

He stopped her. "It's too late."

"But you don't understand."

"What don't I understand? I understood then; I understand now."

Tears now traveled down the lines in her face, but when she spoke her voice was clear. "I thought you knew. I had ten children. I had to give all of them what they needed most." She nodded. "I paid more mind to GL. I had to. GL could-a ended up swinging if I hadn't. But you was smarter. You was more growed up than GL when you was five and he was ten, and I tried to show you that by letting you do what you wanted to do."

"That's not true, Mama. You know it. GL was light-skinned and had good hair and looked almost white and you loved him for that."

"Charles, no. No, son. I didn't love any one of you more than any other."

"That can't be true." His father was standing now, his fists clenched tight. "Admit it, Mama . . . please!" Chig looked at him, shocked; the man was actually crying.

"It may not-a been right what I done, but I ain't no liar." Chig knew she did not really understand what had happened, what he wanted of her. "I'm not lying to you, Charles."

Chig's father had gone pale. He spoke very softly. "You're about thirty years too late, Mama." He bolted from the table. Silverware and dishes rang and jumped. Chig heard him hurrying up to their room.

They sat in silence for awhile and then heard a key in the front door. A man with a new, lacquered straw hat came in. He was wearing brown and white two-tone shoes with very pointed toes and a white summer suit. "Say now! Man! I heard my brother was in town. Where he at? Where that rascal?"

He stood in the doorway, smiling broadly, an engaging, open, friendly smile, the innocent smile of a five-year-old.

Meaning

1. What reason does Chig's father give for having left home when he was fifteen? What was the real reason?
2. What kind of man has Charles Dunford become? How does his personality change when he is with his mother?
3. What reason does Dr. Dunford offer for his mother's treatment of GL? What reason does the mother give?
4. Something that turns out to be the reverse of what is expected is said to be *ironic*. Give three examples of irony in this story.

Method

1. What methods does the author use to arouse suspense in the first two paragraphs of the story?
2. An *anecdote* is a short account of an event or happening. Why does the author include the anecdote about GL and the horse? What function does it serve in the story?
3. How does the author make us aware of GL before he appears at the end of the story?

Language: Nonstandard English and Dialect

Standard English is a general term meaning the type of English which is spoken by most educated people in this country. *Nonstandard English* includes *dialect,* which is the form of a language which is characteristic of a particular place or group of people. It includes differences in word choice, grammar, sentence structure, and pronunciation, especially the distinct intonation given to particular sounds, syllables, and words. The Irish dialect in "The Quiet Man" and the black dialect in "A Visit to Grandmother" give each story an authentic quality.

Reread the following sentences from "A Visit to Grandmother." Decide how each sentence would be written in standard English. Notice how the use of dialect carries out the author's purpose in communicating character and meaning.

1. "... I was sure that boy'd come by that animal ungainly."
2. "I should-a figured how Essie's eyes ain't never been so good."
3. "It may not-a been right what I done, but I ain't no liar."
4. "Well, I'm a-looking at this horse and noticing how he be looking more and more wide awake every minute..."

Discussion and Composition

1. Write a character sketch of the grandmother. Was she kind, proud, honest, loving, unfair, resourceful, dense? Refer to specifics in the story to illustrate your characterization.

2. Like Chig's father, many of us have sometimes felt we were being treated unfairly. If you have had such feelings, write a brief account of the circumstances and how your life was affected.

3. Who has had the most effect on your life so far? Your father, your mother, another relative or person? Write or discuss how one person has affected you in a way that you think may last all of your life.

4. According to one psychological theory, there is a child, more or less hidden, in every adult. What childlike qualities seem good to you and worth keeping as an adult? What childlike qualities might cause pain and embarrassment to you as an adult?

ERNEST HEMINGWAY
(1898–1961)

One of the most influential writers of the twentieth century was Ernest Hemingway, whose style seems simple, yet is remarkably suited to his characters. His love for adventure and his obsession with death are reflected in his fiction, which often depicts strong people facing ordeals that test their courage.

Hemingway was born in Oak Park, Illinois, the oldest of seven children. His father, a doctor, introduced him to hunting and fishing, which became lifelong interests. Hemingway played football and boxed in high school, where he also began to write stories. Eager to serve in World War I, Hemingway refused to go to college, but his father would not let him enlist. Instead, Hemingway worked as a reporter on the Kansas City *Star.* In 1918, he went to Italy as an ambulance driver for the Red Cross. He was wounded and received a medal for heroism.

After the war, Hemingway worked as a newspaper correspondent in Paris, where the American colony of artists and writers encouraged him to write. His first collection of stories, *In Our Time,* was published in 1925. *The Sun Also Rises* (1926), his first novel, and *A Farewell to Arms* (1929) established him as a success. He won the Pulitzer Prize in 1953, and the Nobel Prize for literature in 1954.

Fascinated by war, big-game hunting, deep-sea fishing, and bullfighting, Hemingway's life and work were filled with adventure. In his early sixties, depressed and ill, Hemingway took his own life or was killed accidentally while cleaning a shotgun.

IN ANOTHER COUNTRY

In the fall the war was always there, but we did not go to it any more. It was cold in the fall in Milan and the dark came very early. Then the electric lights came on, and it was pleasant along the streets looking in the windows. There was much game hanging outside the shops, and the snow powdered in the fur of the foxes and the wind blew their tails. The deer hung still and heavy and empty, and small birds blew in the wind and the wind turned their feathers. It was a cold fall and the wind came down from the mountains.

We were all at the hospital every afternoon, and there were different ways of walking across the town through the dusk to the hospital. Two of the ways were alongside canals, but they were long. Always, though, you crossed a bridge across a canal to enter the hospital. There was a choice of three bridges. On one of them a woman sold roasted chestnuts. It was warm, standing in front of her charcoal fire, and the chestnuts were warm afterward in your pocket. The hospital was very old and very beautiful, and you entered through a gate and walked across a courtyard and out a gate on the other side. There were usually funerals starting from the courtyard. Beyond the old hospital were the new brick pavilions, and there we met every afternoon and were all very polite and interested in what was the matter, and sat in the machines that were to make so much difference.

The doctor came up to the machine where I was sitting and said: "What did you like best to do before the war? Did you practice a sport?"

I said: "Yes, football."

"Good," he said. "You will be able to play football again better than ever."

My knee did not bend and the leg dropped straight from the knee to the ankle without a calf, and the machine was to bend the knee and make it move as in riding a tricycle. But it did not bend yet, and instead the machine lurched when it came to the bending part. The doctor said: "That will all pass. You are a fortunate young man. You will play football again like a champion."

In the next machine was a major who had a little hand like a baby's. He winked at me when the doctor examined his hand, which was between two leather straps that bounced up and down and flapped the stiff fingers, and said: "And will I, too, play football, captain-doctor?" He had been a very great fencer, and before the war the greatest fencer in Italy.

The doctor went to his office in a back room and brought a photograph which showed a hand that had been withered almost as small as the major's, before it had taken a machine course, and after was a little larger. The major held the photograph with his good hand and looked at it very carefully. "A wound?" he asked.

"An industrial accident," the doctor said.

"Very interesting, very interesting," the major said, and handed it back to the doctor.

"You have confidence?"

"No," said the major.

There were three boys who came each day who were about the same age I was. They were all three from Milan, and one of them was to be a lawyer, and one was to be a painter, and one had intended to be a soldier, and after we were finished with the machines, sometimes we walked back together to the Café Cova, which was next door to the Scala.[1] We walked the short way through the Communist quarter because we were four together. The people hated us because we were officers, and from a wineshop someone would call out, *"A basso gli ufficiali!"*[2] as we passed. Another boy who walked with us sometimes and made five wore a black silk handkerchief across his face because he had no nose then and his face was to be rebuilt. He had gone out to the front from the military academy and been wounded within an hour after he had gone into the front line for the first time. They rebuilt his face, but he came from a very old family and they could never get the nose exactly right. He went to South America and worked in a bank. But this was a long time ago, and then we did not any of us know how it was going to be afterward. We only knew then that there was always the war, but that we were not going to it any more.

We all had the same medals, except the boy with the black silk bandage across his face, and he had not been at the front long enough to get any medals. The tall boy with a very pale face who was to be a lawyer had been a lieutenant of Arditi and had three medals of the sort we each had only one of. He had lived a very long time with death and was a little detached. We were all a little detached, and there was nothing that held us together except that we met every afternoon at the hospital. Although, as we walked to the Cova through the tough part of town, walking in the dark, with light and singing coming out of wineshops, and sometimes having to walk into the street when the men and women would crowd together on the sidewalk so that we would have had to jostle them to get by, we felt held together by there being something that had happened that they, the people who disliked us, did not understand.

We ourselves all understood the Cova, where it was rich and

1. **Scala** (skä′lə): the opera house in Milan.
2. **A basso gli ufficiali!:** Down with officers.

warm and not too brightly lighted, and noisy and smoky at certain hours, and there were always girls at the tables and the illustrated papers on a rack on the wall. The girls at the Cova were very patriotic, and I found that the most patriotic people in Italy were the café girls—and I believe they are still patriotic.

The boys at first were very polite about my medals and asked me what I had done to get them. I showed them the papers, which were written in very beautiful language and full of *fratellanza*[3] and *abnegazione*,[4] but which really said, with the adjectives removed, that I had been given the medals because I was an American. After that their manner changed a little toward me, although I was their friend against outsiders. I was a friend, but I was never really one of them after they had read the citations, because it had been different with them and they had done very different things to get their medals. I had been wounded, it was true; but we all knew that being wounded, after all, was really an accident. I was never ashamed of the ribbons, though, and sometimes, after the cocktail hour, I would imagine myself having done all the things they had done to get their medals; but walking home at night through the empty streets with the cold wind and all the shops closed, trying to keep near the streetlights, I knew that I would never have done such things, and I was very much afraid to die, and often lay in bed at night by myself, afraid to die and wondering how I would be when I went back to the front again.

The three with the medals were like hunting-hawks; and I was not a hawk, although I might seem a hawk to those who had never hunted; they, the three, knew better and so we drifted apart. But I stayed good friends with the boy who had been wounded his first day at the front, because he would never know now how he would have turned out; so he could never be accepted either, and I liked him because I thought perhaps he would not have turned out to be a hawk either.

The major, who had been the great fencer, did not believe in bravery and spent much time while we sat in the machines correcting my grammar. He had complimented me on how I spoke Italian, and we talked together very easily. One day I had said that Italian seemed such an easy language to me that I could not take a great interest in it; everything was so easy to say. "Ah, yes," the major said. "Why, then, do you not take up the use of grammar?" So we took up the use of

3. **fratellanza** (fra•təl•lantżə): brotherliness, as between allies in combat.
4. **abnegazione** (ab′•nə•gat′•zī•ō•nā): self-sacrificing.

grammar, and soon Italian was such a difficult language that I was afraid to talk to him until I had the grammar straight in my mind.

The major came very regularly to the hospital. I do not think he ever missed a day, although I am sure he did not believe in the machines. There was a time when none of us believed in the machines, and one day the major said it was all nonsense. The machines were new then and it was we who were to prove them. It was an idiotic idea, he said, "a theory, like another." I had not learned my grammar, and he said I was a stupid impossible disgrace, and he was a fool to have bothered with me. He was a small man and he sat straight up in his chair with his right hand thrust into the machine and looked straight ahead at the wall while the straps thumped up and down with his fingers in them.

"What will you do when the war is over if it is over?" he asked me. "Speak grammatically!"

"I will go to the States."

"Are you married?"

"No, but I hope to be."

"The more of a fool you are," he said. He seemed very angry. "A man must not marry."

"Why, Signor Maggiore?"

"Don't call me 'Signor Maggiore.' "

"Why must not a man marry?"

"He cannot marry. He cannot marry," he said angrily. "If he is to lose everything, he should not place himself in a position to lose that. He should not place himself in a position to lose. He should find things he cannot lose."

He spoke very angrily and bitterly, and looked straight ahead while he talked.

"But why should he necessarily lose it?"

"He'll lose it," the major said. He was looking at the wall. Then he looked down at the machine and jerked his little hand out from between the straps and slapped it hard against his thigh. "He'll lose it," he almost shouted. "Don't argue with me!" Then he called to the attendant who ran the machines. "Come and turn this damned thing off."

He went back into the other room for the light treatment and the massage. Then I heard him ask the doctor if he might use his telephone and he shut the door. When he came back into the room, I was sitting in another machine. He was wearing his cape and had his cap on, and he came directly toward my machine and put his arm on my shoulder.

"I am so sorry," he said, and patted me on the shoulder with his good hand. "I would not be rude. My wife has just died. You must forgive me."

"Oh—" I said, feeling sick for him. "I am so sorry."

He stood there, biting his lower lip. "It is very difficult," he said. "I cannot resign myself."

He looked straight past me and out through the window. Then he began to cry. "I am utterly unable to resign myself," he said and choked. And then crying, his head up looking at nothing, carrying himself straight and soldierly, with tears on both his checks and biting his lips, he walked past the machines and out the door.

The doctor told me that the major's wife, who was very young and whom he had not married until he was definitely invalided out of the war, had died of pneumonia. She had been sick only a few days. No one expected her to die. The major did not come to the hospital for three days. Then he came at the usual hour, wearing a black band on the sleeve of his uniform. When he came back, there were large framed photographs around the wall, of all sorts of wounds before and after they had been cured by the machines. In front of the machine the major used were three photographs of hands like his that were completely restored. I do not know where the doctor got them. I always understood we were the first to use the machines. The photographs did not make much difference to the major because he only looked out of the window.

Meaning and Method

1. What do all of the characters in this story have in common? What is the difference between the narrator and the other boys of his age in the story?
2. Why does the major not have much faith in the new machines?
3. The central incident of "In Another Country" is told primarily through *dialogue,* the conversation of characters in a story or play. Notice that *dialogue tags,* phrases that identify the speaker and tell how a statement is made ("she whispered quickly," for example) either are not included or are quite simple in this story. Why do you think Hemingway sometimes chose not to identify who was

speaking? What is the effect of his use of simple, spare dialogue tags?

4. This story is an example of *first-person narration.* The author tells the story from the point of view of one character and uses the pronoun *I* frequently. What are the advantages of this method of telling a story? If Hemingway had chosen to tell this story in the third-person omniscient point of view, what other changes would he have had to make?
5. Hemingway repeats several times that the major looked out the window. What is the purpose of this repetition? Reread the last paragraph of the story, and tell why you think it is a strong or weak ending.

Language: Tone

An author's choice of words and arrangement of sentences creates a *tone* or *mood* that determines how the reader will react to every character and event in a story. Writing that clearly and obviously reveals an author's personal beliefs or feelings is called *subjective.* As you read Maurice Walsh's "A Quiet Man" and William Melvin Kelley's "A Visit to Grandmother," you know how the authors feel about the characters they have created. It is clear, for example, that Walsh does not want his readers to like Liam O'Grady. Every detail that he includes about Liam places the character in an unfavorable light. Kelley's characters are more *complicated*—that is, some of them have both good qualities and bad qualities, just as people have in real life, but it is clear that Kelley admires Grandmother and sympathizes with Charles Dunford.

Hemingway, on the other hand, is a master of *objective* writing. His short, simply constructed sentences include physical details, but do not directly reveal his own feelings. Like a good newspaper reporter, he tells what happened, using strong verbs and a minimum of adjectives and adverbs. Although his tone is matter-of-fact, he communicates a strong impression by repeating important details over and over. We are told little or nothing about how Hemingway feels about his characters, but because we see and hear them in action, we know them first-hand, and they seem quite real to us.

Identify the following sentences as either objective or subjective. Make the subjective sentences objective.

1. Our cozy cabin stood at the edge of the beautiful forest.
2. Shane was quiet and strong, a magnificent giant.

3. She weighed 100 pounds and had red hair.
4. The woman at the door was carrying a suitcase.
5. As the brave astronauts landed, the crowd roared their approval.

Discussion and Composition

1. What qualities of a hawk make it a good symbol for the differences among the soldiers in this story?

2. Make up a brief dialogue between two people that reveals some aspect of at least one of the speakers' personalities. You may introduce the dialogue with a short paragraph that describes the situation, or you may begin with the dialogue.

3. The *theme* is the main idea on which a story is based. It may convey the author's feeling about an important idea or value. Try stating in a sentence or two the theme of "In Another Country." What relationship does the title have to the theme?

ANTON CHEKHOV

(1860–1904)

The short stories and plays of Anton Pavlovich Chekhov portray realistic characters and situations. He once wrote to his brother, "Don't invent sufferings which you have not experienced . . . a lie in a story is a hundred times more boring than in a conversation."

Born in Russia, Chekhov was the grandson of a liberated serf. He worked as a clerk in his father's grocery store and won a scholarship to study medicine at the University of Moscow. To help pay for his studies, he began writing humorous sketches for magazines. Although he earned a medical degree in 1884, he devoted most of his time to writing after his first collection of short stories, *Particolored Stories,* was published when he was twenty-six.

Chekhov wrote more than four hundred short stories and twelve plays about the Russian people and their lives. *The Three Sisters* (1901) and *The Cherry Orchard* (1904), plays that he wrote toward the end of his life, when he was ill with tuberculosis, are considered his masterpieces.

THE BET

It was a dark autumn night. The old banker was walking up and down his study and remembering how, fifteen years before, he had given a party one autumn evening. There had been many clever men there, and there had been interesting conversations. Among other things, they had talked of capital punishment. The majority of the guests, among whom were many journalists and intellectual men, disapproved of the death penalty. They considered that form of punishment out of date, immoral, and unsuitable for Christian states. In the opinion of some of them the death penalty ought to be replaced everywhere by imprisonment for life.

"I don't agree with you," said their host the banker. "I have not tried either the death penalty or imprisonment for life, but if one may judge *a priori,* the death penalty is more moral and more humane than imprisonment for life. Capital punishment kills a man at once, but lifelong imprisonment kills him slowly. Which executioner is the more humane, he who kills you in a few minutes or he who drags the life out of you in the course of many years?"

"Both are equally immoral," observed one of the guests, "for they both have the same object—to take away life. The State is not God. It has not the right to take away what it cannot restore when it wants to."

Among the guests was a young lawyer, a young man of five-and-twenty. When he was asked his opinion, he said:

"The death sentence and the life sentence are equally immoral, but if I had to choose between the death penalty and imprisonment for life, I would certainly chose the second. To live anyhow is better than not at all."

A lively discussion arose. The banker, who was younger and more nervous in those days, was suddenly carried away by excitement; he struck the table with his fist and shouted at the young man:

"It's not true! I'll bet you two millions[1] you wouldn't stay in solitary confinement for five years."

"If you mean that in earnest," said the young man, "I'll take the bet, but I would stay not five but fifteen years."

"Fifteen? Done!" cried the banker. "Gentlemen, I stake two millions!"

"Agreed! You stake your millions and I stake my freedom!" said the young man.

And this wild, senseless bet was carried out! The banker, spoiled and frivolous, with millions beyond his reckoning, was delighted at the bet. At supper he made fun of the young man, and said:

"Think better of it, young man, while there is still time. To me two millions are a trifle, but you are losing three or four of the best years of your life. I say three or four, because you won't stay longer. Don't forget either, you unhappy man, that voluntary confinement is a great deal harder to bear than compulsory. The thought that you have the right to step out in liberty at any moment will poison your whole existence in prison. I am sorry for you."

And now the banker, walking to and fro, remembered all this, and asked himself: "What was the object of that bet? What is the good of that man's losing fifteen years of his life and my throwing away two millions? Can it prove that the death penalty is better or worse than imprisonment for life? No, no. It was all nonsensical and

1. millions: refers to rubles. A ruble in pre-Revolutionary Russia was worth about fifty cents in American money.

meaningless. On my part it was the caprice of a pampered man, and on his part simple greed for money. . . ."

Then he remembered what followed that evening. It was decided that the young man should spend the years of his captivity under the strictest supervision in one of the lodges in the banker's garden. It was agreed that for fifteen years he should not be free to cross the threshold of the lodge, to see human beings, to hear the human voice, or to receive letters and newspapers. He was allowed to have a musical instrument and books, and was allowed to write letters, to drink wine, and to smoke. By the terms of the agreement, the only relations he could have with the outer world were by a little window made purposely for that object. He might have anything he wanted—books, music, wine, and so on—in any quantity he desired, by writing an order, but could receive them only through the window. The agreement provided for every detail and every trifle that would make his imprisonment strictly solitary, and bound the young man to stay there *exactly* fifteen years, beginning from twelve o'clock of November 14, 1870, and ending at twelve o'clock of November 14, 1885. The slightest attempt on his part to break the conditions, if only two minutes before the end, released the banker from the obligation to pay him two millions.

For the first year of his confinement, as far as one could judge from his brief notes, the prisoner suffered severely from loneliness and depression. The sounds of the piano could be heard continually day and night from his lodge. He refused wine and tobacco. Wine, he wrote, excites the desires, and desires are the worst foes of the prisoner; and besides, nothing could be more dreary than drinking good wine and seeing no one. And tobacco spoiled the air of his room. In the first year the books he sent for were principally of a light character; novels with a complicated love plot, sensational and fantastic stories, and so on.

In the second year the piano was silent in the lodge, and the prisoner asked only for the classics. In the fifth year music was audible again, and the prisoner asked for wine. Those who watched him through the window said that all that year he spent doing nothing but eating and drinking and lying on his bed, frequently yawning and talking angrily to himself. He did not read books. Sometimes at night he would sit down to write; he would spend hours writing, and in the morning tear up all that he had written. More than once he could be heard crying.

In the second half of the sixth year the prisoner began zealously studying languages, philosophy, and history. He threw himself eagerly into these studies—so much so that the banker had enough to do to get him the books he ordered. In the course of four years some six hundred volumes were procured at his request. It was during this period that the banker received the following letter from his prisoner:

"My dear Jailer, I write you these lines in six languages. Show them to people who know the languages. Let them read them. If they find not one mistake, I implore you to fire a shot in the garden. That shot will show me that my efforts have not been thrown away. The geniuses of all ages and of all lands speak different languages, but the same flame burns in them all. Oh, if you only knew what unearthly happiness my soul feels now from being able to understand them!" The prisoner's desire was fulfilled. The banker ordered two shots to be fired in the garden.

Then, after the tenth year, the prisoner sat immovably at the table and read nothing but the Gospel. It seemed strange to the banker that a man who in four years had mastered six hundred learned volumes should waste nearly a year over one thin book easy of comprehension. Theology and histories of religion followed the Gospels.

In the last two years of his confinement the prisoner read an immense quantity of books quite indiscriminately. At one time he was busy with the natural sciences, then he would ask for Byron or Shakespeare. There were notes in which he demanded at the same time books on chemistry, and a manual of medicine, and a novel, and some treatise on philosophy or theology. His reading suggested a man swimming in the sea among the wreckage of his ship, and trying to save his life by greedily clutching first at one spar and then at another.

The old banker remembered all this, and thought:

"Tomorrow at twelve o'clock he will regain his freedom. By our agreement I ought to pay him two millions. If I do pay him, it is all over with me: I shall be utterly ruined."

Fifteen years before, his millions had been beyond his reckoning; now he was afraid to ask himself which were greater, his debts or his assets. Desperate gambling on the Stock Exchange, wild speculation, and the excitability which he could not get over even in advancing years, had by degrees led to the decline of his fortune, and the proud, fearless, self-confident millionaire had become a banker of middling rank, trembling at every rise and fall in his investments. "Cursed bet!" muttered the old man, clutching his head in despair. "Why didn't the man die? He is only forty now. He will take my last penny from me, he will marry, will enjoy life, will gamble on the Exchange; while I shall look at him with envy like a beggar, and hear from him every day the same sentence: 'I am indebted to you for the happiness of my life, let me help you!' No, it is too much! The one means of being saved from bankruptcy and disgrace is the death of that man!"

It struck three o'clock. The banker listened; everyone was asleep in the house, and nothing could be heard outside but the rustling of the chilled trees. Trying to make no noise, he took from a fireproof safe the key of the door which had not been opened for fifteen years, put on his overcoat, and went out of the house.

It was dark and cold in the garden. Rain was falling. A damp, cutting wind was racing about the garden, howling and giving the trees no rest. The banker strained his eyes, but could see neither the earth nor the white statues, nor the lodge, nor the trees. Going to the spot where the lodge stood, he twice called the watchman. No answer followed. Evidently the watchman had sought shelter from the weather, and was now asleep somewhere either in the kitchen or in the greenhouse.

"If I had the pluck to carry out my intention," thought the old man, "suspicion would fall first upon the watchman."

He felt in the darkness for the steps and the door, and went into the entry of the lodge. Then he groped his way into a little passage and lighted a match. There was not a soul there. There was a bedstead with no bedding on it, and in the corner there was a dark cast-iron stove. The seals on the door leading to the prisoner's rooms were intact.

When the match went out the old man, trembling with emotion, peeped through the little window. A candle was burning dimly in the prisoner's room. He was sitting at the table. Nothing could be seen but his back, the hair on his head, and his hands. Open books were lying on the table, on the two easy chairs, and on the carpet near the table.

Five minutes passed and the prisoner did not once stir. Fifteen years' imprisonment had taught him to sit still. The banker tapped at the window with his finger, and the prisoner made no movement whatever in response. Then the banker cautiously broke the seals off the door and put the key in the keyhole. The rusty lock gave a grating sound and the door creaked. The banker expected to hear at once footsteps and a cry of astonishment, but three minutes passed and it was as quiet as ever in the room. He made up his mind to go in.

At the table a man unlike ordinary people was sitting motionless. He was a skeleton with the skin drawn tight over his bones, with long curls like a woman's, and a shaggy beard. His face was yellow with an earthy tint in it, his cheeks were hollow, his back long and narrow, and the hand on which his shaggy head was propped was so thin and delicate that it was dreadful to look at it. His hair was already streaked with silver, and seeing his emaciated,[2] aged-looking face, no one would have believed that he was only forty. He was asleep. . . . In front of his bowed head there lay on the table a sheet of paper, on which there was something written in fine handwriting.

"Poor creature!" thought the banker, "he is asleep and most likely dreaming of the millions. And I have only to take this half-dead man, throw him on the bed, stifle him a little with the pillow, and the most conscientious expert would find no sign of a violent death. But let us first read what he has written here. . . ."

The banker took the page from the table and read as follows:

"Tomorrow at twelve o'clock I regain my freedom and the right to associate with other men, but before I leave this room and see the sunshine, I think it necessary to say a few words to you. With a clear conscience I tell you, as before God, who beholds me, that I despise freedom and life and health, and all that your books call the good things of the world.

"For fifteen years I have been intently studying earthly life. It is true I have not seen the earth nor men, but in your books I have drunk fragrant wine, I have sung songs, I have hunted stags and wild boars in the forests, have loved women. . . . Beauties as ethereal as clouds, created by the magic of your poets and geniuses, have visited me at night, and have whispered in my ears wonderful tales that have set my brain in a whirl. In your books I have climbed to the peaks of Elburz and Mont Blanc, and from there I have seen the sun rise and have watched it at evening flood the sky, the ocean, and the mountaintops with gold and crimson. I have watched from there the lightning flashing over my head and cleaving[3] the storm clouds. I have seen green forests, fields, rivers, lakes, towns. I have heard the singing of the sirens, and the strains of the shepherds' pipes; I have touched the wings of comely devils who flew down to converse with

2. emaciated (ĭ·mā′shē·ā′tĭd): very thin; wasted away.
3. cleaving (klēv′ĭng): splitting.

me of God. . . . In your books I have flung myself into the bottomless pit, performed miracles, slain, burned towns, preached new religions, conquered whole kingdoms. . . .

"Your books have given me wisdom. All that the unresting thought of man has created in the ages is compressed into a small compass in my brain. I know that I am wiser than all of you.

"And I despise your books, I despise wisdom and the blessings of this world. It is all worthless, fleeting, illusory, and deceptive, like a mirage. You may be proud, wise, and fine, but death will wipe you off the face of the earth as though you were no more than mice burrowing under the floor, and your posterity, your history, your immortal geniuses will burn or freeze together with the earthly globe.

"You have lost your reason and taken the wrong path. You have taken lies for truth, and hideousness for beauty. You would marvel if, owing to strange events of some sort, frogs and lizards suddenly grew on apple and orange trees instead of fruit, or if roses began to smell like a sweating horse; so I marvel at you who exchange heaven for earth. I don't want to understand you.

"To prove to you in action how I despise all that you live by, I renounce the two millions of which I once dreamed as of paradise and which now I despise. To deprive myself of the right to the money I shall go out from here five minutes before the time fixed, and so break the compact. . . ."

When the banker had read this he laid the page on the table, kissed the strange man on the head, and went out of the lodge, weeping. At no other time, even when he had lost heavily on the Stock Exchange, had he felt so great a contempt for himself. When he got home he lay on his bed, but his tears and emotion kept him for hours from sleeping.

Next morning the watchmen ran in with pale faces, and told him they had seen the man who lived in the lodge climb out of the window into the garden, go to the gate, and disappear. The banker went at once with the servants to the lodge and made sure of the flight of his prisoner. To avoid arousing unnecessary talk, he took from the table the writing in which the millions were renounced, and when he got home locked it up in the fireproof safe.

Meaning

1. What are the terms of the bet made between the young lawyer and the middle-aged banker?
2. How does the lawyer change during his fifteen years of imprisonment? How does the banker change?
3. What is ironic about the outcome of the bet?
4. Which of the following themes do you consider to be most appropriate for this story? Give reasons for your answer.
   a. Life imprisonment is worse than capital punishment.
   b. The fewer one's material needs and illusions, the greater one's freedom.
   c. One way or another, all human beings discover the vanities of life.
   d. What actually takes place in life often falls far short of our expectations.
   e. Life is a game of chance.

Method

1. This story is told from the third-person omniscient point of view. Explain this method briefly in your own words.
2. The *flashback* is a technique by which an author focuses on, or flashes back to, an episode or incident that took place prior to the opening situation of a story. What is the purpose of the flashback in this story?
3. Dialogue is one means of portraying character. Quote lines from the banker's and lawyer's conversations at the dinner party that reveal their temperaments and attitudes.
4. An author sometimes uses setting and atmosphere to reflect a person's state of mind, as in the following: "It was dark and cold in the garden. Rain was falling. A damp, cutting wind was racing about the garden, howling and giving the trees no rest. The banker strained his eyes, but could see neither the earth nor the white statues, nor the lodge, nor the trees."

   How does this description of the garden reflect the banker's mood as he heads for the lodge where the lawyer is confined?

Language: Words and Phrases from Latin

During the discussion of capital punishment at the dinner party, the banker speaks of reasoning *a priori*. This phrase comes directly from two Latin words: *a* (from) and *prior* (former or first), and literally means "from the preceding." If something is known *a priori*, it is known simply by reasoning from what is self-evident. It does not have to be supported by facts or experience. For example, the banker says, "I have not tried either the death penalty or imprisonment for life, but if one may judge *a priori*, the death penalty is more moral and more humane than imprisonment for life."

Many English words and phrases are derived directly from Latin. Check your dictionary to find the meaning of the Latin word or phrase which is the basis for each of the following:

1. capital
2. *bona fide*
3. executioner
4. conscience
5. *ipso facto*
6. *summa cum laude*
7. voluntary
8. miracle
9. *obiter dictum*
10. *prima facie*

Discussion and Composition

1. Support or refute the following statement by giving reasons, examples, comparisons, and contrasts: "To live, regardless of how, is better than not to live at all."

2. As the basis for a composition or a debate, use the topic sentence "Capital punishment should (or should not) be abolished." As preparation for this assignment, write an outline in which you state **a.** the problem, **b.** the pros and cons, and **c.** your recommendations and solutions.

3. If you had to be isolated for three months, what books would you choose to take with you? Give a reason for each choice.

4. You have seen how setting can be used to develop and emphasize a tone or mood. Choose a mood, and write a paragraph in which you describe a setting that reflects it. Here are some ideas for moods:

happy
sad
bored
angry
impatient
humorous
loving
dream-like
tense
fearful

JESSAMYN WEST
(born 1907)

Gentle humor and good will pervade the work of Jessamyn West. Most of her stories are set in Indiana, where she was born. For her first book, *The Friendly Persuasion* (1945), from which the following selection is taken, she drew upon the legends she had heard from childhood about her Irish Quaker ancestors in Indiana. Eliza, the mother, is a composite of Miss West's own grandmothers, both of whom were Quaker preachers.

Miss West has lived in California most of her life. She attended Whittier College in California and studied for a year at Oxford, England. While studying for her doctorate at the University of California, she became so ill with tuberculosis that she was not expected to recover. While her mother nursed her back to health, Miss West began writing down the family stories that her mother told her; this marked the start of her writing career. *The Woman Said Yes* (1976) tells of her fight for life, and also contains biographical material about her mother and sister.

Miss West has written several novels and movie scripts. Her stories appear frequently in magazines, and she often lectures on writing at college campuses and writing conferences.

THE PACING GOOSE

Jess sat in the kitchen at the long table by the west window where in winter he kept his grafting tools: the thin-bladed knife, the paper sweet with the smell of beeswax and the resin, the boxes of roots and scions.[1] Jess was a nurseryman and spring meant for him not only spirits flowering—but the earth's. A week more of moderating weather and he'd be out, still in gum boots, but touching an earth that had thawed, whose riches were once again fluid enough to be

1. **scions** (sī′ənz): twigs or shoots prepared for grafting.

sucked upward, toward those burgeonings[2] which by summer would have swelled into Early Harvests, Permains, and Sweet Bows.[3]

Spring's a various season, Jess thought, no two years the same: comes in with rains, mud deep enough to swallow horse and rider; comes in cold, snow falling so fast it weaves a web; comes in with a warm wind blowing about thy ears and bringing a smell of something flowering, not here, but southaways, across the Ohio, maybe, in Kentucky. Nothing here now but a smell of melting snow—which is no smell at all, but a kind of prickle in the nose, like a bygone sneeze. Comes in so various, winter put by and always so welcome.

"And us each spring so much the same."

"Thee speaking to me, Jess?"

"Nothing thee'd understand, Eliza."

Spring made Jess discontented with the human race—and with women, if anything more than men. It looked as if spring put them all in the shade: the season so resourceful and they each year meeting it with nothing changed from last year, digging up roots from the same sassafras thicket, licking sulfur and molasses[4] from the big-bowled spoon.

Behind him the table was set for supper, plates neatly turned to cover the bone-handled knives and forks, spoon vase aglitter with steel well burnished by brick dust, dishes of jam with more light to them than the sun, which was dwindling away, peaked and overcast, outside his window.

"Spring opening up," he said, "and nobody in this house so much as putting down a line of poetry."

Eliza, who was lifting dried-peach pies from a hot oven, said nothing. She set the four of them in a neat row on the edge of her kitchen cabinet to cool, and slid her pans of cornbread into the oven. Then she turned to Jess, her cheeks red with heat and her black eyes warm with what she had to say: "Thee'd maybe relish a nice little rhyme for thy supper, Jess Birdwell."

Jess sighed, then sniffed the pies, so rich with ripe peach flavor that the kitchen smelled like a summer orchard, nothing lacking but the sound of bees. "Now, Eliza," he said, "thee knows I wouldn't have thee anyways altered. Thee . . ."

2. **burgeonings** (bûr′jən•ingz): buds or sprouts.

3. **Early . . . Bows:** varieties of apples.

4. **sulfur and molasses:** an old-fashioned "spring tonic." In theory this medication would alter the thickness of the blood as required for different seasons.

"Thee," Eliza interrupted him, "is like all men. Thee wants to have thy poetry and eat it too."

Jess wondered how what he'd felt about spring, a season with the Lord's thumbprint fresh on it, could've led to anything so unspring-like as an argument about a batch of dried-peach pies.

"Eliza," he said firmly, "I didn't mean thee. Though it's crossed my mind sometimes as strange that none of the boys have ever turned, this time of year, to rhyming."

"Josh writes poems," Eliza said.

"Thee ever read what Josh writes, Eliza?"

Eliza nodded.

Ah, well, Jess thought, no use at this late date to tell her what's the difference.

Eliza looked her husband over carefully. "Jess Birdwell," she said, "thee's full of humors.[5] Thy blood needs thinning. I'll boil thee up a good cup of sassafras tea."

Jess turned away from the green and gold sunset and the patches of snow it was gilding and fairly faced the dried-peach pies and Eliza, who was dropping dumplings into a pot of beans.

"That's just it, Eliza," he said. "That's just the rub."

Eliza gave him no encouragement, but he went on anyway. "Earth alters, season to season, spring comes in never two times the same, only us pounding on steady as pump bolts and not freshened by so much as a grass blade."

"Jess, thee's got spring fever."

"I could reckon time and temperature, each spring, by the way thee starts honing[6] for geese. 'Jess, don't thee think we might have a few geese?' It's a tardy spring," Jess said. "Snow still on the ground and not a word yet from thee about geese."

Eliza pulled a chair out from the table and sat. "Jess, why's thee always been so set against geese?"

"I'm not set against geese. It's geese that's set against farming. They can mow down a half-acre of sprouting corn while thee's trying to head them off—and in two minutes they'll level a row of pie plant it's taken two years to get started. No, Eliza, it's the geese that's against me."

"If thee had tight fences . . ." Eliza said.

"Eliza, I got tight fences, but the goose's never been hatched

5. **humors:** moods, whims.
6. **honing** (hōn′ĭng): *dialect,* yearning.

that'll admit fences exist. And an old gander'd just as soon go through a fence as hiss—and if he can't find a hole or crack in a fence he'll lift the latch."

"Jess," said Eliza flatly, "thee don't like geese."

"Well," said Jess, "I wouldn't go so far's to say I didn't like them, but I will say that if there's any meaner, dirtier animal, or one that glories in it more, I don't know it. And a thing I've never been able to understand about thee, Eliza, is what thee sees in the shifty-eyed birds."

"Geese," said Eliza, with a dreaminess unusual to her, "march along so lordly like . . . they're pretty as swans floating down a branch . . . in fall they stretch out their necks and honk to geese passing overhead as if they's wild. My father never had any trouble raising geese and I've heard him say many a time that there's no better food for a brisk morning than a fried goose egg."

Jess knew, with spring his topic, he'd ought to pass over Eliza's father and his fried goose egg, but he couldn't help saying. "A fried goose egg always had a kind of bloated look to me, Eliza"—but then he went on fast. "The season's shaping up," he said, "I can see thee's all primed to say, 'Jess, let's get a setting of goose eggs.' "

Eliza went over to the bean kettle and began to lift out dumplings. "It's a forwarder season than thee thinks, Jess," she said. "I got a setting under a hen now."

Jess looked at his wife. He didn't know what had made him want spring's variety in a human being—nor Eliza's substituting doing for asking. And speaking of it just now, as he had, made opposition kind of ticklish.

"When'd thee set them?" he asked finally.

"Yesterday," said Eliza.

"Where'd thee get the eggs?"

"Overbys'," said Eliza. The Overbys were their neighbors to the south.

"Well, they got enough for a surety," Jess said, "to give a few away."

"The Overbys don't give anything away, as thee knows. I paid for them. With my own money," Eliza added.

"How many?" Jess asked.

"Eight," Eliza said.

Jess turned back to his window. The sun had set, leaving a sad green sky and desolate black and white earth. "Five acres of corn gone," he calculated.

"Thee said," Eliza reminded him, "that what thee wanted was a little variety in me. 'Steady as a pump bolt,' were thy words."

"I know I did," Jess admitted glumly, "I talk too much."

"Draw up thy chair," Eliza said placidly, not contradicting him; "here's Enoch and the boys."

Next morning after breakfast Jess and Enoch left the kitchen together. The sun was the warmest the year had yet produced and the farm roofs were steaming; south branch, swollen by melting snow, was running so full the soft lap of its eddies could be heard in the barnyard; a rooster tossed his voice into the bright air, loud and clear, as if aiming to be heard by every fowl in Jennings County.

"Enoch," said Jess to his hired man, "what's thy feeling about geese?"

Enoch was instantly equipped, for the most part, with feelings on every subject. Geese was a homelier topic than he'd choose himself to enlarge upon, not one that could be much embellished nor one on which Mr. Emerson,[7] so far's he could recall, had ever expressed an opinion. "In the fall of the year," he said, "long about November or December, there's nothing tastier on the table than roast goose."

"Goose on the table's not what I mean," Jess said. "I was speaking of goose on the hoof. Goose nipping off a stand of corn, Enoch, goose roistering around, honking and hissing so's thee can't hear thyself think, goose eying thee like a snake on stilts."

Enoch gazed at his employer for a few seconds. "Mr. Birdwell," he said, "I think that if they's an ornery bird it's a goose. Ornery and undependable."

"I'm glad we's so like minded about them," Jess said. "Otherwise, I'd not like to ask thee to do this little job." He pulled a long darning needle from beneath the lapel of his coat.

Enoch eyed it with some mistrust. "I can't say's I've ever been handy with a needle, Mr. Birdwell."

"Thee'll be handy enough for this," Jess said with hearty conviction. "To come to it, Enoch, Eliza's set eight goose eggs. Next year with any luck she'd have two dozen. And so on. More and more. Feeling the way thee does, Enoch, about geese, it's no more'n fair to give thee a chance to put a stop to this before it goes too far. One little puncture in each egg with this and the goose project's nipped in the bud and Eliza none the wiser."

7. Mr. Emerson: Ralph Waldo Emerson, American essayist and poet (1803–1882).

"I'm mighty awkward with my hands," said Enoch, "doing fine work. Ticklish job like this I might drop an egg and break it."

"Enoch," said Jess, "thee's not developing a weakness for geese, is thee?"

"It ain't the geese," said Enoch frankly, "it's your wife. She's been mighty clever[8] to me and if she's got her heart set on geese, it'd go against the grain to disappoint her. Whyn't you do it, Mr. Birdwell?"

"Same reason," said Jess, "only more of them—and if Eliza ever asks if I tampered with that setting of eggs I figure on being able to say no." Jess held the needle nearer Enoch, who looked at it but still made no motion to take it.

"Likely no need to do a thing," Enoch said. "Two to one those eggs'll never hatch anyways. Overbys're such a fox-eared tribe they more'n likely sold her bad eggs to begin with."

"Thee's knowed about this," Jess asked, "all along?"

"Yes," Enoch said.

"Here's the needle," Jess said.

"You look at this," Enoch inquired, "not so much as a favor asked as a part of the day's work with orders from you?"

"Yes," Jess said, "that's about the way I look at it."

Enoch took the needle, held it somewhat gingerly, and with the sun glinting across its length walked slowly toward the chicken house.

It takes thirty days for a goose egg to hatch, and the time, with spring work to be done, went fast. The hen Eliza had picked was a good one and kept her mind strictly on her setting. Eliza kept her mind on the hen, and Jess and Enoch found their minds oftener than they liked on Eliza and her hoped-for geese.

At breakfast on the day the geese were due to break their shells Jess said, "If I's thee, Eliza, I wouldn't bank too much on them geese. I heard Enoch say a while back he wouldn't be surprised if not an egg hatched. Thought the eggs were likely no good."

Enoch was busy pouring coffee into a saucer, then busy cooling it, but Eliza waited until he was through. "Did thee say that, Enoch?"

Enoch looked at Jess. "Yes," he said, "I kind of recollect something of the sort."

8. clever: *dialect,* good-natured, kind.

"What made thee think so, Enoch?"

"Why," said Jess, for Enoch was busy with his coffee again, "it was the Overbys. Enoch's got a feeling they's kind of unreliable. Fox-eared, I think thee said, Enoch, didn't thee?"

Enoch's work took him outside almost at once, and Jess himself said, "If thee'll just give me a little packet of food, Eliza, I won't trouble thee for anything at noon. I'm going to be over'n the south forty and it'll save time coming and going."

Eliza was surprised, for Jess'd usually come twice as far for a hot dinner at midday, but she made him fried ham sandwiches and put them and some cold apple turnovers in a bag.

"It's a pity thee has to miss thy dinner," she told him, but Jess only said, "Press of work, press of work," and hurriedly departed.

Jess came home that evening through the spring twilight, somewhat late, and found a number of things to do at the barn before he went up to the house. When he entered the kitchen nothing seemed amiss—lamps ruddy, table set, stove humming, and beside the stove a small box over which Eliza was bending. Jess stopped to look—and listen; from inside the box was coming a kind of birdlike peeping, soft and not unpleasant. Reluctantly he walked to Eliza's side. There, eating minced boiled egg, and between bites lifting its beak to Eliza, it seemed, and making those chirping sounds he'd heard, was a gray-gold gosling.

Eliza looked up pleasantly. "Enoch was right," she said. "The eggs were bad. Only one hatched. I plan to call it Samantha," she told Jess. "It's a name I've always been partial to."

"Samantha," said Jess, without any enthusiasm whatever for either name or gosling. "How's thee know it's a she?"

"I don't," said Eliza, "but if it's a gander it's a name easily changed to Sam."

Enoch came in just then with a load of wood for the kitchen woodbox. "Enoch," said Jess, "has thee seen Samantha—or Sam?"

Enoch mumbled but Jess understood him to say he had.

"It was my understanding, Enoch, that thy opinion was that all those eggs were bad."

"Well, Mr. Birdwell," said Enoch, "a man could make a mistake. He could count wrong."

"A man ought to be able to count to eight without going astray," said Jess.

Eliza was paying no attention to either of them; she was making little tweeting sounds herself, bending over the chirping gosling. "Does thee know," she asked Jess, "that this is the first pet I ever had in my life?"

"Thee's got Ebony," Jess said.

"I don't mean a caged pet," Eliza said, "but one to walk beside thee. I'm reconciled the others didn't hatch. With eight I'd've had to raise geese for the table. With one only I can make Samantha a pure pet."

A pure pet was what she made of her: Samantha ate what the family ate, with the exception of articles which Eliza thought might be indigestible and would risk on humans but not on her goose. Cake, pie, corn on the cob, there was nothing too good for Samantha. From a big-footed, gold-downed gosling she swelled, almost at once, like a slack sail which gets a sudden breeze, into a full-rounded convexity.

"Emphasis on the vexity," Jess said when he thought of this. Samantha was everything he'd disliked in the general run of geese, with added traits peculiar to herself, which vexed him. Because she was fed at the doorstep, she was always underfoot. No shout, however loud, would move her before she's ready to move. If she's talked to too strong she'd flail you with her wings and pinch the calf of your leg until for some days it would look to be mortifying. She'd take food out of children's hands, and the pansies Jess had planted in a circle at the base of the Juneberry tree she sheared so close that there was not a naked stem left to show for all his work. And when not being crossed in any way, Jess simply looking at her and meditating, trying to fathom Samantha's fascination for Eliza, the goose would suddenly extend her snakelike neck and, almost touching Jess, hiss with such a hint of icy disapprobation that Jess would involuntarily recoil.

But she was Eliza's pure pet, no two ways about that, and would lift her head for Eliza to scratch, and walk beside her with the lordly roll of the known elect.

"There was some goddess," Enoch remembered, "who always had a big bird with her." Jess supposed Enoch was thinking of Juno and her peacock, but the reference didn't convince him that a goose was a suitable companion for any goddess—let alone Eliza, and he couldn't honestly feel much regret when one evening toward the end of November Eliza told him Samantha was missing. "She'll turn up," Jess said. "That bird's too ornery to die young."

Eliza said nothing, but next evening she proved Jess was right. "Samantha's over at Overbys'," she said.

"Well, did thee fetch her home?" Jess asked.

"No," said Eliza with righteous indignation, "they wouldn't let me. They said they had forty geese—and forty's what they got now, and they don't think Samantha's there. They provoked me so, Jess, I told them they'd sold me seven bad eggs and now they try to take the eighth away from me."

Jess felt a little abashed at this, but he asked, "How can thee be so sure Samantha's there? She might've been carried off by a varmint."

Eliza was scornful. "Thee forgets I hand-raised Samantha from a gosling. I'd know her among four hundred—let alone forty."

"Whyn't thee buy her back then," Jess asked, "if that's the only way?"

"After what I said about their eggs," Eliza answered sadly, "the Overbys say they don't want any more dealings with me."

Eliza mourned so for the lost Samantha that first Enoch and then Jess went over to the Overbys', but no one there would admit the presence of a visiting goose—forty they had, and forty you could see by counting was what they had now. Short of force, there didn't seem any way of getting Samantha home again.

When Eliza heard the Overbys were going to sell geese for Christmas eating she was frantic. "Jess," she said, "I just can't bear to think of Samantha plucked naked and resting on a table waiting to be carved. She used to sing as sweet as any bird when she was little, and she'd walk by my side taking the air. She's the only goose I ever heard of," Eliza remembered mournfully, "who'd drink tea."

In Jess's opinion a goose'd eat anything at either end of the scale, but he didn't suppose this was a suitable time to mention it to Eliza. "Eliza," he said, "short of me and Enoch's going over there and using force on old man Overby—or sneaking over at night and breaking into their chicken pen, I don't know how in the world we're going to get Samantha back for thee."

"We could sue," said Eliza.

"Thee mean go to law?" Jess asked, astounded. Quakers stayed out of courts, believing in amicable settlements without recourse to law.

"Yes," said Eliza. "I'd do it for Samantha. I'd think it my duty. Going to law'd be a misery for us . . . but not so lasting a misery as being roasted would be for Samantha."

Jess couldn't deny this, but he said, "I'd have to think it over. I've never been to law yet in my life and suing for a gone goose don't seem to me a very likely place to start."

Next morning Eliza served a good but silent breakfast, not sitting herself to eat with the rest of her family.

"Thee feeling dauncy,[9] Eliza?" Jess asked.

"I just can't eat," she said, "for thinking of Samantha."

Labe and Mattie had tears in their eyes. Little Jess was mournfully bellowing. Enoch looked mighty glum. Jess felt ashamed to be swallowing victuals in the midst of so much sorrow. Eliza stood at the end of the stove where the gosling's box had rested for the first few weeks of its life, looking down, as if remembering how it had sung and lifted its beak to her.

Jess couldn't stand it. "Eliza," he said, "if thee wants to go through with it I'll go to Vernon and fee a lawyer for thee. Thee'll have to go to court, be on the witness stand—and even then I misdoubt thee'll ever get thy goose back. Does thee still want me to do it?"

Eliza came to the table and stood with her hand on Jess's shoulder. "Yes, Jess," she said, "I want thee to do it."

Jess went to Vernon, fee'd a lawyer, had a restraining order put on the Overbys so they couldn't sell or kill the goose Eliza said was Samantha, and awaited with misgivings the day of the trial. It came in mid-December.

Eliza, Jess, and Enoch rode to the trial through a fall of light, fresh snow. Brilliant sunlight, crisp air, glittering snow, and Rome's[10] spirited stepping made the occasion, in spite of its purpose, seem festive. Eliza made it seem festive. Jess, who did not forget its purpose, regarded her with some wonder. He couldn't say what it was about her—dress and bonnet appeared to be simply her First Day[11] best—but she had a holiday air.

He considered it his duty to warn her. "Eliza," he said, "thee understands thee's not going to Meeting?[12] They're not going to sit silent while thee tells them how much thee loves Samantha and how she sang when young and drank tea. Old man Overby'll have his say and he's got a lawyer hired for no other purpose than to trip thee up."

9. **dauncy:** *dialect,* sick.
10. **Rome:** the Birdwells' carriage horse.
11. **First Day:** the Quaker term for Sunday.
12. **Meeting:** the Quaker church service.

Eliza was unimpressed. "What's our lawyer fee'd for, Jess?" she asked.

Jess took another tack. "Eliza," he told her, "I don't figger thee's got a chance in a thousand to get Samantha back."

"This is a court of justice, isn't it?" Eliza asked.

"Yes," Jess said.

"Then there's no need for thee to fash[13] thyself, Jess Birdwell. I'll get Samantha back."

Not getting Samantha back wasn't what fashed Jess—he reckoned he could bear up under that mighty well. What fashed him was the whole shooting match. . . . In some few cases, matters of life and death, going to court might be necessary, and he could imagine such. But a suit over a goose named Samantha wasn't one of them. And poor Eliza. Law to her was all Greek and turkey tracks . . . and here she was bound for court as chipper as if she was Chief Justice Taney[14] himself. Jess sighed and shook his head. Getting shut of Samantha would be no hardship for him, but he was downcast for Eliza's sake and the way she'd have to turn homeward empty-handed.

In the courtroom, hard clear light reflected upward from the snow fell onto what Jess thought were hard faces: courthouse hangers-on; farmers whose slackening work made the diversion of a trial an inviting possibility; lovers of oddity who figured a tilt between a Quaker female, preacher to boot, and an old sinner like Milt Overby over the ownership of a goose ought to produce some enlivening quirks. They stared at Eliza, exchanged salutes with Milt Overby, and inspected Samantha, who in her crate awaited the court's decision.

The two lawyers Jess considered to be on a par. Nothing fancy, either one . . . old roadsters both, gone gray in service and with a knowledge of their business. The circuit judge was something else, unaccountably young, jug-eared and dressed more sprightly than a groom for his own wedding. A city whippersnapper, born and trained north of the Mississinewa,[15] and now, in Jess's opinion, setting a squeamish foot in backwoods provinces, and irked to find himself trying so trifling a case. Didn't know a goose from a guinea hen, like as not, and would consider tossing a coin a more suitable manner of

13. fash: vex, annoy, bother.

14. Taney (tā′nē): Roger B. Taney, Chief Justice of the Supreme Court (1836–1864).

15. Mississinewa (mĭs′ə·sĭn′e·wä): a small river in Indiana flowing into the Wabash River.

settling such a matter—just as near right in the end—and his valuable time saved.

Eliza, Jess saw, was of no such opinion. She, too, was scanning the young judge, and Jess, who knew her, saw from the look on her face that she was taken by him. A neat, thin, pious boy—far from home—he looked, no doubt, to her; a young man who could do with better cooking and more regular eating.

The young man rapped the court to order. Spitting and shuffling slackened and in a high, precise voice he read, "Birdwell versus Overby. Charge, petty larceny. Appropriation and willful withholding of goose named Samantha." The name Samantha seemed to somewhat choke him, but he got it out.

"Ready for Birdwell," said Mr. Abel Samp, Eliza's lawyer.

"Ready for Overby," said the defendant's lawyer.

Eliza was the first witness on the stand. Jess sometimes forgot what a good-looking woman Eliza was, but the interest shown on lifted faces all about him refreshed his memory.

"Swear the plaintiff in," the judge said.

Eliza, in her sweet voice, spoke directly to the judge. "I don't swear," she said.

The judge explained that profanity was not asked for. "I understood," said Eliza, "that thee wasn't asking for profanity. No one would think that of thee. But we Quakers do not take oaths in court. We affirm."

"Permit Mrs. Birdwell to affirm," said the judge. Eliza affirmed.

Mr. Samp then proceeded to question Eliza as to Samantha's birth and habits.

"Judge," Eliza began.

"Address the judge," Mr. Samp said, "as Your Honor."

"We Quakers," Eliza told the judge, gently, "do not make use of such titles. What is thy name? I think thee'll go far in our state and thy name's one I'd like to know."

The judge appeared somewhat distraught, undecided as to whether to make the tone of the court brisk and legal (if possible) or to follow Eliza's lead of urbane sociability.

"Pomeroy," he said and made a slight bow in Eliza's direction.

Eliza returned the bow, deeper and with more grace. "Friend Pomeroy," she said, "it is indeed a pleasure to know thee."

Samantha's story as Eliza told it to Friend Pomeroy was surprisingly terse. Affecting, and losing nothing by Eliza's telling, but to the point.

"Mrs. Birdwell," said Samp, "how long have you had an acquaintanceship with geese and their habits?"

"Since I was a child," Eliza said. "My father was a great fancier of geese."

"And you think you could identify this goose Samantha, which you admit in looks was similar to the defendant's?"

"I could," Eliza said with much authority.

Mr. Samp, to Jess's surprise, left the matter there. "Take the witness," he said to Overby's lawyer—but the counsel for the defendant was in no hurry to cross-examine Eliza. Instead he put his client on the stand.

"Farewell, Samantha," Jess said to Enoch.

"You relieved?" Enoch asked.

"Putting Eliza first," Jess said, "as I do, no."

Milt Overby, whose natural truculence was somewhat stimulated by a nip he'd had to offset snappy weather, bellowed his way through his testimony. At one juncture he set the judge aright when he asked some elementary questions concerning the habits and configurations of geese. "Where in tarnation you from?" he snorted. "What they mean sending us judges down here who don't know Toulouse from Wyandotte,[16] or goose from gander?"

The young judge used voice and gavel to quiet the guffawing that filled the courtroom, and the trial proceeded. A number of witnesses for both sides were brought to the stand and while it was shown that Overbys had maybe eaten a goose or two and neglected out of pure fondness for the creatures to count them as among the departed, still nobody had been able to positively identify Samantha.

Mr. Overby's lawyer seemed somewhat loath to cross-examine Eliza, but he put her on the stand. She'd said she knew geese and her testimony had been direct and positive. "Mrs. Birdwell," he said, "how can you be so sure your goose was with my client's geese?"

Eliza's black eyes rested confidingly upon the judge. "Friend Pomeroy," she said, "I raised Samantha from a gosling."

Jess sighed. "Here it comes," he said, "how that goose could sing and drink tea."

Eliza continued, "And there's one thing about her that always set her apart from every other goose."

"Yes, Mrs. Birdwell," said Judge Pomeroy, who was inclined to forget, with Eliza on the stand, that he was in a courtroom.

16. Toulouse (to͞o•lo͞oz′) . . . **Wyandotte** (wī′ən•dŏt): breeds of fowl.

"Samantha," said Eliza, with much earnestness, "from the day she was born had a gait unlike any other goose I ever saw and one that set her apart from all her Overby connections. I picked her out at once when I went over there, because of it. Thee couldn't've missed it, Friend Pomeroy."

"Yes, Mrs. Birdwell," said the judge, with interest in his voice.

"Samantha," said Eliza, "was a born pacer. Thee knows what a pacer is?"

"Certainly," said Judge Pomeroy. "A pacer," he repeated with no surprise—and with obvious pleasure that Eliza'd hit upon so clear and differentiating an aspect of her goose and one that made identification possible.

A titter was mounting through the courtroom—Judge Pomeroy lifted his head. He had no desire to be further instructed as to the history, habits, and breeds of geese, and he liked to see a trial settled by some such little and too often overlooked subtlety. Judge Pomeroy brought down his gavel. "The court awards decision in favor of the plaintiff. Case dismissed." While the silence that followed on his words still prevailed Judge Pomeroy stepped briskly and with obvious pleasure out through the rear door.

Jess was also brisk about departure. No use lingering until friend Pomeroy had been more thoroughly informed as to gaits in general and geese in particular. Midafternoon's a quiet time in any season. In winter, with snow on the ground, no leaves to rustle, and bare limbs rigid as rock against a cloudless sky, the hush is deepest of all. Nothing broke that hush in the surrey, except the squeak of leather and snow, the muffled footfalls of Rome Beauty. Jess and Eliza, on the front seat, rode without speaking. Enoch, in the back, seemed to meditate. Even Samantha, in her crate at Enoch's feet, was silent.

Maple Grove Nursery was in sight before Jess spoke. "Eliza," he said, "Would thee mind telling me—did thee ever see a trotting goose?"

Enoch ceased to meditate and listened. He had been wondering about this himself.

"Certainly not," said Eliza. "Thee knows as well as I, Jess Birdwell, an animal can't trot without hind feet and forefeet."

"So far, Eliza," Jess said, "we see eye to eye. Now maybe thee'd tell me—did thee ever see a goose that didn't pace?"

Eliza was truly amazed, it seemed. "Why, Jess," she said, "an ordinary goose just walks—but Samantha paces."

Jess was silent for a spell. "What'd thee say the difference is?"

"It's the swing, Jess Birdwell," said Eliza, "same as in a horse that nature's formed for a pacer . . . it's the natural bent, the way the spirit leads the beast to set his feet down. Samantha's a natural pacer."

That seemed as far as they'd likely get on the subject, and Jess joined Enoch in meditation. In the barnyard, before she went up to the house, Eliza said, like an old hand at the business, "Attending court whettens the appetite. It's a little early but I thought if thee'd relish it"—and she looked at Jess and Enoch, never sparing a glance for Samantha, as if her menfolk's welfare was her sole concern—"I'd stir us up a bite to eat. Hot tea and fresh sweetcakes, say. Might fry a little sausage and open some cherry preserves. If thee'd relish it," she repeated.

Jess wasn't taken in, but he'd relish it, and so would Enoch, and they both said so. They hustled with the unhitching so they could uncrate Samantha and note her progress with eyes newly instructed as to what made a pacer. Jess dumped her in the snow, and Enoch tapped her with his hat. Samantha made for the back door.

"By sugar," said Jess, "Eliza's right. She paces." Samantha had the smooth roll of a racker[17]—there were no two ways about it. At heart she was a pacer, and what two legs could do in that line, Samantha accomplished.

"With four legs," Enoch said, "you could enter her in any county fair—rack on," he cried with enthusiasm. As they followed Samantha to the house, Enoch, for whom any event existed chiefly in its afteraspects, as a cud for rumination, asked, "How you feel in respect of court trials now, Mr. Birdwell?"

"I'm still against them," Jess said, "though they's three things this trial's taught me I might never otherwise have learned. Two's about women."

Enoch revered all knowledge and he had a notion that information on this subject might have a more than transcendental[18] value. "What's the two things you learned about women, Mr. Birdwell?"

"Well, Enoch, I learned first, dependability's woman's greatest virtue. Steady as a pump bolt, day in, day out. When thee finds a woman like that, Enoch, don't try to change her. Not even in spring."

"No, sir," said Enoch, "I won't."

"Second, when it's a case of woman and the law—thee don't need to waste any worry on the woman."

17. racker: a horse that paces or single-foots.
18. transcendental: highly abstract; beyond human understanding.

"No, sir," said Enoch again.

When they reached the back steps, Enoch asked, "I understood you to say you'd learned three things, Mr. Birdwell. What's the third about?"

"Hired men," said Jess.

Enoch was taken aback, but he'd asked for it. "Yes, Mr. Birdwell," he said.

"Never hire one," Jess told him, "till thee finds out first if he can count to eight. Save thyself a lot of trouble that way, Enoch."

"How's I to know the eighth'd turn out to be Samantha?" Enoch asked.

Samantha herself, who was waiting at the doorstep for an expected tidbit, reached out and, unhampered by either boots or work pants, nipped Enoch firmly through his thin Sunday best.

"Thee say something, Enoch?" Jess asked.

Enoch had, but he didn't repeat it. Instead he said, "Pacer or no pacer, that's Samantha," and the two of them stepped out of the snow into the warm kitchen, scented with baking sweetcakes and frying sausage.

Meaning

1. Where in the story could friendly disagreements have grown into bitter arguments? What is there about Eliza and Jess that prevents this from happening?
2. The external conflict between Eliza and the Overbys is the primary conflict in the story. What are some of the internal conflicts? What conflict is not resolved at the end of the story?
3. On what basis does Judge Pomeroy decide the case? Do you think his decision is fair? Tell why or why not.

Method

1. What is the advantage of narrating the events in this story from the omniscient point of view?
2. What role does Enoch play in the story? How has the author made this minor character interesting?
3. Most description appeals to the sense of sight. When an author wants to give you a total impression of a place, event, or object, he or she may include details that appeal to your senses of hearing, touch, smell and taste. Reread paragraphs seven through ten,

beginning "Behind him the table . . ." and ending ". . . thee knows I wouldn't have thee anyways altered." Name the words that call to mind a particular sense.

4. A *local color* story is one that captures the particular features of a region and its inhabitants. An author may describe the customs and dress of a people and, in reporting their conversations, use authentic dialect. The quaint dialect formerly used by the Quakers gives "The Pacing Goose" much flavor and charm. The most striking example of this is the use of the pronoun *thee* instead of *you* in addressing a person. Find some additional examples of the use of local color and dialect in this story.

Language: Similes and Metaphors

The figurative language in "The Pacing Goose" creates pictures in your mind by means of similes and metaphors. *Similes* and *metaphors* are comparisons of things that are *unlike* except in one aspect that the writer makes us see, with striking vividness, perhaps for the first time. A simile says that the things are *like* one another. It uses the words *like* or *as.* ("My love is like a red, red rose," or "The dawn came up like thunder.") A metaphor implies that the two things in the comparison are identical. ("It is the East and Juliet is the sun," or "You are my sunshine.")

Reread the following phrases from the story. Decide which are similes and which are metaphors. What elements are being compared in each figure of speech?

1. ". . . snow falling so fast it weaves a web . . ."

2. ". . . the kitchen smelled like a summer orchard . . ."

3. ". . . goose eying thee like a snake on stilts."

4. ". . . she swelled, almost at once, like a slack sail which gets a sudden breeze . . ."

5. ". . . she was Eliza's pure pet . . . and would . . . walk beside her with the lordly roll of the known elect."

6. "The circuit judge was . . . young, jug-eared . . ."

7. ". . . bare limbs rigid as rock against a cloudless sky . . ."

Discussion and Composition

1. Write a one- or two-paragraph description of a pet you have or have had. Be sure to explain any distinctive characteristics or marks by which you could positively distinguish your pet from all other pets of the same kind.

2. Read *The Friendly Persuasion* (Harcourt Brace Jovanovich, 1945), the book from which this selection was taken, and report on some additional episodes from the life of the Birdwells.

3. The author gives a subjective description of a kitchen with its table set for supper. Describe a room (either real or imaginary), using details that will convey either a pleasant or unpleasant impression. Try to include at least one detail that will appeal to each of the five senses.

GRAHAM GREENE
(born 1904)

A master of suspense, Graham Greene divides his work into two groups: "entertainments," such as *This Gun for Hire* (1936), which are fast-moving adventure stories, and "serious" novels, such as *The Power and the Glory* (1940), which have themes emphasizing religious and moral issues. He has also written travel books, short stories, and plays.

Born in Hertfordshire, England, Graham Greene was one of six children, and the son of a school headmaster. Bored and unhappy, Greene ran away from home and tried to take his own life when he was a teenager. At twenty-one, while he was a student at Oxford University, he converted to Roman Catholicism, a step that had a profound influence on his life and writing.

After graduation, he worked as an editor for the *London Times* until his first novel, *The Man Within,* was published in 1929. In later years, he has been a film critic, literary editor, and free-lance writer. His travels through Europe, Mexico, Africa, and Southeast Asia have provided background material for much of his writing. Many of his stories have been made into films.

ACROSS THE BRIDGE

"They say he's worth a million," Lucia said. He sat there in the little hot damp Mexican square, a dog at his feet, with an air of immense and forlorn patience. The dog attracted your attention at once, for it was very nearly an English setter, only something had gone wrong with the tail and the feathering. Palms wilted over his head, it was all shade and stuffiness around the bandstand, radios talked loudly in Spanish from the little wooden sheds where they changed your pesos into dollars at a loss. I could tell he didn't understand a word from the way he read his newspaper—as I did myself, picking out the words which were like English ones. "He's been here a month," Lucia said. "They turned him out of Guatemala and Honduras."

You couldn't keep any secrets for five hours in this border town. Lucia had only been twenty-four hours in the place, but she knew all about Mr. Joseph Calloway. The only reason I didn't know about him (and I'd been in the place two weeks) was that I couldn't talk the language any more than Mr. Calloway could. There wasn't another soul in the place who didn't know the story—the whole story of the Halling Investment Trust and the proceedings for extradition.[1] Any man doing dusty business in any of the wooden booths in the town is better fitted by long observation to tell Mr. Calloway's tale than I am, except that I was in—literally—at the finish. They all watched the drama proceed with immense interest, sympathy, and respect. For after all, he had a million.

Every once in a while through the long steamy day a boy came and cleaned Mr. Calloway's shoes: he hadn't the right words to resist them—they pretended not to know his English. He must have had his shoes cleaned the day Lucia and I watched him at least half a dozen times. At midday he took a stroll across the square to the Antonio Bar and had a bottle of beer, the setter sticking to heel as if they were out for a country walk in England (he had, you may remember, one of the biggest estates in Norfolk[2]). After his bottle of beer, he would walk down between the moneychangers' huts to the Rio Grande and look across the bridge into the United States: people came and went constantly in cars. Then back to the square till lunch time. He was staying in the best hotel, but you don't get good hotels in this border town: nobody stays in them more than a night. The good hotels were on the other side of the bridge: you could see their electric signs twenty stories high from the little square at night, like lighthouses marking the United States.

You may ask what I'd been doing in so drab a spot for a fortnight.[3] There was no interest in the place for anyone; it was just damp and dust and poverty, a kind of shabby replica of the town across the river: both had squares in the same spots; both had the same number of cinemas. One was cleaner than the other, that was all, and more expensive, much more expensive. I'd stayed across there a couple of nights waiting for a man a tourist bureau said was driving down from Detroit to Yucatán[4] and would sell a place in his car for

1. extradition: the turning over of an accused individual by one state, country, or authority to another.

2. Norfolk (nôr′fək)**:** a county in England.

3. fortnight: two weeks.

4. Yucatán (yo͞o′kə·tăn′)**:** a state in southeastern Mexico.

some fantastically small figure—twenty dollars, I think it was. I don't know if he existed or was invented by the optimistic half-caste in the agency; anyway, he never turned up, and so I waited, not much caring, on the cheap side of the river. It didn't much matter; I was living. One day I meant to give up the man from Detroit and go home or go south, but it was easier not to decide anything in a hurry. Lucia was just waiting for a car going the other way, but she didn't have to wait so long. We waited together and watched Mr. Calloway waiting—for God knows what.

I don't know how to treat this story—it was a tragedy for Mr. Calloway, it was poetic retribution,[5] I suppose, in the eyes of the shareholders he'd ruined with his bogus transactions, and to Lucia and me, at this stage, it was pure comedy—except when he kicked the dog. I'm not a sentimentalist about dogs, I prefer people to be cruel to animals rather than to human beings, but I couldn't help being revolted at the way he'd kick that animal—with a hint of cold-blooded venom, not in anger but as if he were getting even for some trick it had played him a long while ago. That generally happened when he returned from the bridge: it was the only sign of anything resembling emotion he showed. Otherwise he looked a small, set, gentle creature, with silver hair and a silver moustache, and gold-rimmed glasses, and one gold tooth like a flaw in character.

Lucia hadn't been accurate when she said he'd been turned out of Guatemala and Honduras; he'd left voluntarily when the extradition proceedings seemed likely to go through, and moved north. Mexico is still not a very centralized state, and it is possible to get around governors as you can't get around cabinet ministers or judges. And so he waited there on the border for the next move. That earlier part of the story is, I suppose, dramatic, but I didn't watch it and I can't invent what I haven't seen—the long waiting in anterooms, the bribes taken and refused, the growing fear of arrest, and then the flight—in gold-rimmed glasses—covering his tracks as well as he could, but this wasn't finance and he was an amateur at escape. And so he'd washed up here, under my eyes and Lucia's eyes, sitting all day under the bandstand, nothing to read but a Mexican paper, nothing to do but look across the river at the United States, quite unaware, I suppose, that everyone knew everything about him, once a day kicking his dog. Perhaps in its semi-setter way it reminded him too much

5. poetic retribution: in plays, short stories, and poems, an outcome in which vice is punished and virtue rewarded in an ideal or appropriate manner.

of the Norfolk estate—though that too, I suppose, was the reason he kept it.

And the next act again was pure comedy. I hesitate to think what this man worth a million was costing his country as they edged him out from this land and that. Perhaps somebody was getting tired of the business, and careless; anyway, they sent across two detectives, with an old photograph. He'd grown his silvery moustache since that had been taken, and he'd aged a lot, and they couldn't catch sight of him. They hadn't been across the bridge two hours when everybody knew that there were two foreign detectives in town looking for Mr. Calloway—everybody knew, that is to say, except Mr. Calloway, who couldn't talk Spanish. There were plenty of people who could have told him in English, but they didn't. It wasn't cruelty, it was a sort of awe and respect: like a bull, he was on show, sitting there mournfully in the plaza with his dog, a magnificent spectacle for which we all had ringside seats.

I ran into one of the policemen in the Bar Antonio. He was disgusted; he had had some idea that when he crossed the bridge life was going to be different, so much more color and sun, and—I suspect—love, and all he found were wide mud streets where the nocturnal rain lay in pools, and mangy dogs, smells and cockroaches in his bedroom, and the nearest to love, the open door of the Academia Comercial, where pretty mestizo[6] girls sat all the morning learning to typewrite. Tip-tap-tip-tap-tip—perhaps they had a dream, too—jobs on the other side of the bridge, where life was going to be so much more luxurious, refined, and amusing.

We got into conversation; he seemed surprised that I knew who they both were and what they wanted. He said, "We've got information this man Calloway's in town."

"He's knocking around somewhere," I said.

"Could you point him out?"

"Oh, I don't know him by sight," I said.

He drank his beer and thought awhile. "I'll go out and sit in the plaza. He's sure to pass sometime."

I finished my beer and went quickly off and found Lucia. I said, "Hurry, we're going to see an arrest." We didn't care a thing about Mr. Calloway; he was just an elderly man who kicked his dog and

6. mestizo (mĕs·tē′zō): of mixed blood; in Mexico and the western United States, of Spanish and Indian ancestry.

swindled the poor, and who deserved anything he got. So we made for the plaza; we knew Calloway would be there, but it had never occurred to either of us that the detectives wouldn't recognize him. There was quite a surge of people around the place; all the fruit sellers and bootblacks in town seemed to have arrived together; we had to force our way through, and there in the little green stuffy center of the place, sitting on adjoining seats, were the two plainclothes men and Mr. Calloway. I've never known the place so silent; everybody was on tiptoe, and the plainclothes men were staring at the crowd, looking for Mr. Calloway, and Mr. Calloway sat on his usual seat staring out over the moneychanging booths at the United States.

"It can't go on. It just can't," Lucia said. But it did. It got more fantastic still. Somebody ought to write a play about it. We sat as close as we dared. We were afraid all the time we were going to laugh. The semi-setter scratched for fleas, and Mr. Calloway watched the U.S.A. The two detectives watched the crowd, and the crowd watched the show with solemn satisfaction. Then one of the detectives got up and went over to Mr. Calloway. That's the end, I thought. But it wasn't, it was the beginning. For some reason they had eliminated him from their list of suspects. I shall never know why.

The man said, "You speak English?"

"I *am* English," Mr. Calloway said.

Even that didn't tear it, and the strangest thing of all was the way Mr. Calloway came alive. I don't think anybody had spoken to him like that for weeks. The Mexicans were too respectful—he was a man with a million—and it had never occurred to Lucia and me to treat him casually like a human being; even in our eyes he had been magnified by the colossal theft and the worldwide pursuit.

He said, "This is rather a dreadful place, don't you think?"

"It is," the policeman said.

"I can't think what brings anybody across the bridge."

"Duty," the policeman said gloomily. "I suppose you are passing through?"

"Yes," Mr. Calloway said.

"I'd have expected over here there'd have been—you know what I mean—life. You read things about Mexico."

"Oh, life," Mr. Calloway said. He spoke firmly and precisely, as if to a committee of shareholders. "That begins on the other side."

"You don't appreciate your own country until you leave it."

"That's very true," Mr. Calloway said. "Very true."

At first it was difficult not to laugh, and then after awhile there didn't seem to be much to laugh at; an old man imagining all the fine things going on beyond the international bridge. I think he thought of the town opposite as a combination of London and Norfolk—theaters and cocktail bars, a little shooting and a walk around the field at evening with the dog—that miserable imitation of a setter—poking the ditches. He'd never been across—he couldn't know that it was just the same thing over again—even the same layout; only the streets were paved and the hotels had ten more stories, and life was more expensive, and everything was a little bit cleaner. There wasn't anything Mr. Calloway would have called living—no galleries, no bookshops, just *Film Fun* and the local paper, and *Click* and *Focus* and the tabloids.

"Well," said Mr. Calloway, "I think I'll take a stroll before lunch. You need an appetite to swallow the food here. I generally go down and look at the bridge about now. Care to come too?"

The detective shook his head. "No," he said, "I'm on duty. I'm looking for a fellow." And that, of course, gave *him* away. As far as Mr. Calloway could understand, there was only one "fellow" in the world anyone was looking for—his brain had eliminated friends who were seeking their friends, husbands who might be waiting for their wives, all objectives of any search but just the one. The power of elimination was what had made him a financier—he could forget the people behind the shares.

That was the last we saw of him for awhile. We didn't see him going into the Botica[7] Paris to get his aspirin, or walking back from the bridge with his dog. He simply disappeared, and when he disappeared people began to talk, and the detectives heard the talk. They looked silly enough, and they got busy after the very man they'd been sitting next to in the garden. Then they too disappeared. They, as well as Mr. Calloway, had gone to the state capital to see the Governor and the Chief of Police, and it must have been an amusing sight there too, as they bumped into Mr. Calloway and sat with him in the waiting rooms. I suspect Mr. Calloway was generally shown in first, for everyone knew he was worth a million. Only in Europe is it possible for a man to be a criminal as well as a rich man.

Anyway, after about a week the whole pack of them returned by the same train. Mr. Calloway traveled Pullman, and the two

7. **Botica** (bō•tē′cā): *Spanish,* drugstore.

policemen traveled in the day coach. It was evident that they hadn't got their extradition order.

Lucia had left by that time. The car came and went across the bridge. I stood in Mexico and watched her get out at the United States Customs. She wasn't anything in particular but she looked beautiful at a distance as she gave me a wave out of the United States and got back into the car. And I suddenly felt sympathy for Mr. Calloway, as if there were something over there which you couldn't find here, and turning around I saw him back on his old beat, with the dog at his heels.

I said "Good afternoon," as if it had been all along our habit to greet each other. He looked tired and ill and dusty, and I felt sorry for him—to think of the kind of victory he'd been winning, with so much expenditure of cash and care—the prize this dirty and dreary town, the booths of the moneychangers, the awful little beauty parlors with their wicker chairs and sofas looking like the reception rooms of brothels, that hot and stuffy garden by the bandstand.

He replied gloomily, "Good morning," and the dog started to sniff at some ordure and he turned and kicked it with fury, with depression, with despair.

And at that moment a taxi with the two policemen in it passed us on its way to the bridge. They must have seen that kick; perhaps they were cleverer than I had given them credit for, perhaps they were just sentimental about animals, and thought they'd do a good deed, and the rest happened by accident. But the fact remains—those two pillars of the law set about the stealing of Mr. Calloway's dog.

He watched them go by. Then he said, "Why don't you go across?"

"It's cheaper here," I said.

"I mean just for an evening. Have a meal at that place we can see at night in the sky. Go to the theater."

"There isn't a chance."

He said angrily, sucking his gold tooth, "Well, anyway, get away from here." He stared down the hill and up the other side. He couldn't see that that street climbing up from the bridge contained only the same moneychangers' booths as this one.

I said, "Why don't *you go*?"

He said evasively, "Oh—business."

I said, "It's only a question of money. You don't *have* to pass by the bridge."

He said with faint interest, "I don't talk Spanish."

"There isn't a soul here," I said, "who doesn't talk English."

He looked at me with surprise. "Is that so?" he said. "Is that so?"

It's as I have said; he'd never tried to talk to anyone, and they respected him too much to talk to him—he was worth a million. I don't know whether I'm glad or sorry that I told him that. If I hadn't, he might be there now, sitting by the bandstand having his shoes cleaned—alive and suffering.

Three days later his dog disappeared. I found him looking for it, calling it softly and shamefacedly among the palms of the garden. He looked embarrassed. He said in a low, angry voice, "I *hate* that dog. The beastly mongrel," and called "Rover, Rover" in a voice which didn't carry five yards. He said, "I bred setters once. I'd have shot a dog like that." It reminded him, I *was* right, of Norfolk, and he lived in the memory, and he hated it for its imperfection. He was a man without a family and without friends, and his only enemy was that dog. You couldn't call the law an enemy; you have to be intimate with an enemy.

Late that afternoon someone told him they'd seen the dog walking across the bridge. It wasn't true, of course, but we didn't know that then—they'd paid a Mexican five pesos to smuggle it across. So all that afternoon and the next Mr. Calloway sat in the garden having his shoes cleaned over and over again, and thinking how a dog could just walk across like that, and a human being, an immortal soul, was bound here in the awful routine of the little walk and the unspeakable meals and the aspirin at the *botica*. That dog was seeing things he couldn't see—that hateful dog. It made him mad—I think literally mad. You must remember the man had been going on for months. He had a million and he was living on two pounds a week, with nothing to spend his money on. He sat there and brooded on the hideous injustice of it. I think he'd have crossed over one day in any case, but the dog was the last straw.

Next day when he wasn't to be seen I guessed he'd gone across, and I went too. The American town is as small as the Mexican. I knew I couldn't miss him if he was there, and I was still curious. A little sorry for him, but not much.

I caught sight of him first in the only drugstore, having a Coca-Cola, and then once outside a cinema, looking at the posters; he had dressed with extreme neatness, as if for a party, but there was no party. On my third time around, I came on the detectives—they were having Coca-Colas in the drugstore, and they must have missed Mr. Calloway by inches. I went in and sat down at the bar.

"Hello," I said, "you still about?" I suddenly felt anxious for Mr. Calloway, I didn't want them to meet.

One of them said, "Where's Calloway?"

"Oh," I said, "he's hanging on."

"But not his dog," he said, and laughed. The other looked a little shocked; he didn't like anyone to *talk* cynically about a dog. Then they got up—they had a car outside.

"Have another?" I said.

"No, thanks. We've got to keep moving."

The man bent close and confided to me, "Calloway's on this side."

"No!" I said.

"And his dog."

"He's looking for it," the other said.

"I'm damned if he is," I said, and again one of them looked a little shocked, as if I'd insulted the dog.

I don't think Mr. Calloway was looking for his dog, but his dog certainly found him. There was a sudden hilarious yapping from the car and out plunged the semi-setter and gamboled[8] furiously down the street. One of the detectives—the sentimental one—was into the car before we got to the door and was off after the dog. Near the bottom of the long road to the bridge was Mr. Calloway—I do believe he'd come down to look at the Mexican side when he found there was nothing but the drugstore and the cinemas and the paper shops on the American. He saw the dog coming and yelled at it to go home—"home, home, home," as if they were in Norfolk. It took no notice at all, pelting toward him. Then he saw the police car coming and ran. After that, everything happened too quickly, but I think the order of events was this—the dog started across the road right in front of the car, and Mr. Calloway yelled, at the dog or the car, I don't know which. Anyway, the detective swerved—he said later, weakly, at the inquiry, that he couldn't run over a dog, and down went Mr. Calloway, in a mess of broken glass and gold rims and silver hair and blood. The dog was on him before any of us could reach him, licking and whimpering and licking. I saw Mr. Calloway put up his hand, and down it went across the dog's neck, and the whimper rose to a stupid bark of triumph, but Mr. Calloway was dead—shock and a weak heart.

"Poor old geezer," the detective said, "I bet he really loved that

8. **gamboled** (găm′bəld): skipped and leaped about.

dog," and it's true that the attitude in which he lay looked more like a caress than a blow. I thought it was meant to be a blow, but the detective may have been right. It all seemed to me a little too touching to be true as the old crook lay there with his arm over the dog's neck, dead with his million between the moneychangers' huts, but it's as well to be humble in the face of human nature. He had come across the river for something, and it may, after all, have been the dog he was looking for. It sat there, baying its stupid and mongrel triumph across his body, like a piece of sentimental statuary. The nearest he could get to the fields, the ditches, the horizon of his home. It was comic and it was pitiable; but it wasn't less comic because the man was dead. Death doesn't change comedy to tragedy, and if that last gesture was one of affection, I suppose it was only one more indication of a human being's capacity for self-deception, our baseless optimism that is so much more appalling than our despair.

Meaning

1. The narrator describes the silver-haired Mr. Calloway as having "one gold tooth like a flaw in his character." What is his fatal flaw? Why is it ironic that he's worth a million?
2. Why does Mr. Calloway want to visit the American town? Why can't he cross the bridge like everyone else?
3. At one point, the narrator says that Mr. Calloway's story was "pure comedy." The classic definition of comedy is that it is a play concerned with humans as social beings rather than as private individuals. In ancient Greece, the writer of comedy wanted to correct the evils of society by making the audience laugh at characters who were immoral or stupid. To what extent does Mr. Calloway's story fit the definition of pure comedy?
4. Explain Mr. Calloway's need to have a setter. What does his mistreatment of the dog reveal about him?

Method

1. The Mexican town is "just damp and dust and poverty." Why are the atmosphere and setting essential to the unfolding of Mr. Calloway's story?

2. What role does the narrator play in the story? What kind of person does he seem to be? Is his attitude toward Mr. Calloway sad and sentimental, amused and sympathetic, or angry and disapproving?
3. A *symbol* is a person, place, event, or object that, besides being itself, also represents or stands for something else. For example, an owl represents wisdom; a sword, power and authority. The reader determines the meaning of each symbol from its context in the story.

   In "Across the Bridge," what elements in Mr. Calloway's life do the moneychangers' huts appear to represent? What does the dog symbolize? the bridge?
4. A *commercial* or *craft* story is one that has stereotyped characters (a *stereotyped* or *stock* character is one who always displays the same traits and always acts in a predictable way), an excess of sentimentality or emotion, a plot that is contrived and filled with coincidences, and often a conventional theme. A *quality* story has true-to-life characters and themes that are thought-provoking and often critical of the established traditions of society. Do you think that "Across the Bridge" is a commercial or a quality story? Tell why.

Language: Abstract and Concrete Terms

Abstract terms are words and phrases that represent ideas, generalities, or characteristics rather than particular objects. They have little or no sense appeal and are difficult to define and analyze. Examples of abstract terms are *patience, optimism,* and *despair.*

Concrete terms stand for objects that can be perceived by the senses or clearly imagined. Examples of concrete terms are *lake, chair,* and *coat.*

Select the abstract terms from among the following words, and define each with a sentence. Modify each concrete term on the list with an adjective so that it will be as specific as possible and appeal to one or more of the senses.

1. affection	**4.** dog	**7.** injustice
2. snow	**5.** triumph	**8.** law
3. death	**6.** bridge	**9.** river

Discussion and Composition

1. Imagine that you are a reporter sent to cover the story of Mr. Calloway's death. Write a human interest or feature story in which you show what the last months of the man who was "worth a million" were really like.

2. Reread the last sentence of the story. Why is Mr. Calloway's story an example of "our baseless optimism"? Do most human beings have a "capacity for self-deception"?

3. If you were suddenly "worth a million"—and the million had been gained honestly—what would you do? Where would you go? How would you change your life?

4. Compare Mr. Calloway's attitude toward animals with that of the narrator and the sentimental detective. With whom do you most agree? Tell why.

SHIRLEY JACKSON
(1919–1965)

The stories of Shirley Jackson typically leave the reader feeling disturbed, if not haunted. The setting and situation are often commonplace, but there is always a meaning, often an unusual one, underlying the deceptively simple plot. Many of her stories contain elements of terror and mystery that reveal her extensive study of the supernatural, especially her interest in ghosts and witchcraft.

Shirley Jackson was born in San Francisco and graduated from Syracuse University. For most of her life she lived in Vermont, where her husband, Stanley Edgar Hyman, a literary critic, taught at Bennington College. Miss Jackson wrote two humorous books about her life as the mother of four lively children: *Life Among the Savages* (1953) and *Raising Demons* (1957).

Miss Jackson wrote novels as well as short stories. "Trial by Combat" is one of the selections in her first short story collection, which was called *The Lottery* (1949).

TRIAL BY COMBAT

When Emily Johnson came home one evening to her furnished room and found three of her best handkerchiefs missing from the dresser drawer, she was sure who had taken them and what to do. She had lived in the furnished room for about six weeks and for the past two weeks she had been missing small things occasionally. There had been several handkerchiefs gone, and an initial pin which Emily rarely wore and which had come from the five-and-ten. And once she had missed a small bottle of perfume and one of a set of china dogs. Emily had known for some time who was taking the things, but it was only tonight that she had decided what to do. She had hesitated about complaining to the landlady because her losses were trivial and because she had felt certain that sooner or later she would know how to deal with the situation herself. It had seemed logical to her from the beginning that the one person in the roominghouse who was home all day was the most likely suspect, and then, one Sunday morning, coming downstairs from the roof, where she had been sitting in the sun, Emily had seen someone come out of her room and go down the stairs, and had recognized the visitor. Tonight, she felt, she knew just what to do. She took off her coat and hat, put her packages down, and, while a can of tamales was heating on her electric plate, she went over what she intended to say.

After her dinner, she closed and locked her door and went downstairs. She tapped softly on the door of the room directly below her own, and when she thought she heard someone say, "Come in," she said, "Mrs. Allen?" then opened the door carefully and stepped inside.

The room, Emily noticed immediately, was almost like her own—the same narrow bed with the tan cover, the same maple dresser and armchair; the closet was on the opposite side of the room, but the window was in the same relative position. Mrs. Allen was sitting in the armchair. She was about sixty. More than twice as old as I am, Emily thought while she stood in the doorway, and a lady still. She hesitated for a few seconds, looking at Mrs. Allen's clean white hair and her neat, dark-blue house coat, before speaking. "Mrs. Allen," she said, "I'm Emily Johnson."

Mrs. Allen put down the *Woman's Home Companion* she had been reading and stood up slowly. "I'm very happy to meet you," she said graciously. "I've seen you, of course, several times, and thought how pleasant you looked. It's so seldom one meets anyone really"—Mrs. Allen hesitated—"really nice," she went on, "in a place like this."

"I've wanted to meet you, too," Emily said.

Mrs. Allen indicated the chair she had been sitting in. "Won't you sit down?"

"Thank you," Emily said. "You stay there. I'll sit on the bed." She smiled. "I feel as if I know the furniture so well. Mine's just the same."

"It's a shame," Mrs. Allen said, sitting down in her chair again. "I've told the landlady over and over, you can't make people feel at home if you put all the same furniture in the rooms. But she maintains that this maple furniture is clean-looking and cheap."

"It's better than most," Emily said. "You've made yours look much nicer than mine."

"I've been here for three years," Mrs. Allen said. "You've only been here a month or so, haven't you?"

"Six weeks," Emily said.

"The landlady's told me about you. Your husband's in the Army."

"Yes. I have a job here in New York."

"My husband was in the Army," Mrs. Allen said. She gestured at a group of pictures on her maple dresser. "That was a long time ago, of course. He's been dead for nearly five years." Emily got up and went over to the pictures. One of them was of a tall, dignified-looking man in Army uniform. Several were of children.

"He was a very distinguished-looking man," Emily said. "Are those your children?"

"I had no children, to my sorrow," the old lady said. "Those are nephews and nieces of my husband's."

Emily stood in front of the dresser, looking around the room. "I see you have flowers, too," she said. She walked to the window and looked at the row of potted plants. "I love flowers," she said. "I bought myself a big bunch of asters tonight to brighten up my room. But they fade so quickly."

"I prefer plants just for that reason," Mrs. Allen said. "But why don't you put an aspirin in the water with your flowers? They'll last much longer."

"I'm afraid I don't know much about flowers," Emily said. "I didn't know about putting an aspirin in the water, for instance."

"I always do, with cut flowers," Mrs. Allen said. "I think flowers make a room look so friendly."

Emily stood by the window for a minute, looking out on Mrs. Allen's daily view: the fire escape opposite, an oblique slice of the street below. Then she took a deep breath and turned around. "Actually, Mrs. Allen," she said, "I had a reason for dropping in."

"Other than to make my acquaintance?" Mrs. Allen said, smiling.

"I don't know quite what to do," Emily said. "I don't like to say anything to the landlady."

"The landlady isn't much help in an emergency," Mrs. Allen said.

Emily came back and sat on the bed, looking earnestly at Mrs. Allen, seeing a nice old lady. "It's so slight," she said, "but someone has been coming into my room."

Mrs. Allen looked up.

"I've been missing things," Emily went on, "like handkerchiefs and little inexpensive jewelry. Nothing important. But someone's been coming into my room and helping themselves."

"I'm sorry to hear it," Mrs. Allen said.

"You see, I don't like to make trouble," Emily said. "It's just that someone's coming into my room. I haven't missed anything of value."

"I see," Mrs. Allen said.

"I just noticed it a few days ago. And then last Sunday I was coming down from the roof and I saw someone coming out of my room."

"Do you have any idea who it was?" Mrs. Allen asked.

"I believe I do," Emily said.

Mrs. Allen was quiet for a minute. "I can see where you wouldn't like to speak to the landlady," she said finally.

"Of course not," Emily said. "I just want it to stop."

"I don't blame you," Mrs. Allen said.

"You see, it means someone has a key to my door," Emily said pleadingly.

"All the keys in this house open all the doors," Mrs. Allen said. "They're all old-fashioned locks."

"It *has* to stop," Emily said. "If it doesn't, I'll have to do something about it."

"I can see that," Mrs. Allen said. "The whole thing is very unfortunate." She rose. "You'll have to excuse me," she went on. "I tire very easily and I must be in bed early. I'm so happy you came down to see me."

"I'm so glad to have met you at last," Emily said. She went to the door. "I hope I won't be bothered again," she said. "Good night."

"Good night," Mrs. Allen said.

The following evening, when Emily came home from work, a pair of cheap earrings was gone, along with two packages of cigarettes which had been in her dresser drawer. That evening she sat alone in her room for a long time, thinking. Then she wrote a letter to her husband and went to bed. The next morning she got up and dressed and went to the corner drugstore, where she called her office from a phone booth and said that she was sick and would not be in that day. Then she went back to her room. She sat for almost an hour with the door slightly ajar before she heard Mrs. Allen's door open and Mrs. Allen come out and go slowly down the stairs. When Mrs. Allen had had time to get out onto the street, Emily locked her door and, carrying her key in her hand, went down to Mrs. Allen's room.

She was thinking, I just want to pretend it's my own room, so that if anyone comes I can say I was mistaken about the floor. For a minute, after she had opened the door, it seemed as though she *were* in her own room. The bed was neatly made and the shade drawn down over the window. Emily left the door unlocked and went over and pulled up the shade. Now that the room was light, she looked around. She had a sudden sense of unbearable intimacy with Mrs. Allen, and thought, This is the way she must feel in my room. Everything was neat and plain. She looked in the closet first, but there was nothing in there but Mrs. Allen's blue house coat and one or two plain dresses. Emily went to the dresser. She looked for a moment at the picture of Mrs. Allen's husband, and then opened the top drawer and looked in. Her handkerchiefs were there, in a neat, small pile, and next to them the cigarettes and the earrings. In one corner the little china dog was sitting. Everything is here, Emily thought, all put away and very orderly. She closed the drawer and opened the next two. Both were empty. She opened the top one again. Besides her things, the drawer held a pair of black cotton gloves, and under the little pile of her handkerchiefs were two plain white ones. There was a box of Kleenex and a small tin of aspirin. For her plants, Emily thought.

Emily was counting the handkerchiefs when a noise behind her made her turn around. Mrs. Allen was standing in the doorway watching her quietly. Emily dropped the handkerchiefs she was holding and stepped back. She felt herself blushing and knew her hands were trembling. Now, she was thinking, now turn around and tell her. "Listen, Mrs. Allen," she began, and stopped.

"Yes?" Mrs. Allen said gently.

Emily found that she was staring at the picture of Mrs. Allen's husband; such a thoughtful-looking man, she was thinking. They must have had such a pleasant life together, and now she has a room like mine, with only two handkerchiefs of her own in the drawer.

"Yes?" Mrs. Allen said again.

What does she want me to say, Emily thought. What could she be waiting for with such a ladylike manner? "I came down," Emily said, and hesitated. My voice is almost ladylike, too, she thought. "I had a terrible headache and I came down to borrow some aspirin," she said quickly. "I had this awful headache and when I found you were out I thought surely you wouldn't mind if I just borrowed some aspirin."

"I'm so sorry," Mrs. Allen said. "But I'm glad you felt you knew me well enough."

"I never would have dreamed of coming in," Emily said, "except for such a bad headache."

"Of course," Mrs. Allen said. "Let's not say any more about it." She went over to the dresser and opened the drawer. Emily, standing next to her, watched her hand pass over the handkerchiefs and pick up the aspirin. "You just take two of these and go to bed for an hour," Mrs. Allen said.

"Thank you." Emily began to move toward the door. "You've been very kind."

"Let me know if there's anything more I can do."

"Thank you," Emily said again, opening the door. She waited for a minute and then turned toward the stairs to her room.

"I'll run up later today," Mrs. Allen said, "just to see how you feel."

Meaning

1. Compare and contrast the lives of Mrs. Allen and Emily at the time the story opens. Why is each woman living in the rooming house?
2. How does Emily try to handle the theft of her belongings? What is her intention when she enters Mrs. Allen's room near the climax of the story?
3. Why was Mrs. Allen stealing from Emily?
4. What is the theme of the story?

Method

1. What is your first impression of Emily? How does your impression change during the story?
2. During the Middle Ages, suspected criminals were judged or "tried" by means of various tests of their innocence. One such test was the *trial by combat*—if the suspected criminal won, he was allowed to go free, for the reasoning went, God would not allow the guilty person to win. How does this meaning of trial by combat apply to the story? What is ironic about the title?
3. In a well written story, the author gives you clues that prepare you for, or *foreshadow,* a surprise ending. What foreshadowings are there that Emily will back down?
4. What is the style (choice and arrangement of words) and tone of "Trial by Combat"?

Language: Objective Details

Shirley Jackson makes few comments about her characters and the situation in the story. Instead, she lets you make your own interpretation, based on the objective details that she provides. Objective details are concerned with the physical qualities of objects—their color, size, shape, material, weight, and location. To help you visualize each scene, she tells you where items are located in relation to one another.

Reread the following sentence and pick out the objective details. Which phrases deal with location?

"Her handkerchiefs were there, in a neat, small pile, and next to them the cigarettes and the earrings. In one corner the little china dog was sitting. . . . Besides her things, the drawer held a pair of black cotton gloves, and under the little pile of her handkerchiefs were two plain white ones. . . ."

Discussion and Composition

1. Write the letter that Emily Johnson might have written to her husband after she had decided on her plan to outwit Mrs. Allen.

2. In her own way, Mrs. Allen is a very strong woman, totally in control of herself and her younger visitor. Describe a strong person you have known, perhaps someone who has had either a positive or negative effect on you. Do this person's physical characteristics reveal or hide inner strength?

3. Describe the contents of a drawer in your house. Provide physical details, especially details that tell where each item is located.

4. Discuss what you think Emily might do next in her conflict with Mrs. Allen. Maintaining the characterization of the author, relate a dialogue between Mrs. Allen and Emily that might take place a few days after the story ends.

WILBUR DANIEL STEELE

(1886–1970)

Wilbur Daniel Steele established his reputation as a master craftsman of storytelling during the 1920s. The son of a college professor, Steele studied art for several years after his graduation from the University of Denver in 1907. He chose writing instead of painting as a career in 1912 when the *Atlantic Monthly* accepted his story "A White Horse Winner."

Steele was born in Greensboro, North Carolina. During World War I, he traveled as a naval correspondent to Europe and North Africa. His plays, novels, and short stories often feature the New England coast, where he studied art, and the West, where he lived for several years. *That Girl from Memphis,* set in 1889 in an Arizona mining town, is his best known novel.

FOOTFALLS

This is not an easy story; not a road for tender or for casual feet. Better the meadows. Let me warn you, it is as hard as that old man's soul and as sunless as his eyes. It has its inception in catastrophe, and its end in an act of almost incredible violence; between them it tells barely how one long blind can become also deaf and dumb.

He lived in one of those old Puritan sea towns where the strain has come down austere and moribund,[1] so that his act would not be quite unbelievable. Except that the town is no longer Puritan and Yankee. It has been betrayed; it has become an outpost of the Portuguese islands.

This man, this blind cobbler himself, was a Portuguese from St. Michael, in the western islands,[2] and his name was Boaz Negro.

He was happy. An unquenchable exuberance lived in him. When he arose in the morning he made vast, as it were uncontrolla-

1. **moribund** (môr′ə•bŭnd): approaching extinction; dying.
2. **St. Michael, in the western islands:** the largest island of the Azores, three groups of islands which are part of Portugal, located in the North Atlantic west of Portugal; in Portuguese, São Miguel.

ble, gestures with his stout arms. He came into his shop singing. His voice, strong and deep as the chest from which it emanated, rolled out through the doorway and along the street, and the fishermen, done with their morning work and lounging and smoking along the wharves, said, "Boaz is to work already." Then they came up to sit in the shop.

In that town a cobbler's shop is a club. One sees the interior always dimly thronged. They sit on the benches watching the artisan at his work for hours, and they talk about everything in the world. A cobbler is known by the company he keeps.

Boaz Negro kept young company. He would have nothing to do with the old. On his own head the gray hairs set thickly.

He had a grown son. But the benches in his shop were for the lusty and valiant young, men who could spend the night drinking, and then at three o'clock in the morning turn out in the rain and dark to pull at the weirs,[3] sing songs, buffet one another among the slippery fish in the boat's bottom, and make loud jokes about the fundamental things—love and birth and death. Harkening to their boasts and strong prophecies, his breast heaved and his heart beat faster. He was a large, full-blooded fellow, fashioned for exploits; the flame in his darkness burned higher even to hear of them.

It is scarcely conceivable how Boaz Negro could have come through this much of his life still possessed of that unquenchable and priceless exuberance; how he would sing in the dawn; how, simply listening to the recital of deeds of gale or brawl, he could easily forget himself a blind man, tied to a shop and a last;[4] easily make of himself a lusty young fellow breasting the sunlit and adventurous tide of life.

He had had a wife, whom he had loved. Fate, which had scourged him with the initial scourge of blindness, had seen fit to take his Angelina away. He had had four sons. Three, one after another, had been removed, leaving only Manuel, the youngest. Recovering slowly, with agony, from each of these recurrent blows, his unquenchable exuberance had lived. And there was another thing quite as extraordinary. He had never done anything but work, and that sort of thing may kill the flame where an abrupt catastrophe fails. Work in the dark. Work, work, work! And accompanied by privation, an almost miserly scale of personal economy. Yes indeed, he had

3. weirs (wîrz)**:** nets set in a waterway to catch fish.

4. last: a metal or wooden form, shaped like a human foot, over which a shoe is made or repaired.

"skinned his fingers," especially in the earlier years. When it tells most.

How he had worked! Not alone in the daytime, but also sometimes, when orders were heavy, far into the night. It was strange for one passing along that deserted street at midnight to hear issuing from the black shop of Boaz Negro the rhythmical tap-tap-tap of hammer on wooden peg.

Nor was that sound all: no man in town could get far past that shop in his nocturnal wandering unobserved. No more than a dozen footfalls, and from the darkness Boaz's voice rolled forth, fraternal, stentorian:[5] "Good night, Antone!" "Good night to you, Caleb Snow!"

To Boaz Negro it was still broad day.

Now because of this, he was what might be called a substantial man. He owned his place, his shop, opening on the sidewalk, and behind it the dwelling house with trellised galleries upstairs and down.

And there was always something for his son, a "piece for the pocket," a dollar, five, even a ten-dollar bill if he had "got to have it." Manuel was "a good boy." Boaz not only said this, he felt that he was assured of it in his understanding, to the infinite peace of his heart.

It was curious that he should be ignorant only of the one nearest to him. Not because he was physically blind. Be certain he knew more of other men and of other men's sons than they or their neighbors did. More, that is to say, of their hearts, their understandings, their idiosyncrasies,[6] and their ultimate weight in the balance pan of eternity.

His simple explanation of Manuel was that Manuel "wasn't too stout." To others he said this, and to himself. Manuel was not indeed too robust. How should he be vigorous when he never did anything to make him so? He never worked. Why should he work, when existence was provided for, and when there was always that "piece for the pocket"? Even a ten-dollar bill on a Saturday night! No, Manuel "wasn't too stout."

In the shop they let it go at that. The missteps and frailties of everyone else in the world were canvassed there with the most shameless publicity. But Boaz Negro was a blind man, and in a sense their host. Those reckless, strong young fellows respected and loved

5. **stentorian** (stĕn•tôr′ē•ən): extremely loud.
6. **idiosyncrasies** (idē•ō•sĭng′krə•sēz): peculiarities.

him. It was allowed to stand at that. Manuel was "a good boy." Which did not prevent them, by the way, from joining later in the general condemnation of that father's laxity—"the ruination of the boy!"

"He should have put him to work, that's what."

"He should have said to Manuel, 'Look here, if you want a dollar, go earn it first.' "

As a matter of fact, only one man ever gave Boaz the advice direct. That was Campbell Wood. And Wood never sat in that shop.

In every small town there is one young man who is spoken of as "rising." As often as not he is not a native, but "from away."

In this town Campbell Wood was that man. He had come from another part of the state to take a place in the bank. He lived in the upper story of Boaz Negro's house, the ground floor now doing for Boaz and the meager remnant of his family. The old woman who came in to tidy up for the cobbler looked after Wood's rooms as well.

Dealing with Wood, one had first of all the sense of his incorruptibility. A little ruthless perhaps, as if one could imagine him, in defense of his integrity, cutting off his friend, cutting off his own hand, cutting off the very stream flowing out from the wellsprings of human kindness. An exaggeration, perhaps.

He was by long odds the most eligible young man in town; good-looking in a spare, ruddy, sandy-haired Scottish fashion; important, incorruptible, "rising." But he took good care of his heart. Precisely that: like a sharp-eyed duenna[7] to his own heart. One felt that here was the man, if ever was the man, who held his destiny in his own hand. Failing, of course, some quite gratuitous[8] and unforeseeable catastrophe.

Not that he was not human, or even incapable of laughter or passion. He was, in a way, immensely accessible. He never clapped one on the shoulder; on the other hand, he never failed to speak. Not even to Boaz.

Returning from the bank in the afternoon, he had always a word for the cobbler. Passing out again to supper at his boarding place, he had another, about the weather, the prospects of rain. And if Boaz were at work in the dark when he returned from an evening at the Board of Trade, there was a "Good night, Mr. Negro!"

7. **duenna** (dōō•ĕn′ə): a chaperon; in Spain and Portugal, an elderly woman who serves as a companion and protector to a young girl. Here, it refers to Wood's careful guarding of himself from close relationships.
8. **gratuitous** (grə•tōō′ə•təs): unearned, uncalled for.

On Boaz's part, his attitude toward his lodger was curious and paradoxical. He did not pretend to anything less than reverence for the young man's position; precisely on account of that position he was conscious toward Wood of a vague distrust. This was because he was an uneducated fellow.

To the uneducated, the idea of large finance is as uncomfortable as the idea of law. It must be said for Boaz that, responsive to Wood's unfailing civility, he fought against this sensation of dim and somehow shameful distrust.

Nevertheless, his whole parental soul was in arms that evening when, returning from the bank and finding the shop empty of loungers, Wood paused a moment to propose the bit of advice already referred to.

"Haven't you ever thought of having Manuel learn the trade?"

A suspicion, a kind of premonition, lighted the fires of defense.

"Shoemaking," said Boaz, "is good enough for a blind man."

"Oh, I don't know. At least it's better than doing nothing at all."

Boaz's hammer was still. He sat silent, monumental. Outwardly. For once his unfailing response had failed him, "Manuel ain't too stout, you know." Perhaps it had become suddenly quite inadequate.

He hated Wood; he despised Wood; more than ever before, a hundredfold more, quite abruptly, he distrusted Wood.

How could a man say such things as Wood had said? And where Manuel himself might hear!

Where Manuel *had* heard! Boaz's other emotions—hatred and contempt and distrust—were overshadowed. Sitting in darkness, no sound had come to his ears, no footfall, no infinitesimal creaking of a floor plank. Yet, by some sixth uncanny sense of the blind, he was aware that Manuel was standing in the dusk of the entry joining the shop to the house.

Boaz made a Herculean effort. The voice came out of his throat, harsh, bitter, and loud enough to have carried ten times the distance to his son's ears.

"Manuel is a good boy!"

"Yes—h'm—yes—I suppose so."

Wood shifted his weight. He seemed uncomfortable.

"Well. I'll be running along. I—ugh! Heavens!"

Something was happening. Boaz heard exclamations, breathings, the rustle of sleeve cloth in large, frantic, and futile graspings—all without understanding. Immediately there was an impact on the floor, and with it the unmistakable clink of metal. Boaz even heard that the metal was minted, and that the coins were gold. He understood. A coin sack, gripped not quite carefully enough for a moment under the other's overcoat, had shifted, slipped, escaped and fallen.

And Manuel had heard!

It was a dreadful moment for Boaz, dreadful in its native sense, as full of dread. Why? It was a moment of horrid revelation, ruthless clarification. His son, his link with the departed Angelina, that "good boy"—Manuel, standing in the shadow of the entry, visible alone to the blind, had heard the clink of falling gold, and—*and Boaz wished that he had not!*

There, amazing, disconcerting, destroying, stood the sudden fact.

Sitting as impassive and monumental as ever, his strong, bleached hands at rest on his work, round drops of sweat came out on Boaz's forehead. He scarcely took the sense of what Wood was saying. Only fragments.

"Government money, understand—for the breakwater workings—huge—too many people know here, everywhere—don't trust the safe—tin safe—'Noah's Ark'—give you my word—Heavens, no!"

It boiled down to this—the money, more money than was good for that antiquated "Noah's Ark" at the bank—and whose contemplated sojourn there overnight was public to too many minds—in short, Wood was not only incorruptible, he was canny. To what one of those minds, now, would it occur that he should take away that money bodily, under casual cover of his cat, to his own lodgings behind the cobbler shop of Boaz Negro? For this one, this important night!

He was sorry the coin sack had slipped, because he did not like to have the responsibility of secret sharer cast upon anyone, even upon Boaz, even by accident. On the other hand, how tremendously fortunate that it had been Boaz and not another. So far as that went, Wood had no more anxiety now than before. One incorruptible knows another.

"I'd trust you, Mr. Negro" (that was one of the fragments which came and stuck in the cobbler's brain), "as far as I would myself. As long as it's only you. I'm just going up here and throw it under the bed. Oh, yes, certainly."

Boaz ate no supper. For the first time in his life food was dry in his gullet. Even under those other successive crushing blows of Fate the full and generous habit of his functionings had carried on unabated; he had always eaten what was set before him. Tonight, over his untouched plate, he watched Manuel with his sightless eyes, keeping track of his every mouthful, word, intonation, breath. What profit he expected to extract from this catlike surveillance it is impossible to say.

When they arose from the supper table Boaz made another Herculean effort: "Manuel, you're a good boy!"

The formula had a quality of appeal, of despair, and of command.

"Manuel, you should be short of money, maybe. Look, what's this? A tenner? Well, there's a piece for the pocket; go and enjoy yourself."

He would have been frightened had Manuel, upsetting tradition, declined the offering. With the morbid contrariness of human imagination, the boy's avid grasping gave him no comfort.

He went out into the shop, where it was already dark, drew to him his last, his tools, mallets, cutters, pegs, leather. And having prepared to work, he remained idle. He found himself listening.

It has been observed that the large phenomena of sunlight and darkness were nothing to Boaz Negro. A busy night was broad day. Yet there was a difference; he knew it with the blind man's eyes, the ears.

Day was a vast confusion, or rather a wide fabric, of sounds: great and little sounds all woven together—voices, footfalls, wheels, far-off whistles and foghorns, flies buzzing in the sun. Night was another thing. Still, there were voices and footfalls, but rarer, emerging from the large, pure body of silence as definite, surprising, and yet familiar entities.

Tonight there was an easterly wind, coming off the water and carrying the sound of waves. So far as other fugitive sounds were concerned it was the same as silence. The wind made little difference to the ears. It nullified, from one direction at least, the other two visual processes of the blind, the sense of touch and the sense of smell. It blew away from the shop, toward the living house.

As has been said, Boaz found himself listening, scrutinizing with an extraordinary attention this immense background of sound. He heard footfalls. The story of that night was written, for him, in footfalls.

He heard them moving about the house, the lower floor, prowling here, there, halting for long spaces, advancing, retreating softly on the planks. About this aimless, interminable perambulation there was something to twist the nerves, something led and at the same time driven, like a succession of frail and indecisive charges.

Boaz lifted himself from his chair. All his impulses called him to make a stir, join battle, cast in the breach the reinforcement of his presence, authority, good will. He sank back again; his hands fell down. The curious impotence of the spectator held him.

He heard footfalls, too, on the upper floor, a little fainter, borne to the inner rather than the outer ear, along the solid causeway of partitions and floor, the legs of his chair, the bony framework of his body. Very faint indeed. Sinking back easily into the background of the wind. They, too, came and went, this room, that, to the passage, the stairhead, and away. About them, too, there was the same quality of being led and at the same time driven.

Time went by. In his darkness it seemed to Boaz that hours must have passed. He heard voices. Together with the footfalls, that abrupt, brief, and (in view of Wood's position) astounding interchange of sentences made up his history of the night. Wood must have opened the door at the head of the stair; by the sound of his voice he would be standing there, peering below perhaps; perhaps listening.

"What's wrong down there?" he called. "Why don't you go to bed?"

After a moment came Manuel's voice. "Ain't sleepy."

"Neither am I. Look here, do you like to play cards?"

"What kind? Euchre? I like euchre all right. Or pitch."[9]

"Well, what would you say to coming up and having a game of euchre then, Manuel? If you can't sleep?"

"That'd be all right."

The lower footfalls ascended to join the footfalls on the upper floor. There was the sound of a door closing.

Boaz sat still. In the gloom he might have been taken for a piece of furniture, of machinery, an extraordinary lay figure[10] perhaps, for the trying on of the boots he made. He seemed scarcely to breathe, only the sweat starting from his brow giving him an aspect of life.

He ought to have run, and leaped up that inner stair, and pounded with his fists on that door. He seemed unable to move. At

9. Euchre (yo͞o′kər) **. . . pitch:** In a game of *euchre,* whoever declares trumps has to make three to five tricks to win a hand; in *pitch,* the first card led or "pitched" by a designated player determines which suit is trump.

10. lay figure: a jointed model of the human body used by artists.

rare intervals feet passed on the sidewalk outside, just at his elbow, so to say, and yet somehow, tonight, immeasurably far away. Beyond the orbit of the moon. He heard Rugg, the policeman, noting the silence of the shop, muttering, "Boaz is to bed tonight," as he passed.

The wind increased. It poured against the shop with its deep, continuous sound of a river. Submerged in its body, Boaz caught the note of the town bell striking midnight.

Once more, after a long time, he heard footfalls. He heard them coming around the corner of the shop from the house, footfalls half swallowed by the wind, passing discreetly, without haste, retreating, merging step by step with the huge, incessant background of the wind.

Boaz's muscles tightened all over him. He had the impulse to start up, to fling open the door, shout into the night, "What are you doing? Stop there! Say! What are you doing and where are you going?"

And as before, the curious impotence of the spectator held him motionless. He had not stirred in his chair. And those footfalls, upon which hinged, as it were, that momentous decade of his life, were gone.

There was nothing to listen for now. Yet he continued to listen. Once or twice, half arousing himself, he drew toward him his unfinished work. And then relapsed into immobility.

As has been said, the wind, making little difference to the ears, made all the difference in the world with the sense of feeling and the sense of smell. From the one important direction of the house. That is how it could come about that Boaz Negro could sit waiting and listening to nothing in the shop and remain ignorant of disaster until the alarm had gone away and come back again, pounding, shouting, clanging.

"Fire!" he heard them bawling in the street. *"Fire! Fire!"*

Only slowly did he understand that the fire was in his own house.

There is nothing stiller in the world than the skeleton of a house in the dawn after a fire. It is as if everything living, positive, violent, had been completely drained in the one flaming act of violence, leaving nothing but negation till the end of time. It is worse than a tomb. A monstrous stillness! Even the footfalls of the searchers cannot disturb it, for they are separate and superficial. In its presence they are almost frivolous.

Half an hour after dawn the searchers found the body, if what was left from that consuming ordeal might be called a body. The discovery came as a shock. It seemed incredible that the occupant of that house, no cripple or invalid but an able man in the prime of youth, should not have awakened and made good his escape. It was the upper floor which had caught; the stairs had stood to the last. It was beyond calculation. Even if he had been asleep!

And he had not been asleep. This second and infinitely more appalling discovery began to be known. Slowly. By a hint, a breath of rumor here, there an allusion, half taken back. The man whose incinerated body still lay curled in its bed of cinders had been dressed at the moment of disaster, even to the watch, the cuff buttons, the studs, the very scarf pin. Fully clothed to the last detail, precisely as those who had dealings at the bank might have seen Campbell Wood any weekday morning for the past eight months. A man does not sleep with his clothes on. The skull of the man had been broken, as if with a blunt instrument of iron. On the charred lacework of the floor lay the leg of an old andiron[11] with which Boaz Negro and his Angelina had set up housekeeping in that new house.

It needed only Mr. Asa Whitelaw, coming up the street from that gaping "Noah's Ark" at the bank, to round out the scandalous circle of circumstance.

"Where is Manuel?"

Boaz Negro still sat in his shop, impassive, monumental, his thick, hairy arms resting on the arms of his chair. The tools and materials of his work remained scattered about him, as his irresolute gathering of the night before had left them. Into his eyes no change could come. He had lost his house, the visible monument of all those years of "skinning his fingers." It would seem that he had lost his son. And he had lost something incalculably precious—that hitherto unquenchable exuberance of the man.

"Where is Manuel?"

When he spoke his voice was unaccented and stale, like the voice of a man already dead.

"Yes, where is Manuel?"

He had answered them with their own question.

"When did you last see him?"

Neither he nor they seemed to take note of that profound irony.

"At supper."

11. andiron (and′ī′ərn): one of a pair of metal supports used to hold wood in an open fireplace.

"Tell us, Boaz; you knew about this money?"

The cobbler nodded his head.

"And did Manuel?"

He might have taken sanctuary in a legal doubt. How did he know what Manuel knew? Precisely! As before, he nodded his head.

"After supper, Boaz, you were in the shop? But you heard something?"

He went on to tell them what he had heard: the footfalls, below and above, the extraordinary conversation which had broken for a moment the silence of the inner hall. The account was bare, the phrases monosyllabic. He reported only what had been registered on the sensitive tympanums[12] of his ears, to the last whisper of footfalls stealing past the dark wall of the shop. Of all the formless tangle of thoughts, suspicions, interpretations, and the special and personal knowledge given to the blind which moved in his brain, he said nothing.

He shut his lips there. He felt himself on the defensive. Just as he distrusted the higher ramifications of finance (his house had gone down uninsured), so before the rites and processes of that inscrutable creature, the Law, he felt himself menaced by the invisible and the unknown, helpless, oppressed; in an abject sense, skeptical.

"Keep clear of the Law!" they had told him in his youth. The monster his imagination had summoned up then still stood beside him in his age.

Having exhausted his monosyllabic and superficial evidence, they could move him no further. He became deaf and dumb. He sat before them, an image cast in some immensely heavy stuff, inanimate. His lack of visible emotion impressed them. Remembering his exuberance, it was only the stranger to see him unmoving and unmoved. Only once did they catch sight of something beyond. As they were preparing to leave he opened his mouth. What he said was like a swan song[13] to the years of his exuberant happiness. Even now there was no color of expression in his words, which sounded mechanical.

"Now I have lost everything. My house. My last son. Even my honor. You would not think I would like to live. But I go to live. I go to work. That *cachorra,* one day he shall come back again, in the dark night, to have a look. I shall go to show you all. That *cachorra!*"

12. tympanums (tĭm′pə•nəms): eardrums; a tympanum is the thin membrane, shaped like the head of a drum, that separates the middle ear from the external ear.

13. swan song: a farewell. An allusion to the fable that a swan sings a final song before dying.

(And from that time on, it was noted, he never referred to the fugitive by any other name than *cachorra,* which is a kind of dog. "That *cachorra!"* As if he had forfeited the relationship not only of the family, but of the very genus, the very race! "That *cachorra!"*)

He pronounced this resolution without passion. When they assured him that the culprit would come back again indeed, much sooner than he expected, "with a rope around his neck," he shook his head slowly.

"No, you shall not catch that *cachorra* now. But one day—"

There was something about its very colorlessness which made it sound oracular. It was at least prophetic. They searched, laid their traps, proceeded with all their placards, descriptions, rewards, clues, trails. But on Manuel Negro they never laid their hands.

Months passed and became years. Boaz Negro did not rebuild his house. He might have done so, out of his earnings, for upon himself he spent scarcely anything, reverting to his old habit of an almost miserly economy. Yet perhaps it would have been harder after all. For his earnings were less and less. In that town a cobbler who sits in any empty shop is apt to want for trade. Folks take their boots to mend where they take their bodies to rest and their minds to be edified.[14]

No longer did the walls of Boaz's shop resound to the boastful recollections of young men. Boaz had changed. He had become not only different, but opposite. A metaphor will do best. The spirit of Boaz Negro had been meadowed hillside giving upon the open sea, the sun, the warm, wild winds from beyond the blue horizon. And covered with flowers, always hungry and thirsty for the sun and the fabulous wind and bright showers of rain. It had become an entrenched camp, lying silent, sullen, verdureless, under a gray sky. He stood solitary against the world. His approaches were closed. He was blind, and he was also deaf and dumb.

Against that, what can young fellows do who wish for nothing but to rest themselves and talk about their friends and enemies? They had come and they had tried. They had raised their voices even higher than before. Their boasts had grown louder, more presumptuous, more preposterous, until, before the cold separation of that unmoving and as if contemptuous presence in the cobbler's chair, they burst of their own air, like toy balloons. And they went and left Boaz alone.

14. edified: instructed and improved, especially in a moral or religious sense.

There was another thing which served, if not to keep them away, at least not to entice them back. That was the aspect of the place. It was not cheerful. It invited no one. In its way that fire-bitten ruin grew to be almost as great a scandal as the act itself had been. It was plainly an eyesore. A valuable property, on the town's main thoroughfare—and an eyesore! The neighboring owners protested.

Their protestations might as well have gone against a stone wall. That man was deaf and dumb. He had become, in a way, a kind of vegetable, for the quality of a vegetable is that, while it is endowed with life, it remains fixed in one spot. For years Boaz was scarcely seen to move foot out of that shop that was left him, a small, square, blistered promontory[15] on the shores of ruin.

He must indeed have carried out some rudimentary sort of domestic program under the debris at the rear (he certainly did not sleep or eat in the shop). One or two lower rooms were left fairly intact. The outward aspect of the place was formless; it grew to be no more than a mound in time; the charred timbers, one or two still standing, lean and naked against the sky, lost their blackness and faded to a silvery gray. It would have seemed strange, had they not grown accustomed to the thought, to imagine that blind man, like a mole, or some slow slug, turning himself mysteriously in the bowels of that gray mound—that time-silvered eyesore.

When they saw him, however, he was in the shop. They opened the door to take in their work (when other cobblers turned them off), and they saw him seated in his chair in the half darkness, his whole person, legs, torso, neck, head, as motionless as the vegetable of which we have spoken—only his hands and his bare arms endowed with visible life. The gloom had bleached the skin to the color of damp ivory, and against the background of his immobility they moved with a certain amazing monstrousness, interminably. No, they were never still. One wondered what they could be at. Surely he could not have had enough work now to keep those insatiable hands so monstrously in motion. Even far into the night. Tap-tap-tap! Blows continuous and powerful. On what? On nothing? On the bare iron last? And for what purpose? To what conceivable end?

Well, one could imagine those arms, growing paler, also grow-

15. promontory (prŏm′ən•tôr′ē): a high point of land projecting into a body of water; here, used figuratively, it means that the shop, being the only piece of Boaz's property left standing, is distinct and noticeable.

ing thicker and more formidable with that unceasing labor; the muscles feeding themselves omnivorously[16] on their own waste, the cords toughening, the bone tissues revitalizing themselves without end. One could imagine the whole aspiration of that mute and motionless man pouring itself out into those pallid arms, and the arms taking it up with a kind of blind greed. Storing it up. Against a day!

"That *cachorra!* One day—"

What were the thoughts of this man? What moved within that motionless cranium covered with long hair? Who can say? Behind everything, of course, stood that bitterness against the world—the blind world—blinder than he would ever be. And against "that *cachorra.*" But this was no longer a thought: it was the man.

Just as all muscular aspiration flowed into his arms, so all the energies of his senses turned to his ears. The man had become, you might say, two arms and two ears. Can you imagine a man listening, intently, through the waking hours of nine years?

Listening to footfalls. Marking with a special emphasis of concentration the beginning, rise, full passage, falling away, and dying of all the footfalls. By day, by night, winter and summer and winter again. Unraveling the skein[17] of footfalls passing up and down the street!

For three years he wondered when they would come. For the next three years he wondered if they would ever come. It was during the last three that a doubt began to trouble him. It gnawed at his huge moral strength. Like a hidden seepage of water, it undermined (in anticipation) his terrible resolution. It was a sign, perhaps, of age, a slipping away of the reckless infallibility of youth.

Supposing, after all, that his ears should fail him. Supposing they were capable of being tricked, without his being able to know it. Supposing that the *cachorra* should come and go, and he, Boaz, living in some vast delusion, some unrealized distortion of memory, should let him pass unknown. Supposing precisely this thing had already happened!

Or the other way around. What if he should hear the footfalls coming, even into the very shop itself? What if he should be as sure of

16. omnivorously (ŏm•nĭv′ər•əs•lē): greedily and indiscriminately.

17. skein (skān): a quantity of yarn or thread wound in a loose coil; here, it refers to the confused, complicated, and tangled mass of footfalls.

them as of his own soul? What, then, if he should strike? And what then if it were not that *cachorra* after all? How many tens and hundreds of millions of people were there in the world? Was it possible for them all to have footfalls distinct and different?

Then they would take him and hang him. And that *cachorra* might then come and go at his own will, undisturbed.

As he sat there, sometimes the sweat rolled down his nose, cold as rain.

Supposing!

Sometimes, quite suddenly, in broad day, in the booming silence of the night, he would start. Not outwardly. But beneath the pale integument[18] of his skin all his muscles tightened and his nerves sang. His breathing stopped. It seemed almost as if his heart stopped.

Was that it? Were those the feet, there, emerging faintly from the distance? Yes, there was something about them. Yes! Memory was in travail.[19] Yes, yes, yes! No! How could he be sure? Ice ran down into his empty eyes. The footfalls were already passing. They were gone, swallowed up already by time and space. Had that been that *cachorra?*

Nothing in his life had been so hard to meet as this insidious[20] drain of distrust in his own powers, this sense of a traitor within the walls. His iron-gray hair turned white. It was always this now, from the beginning of the day to the end of the night: how was he to know? How was he to be inevitably, unshakably, sure?

Curiously, after all this purgatory of doubts, he did know them. For a moment at least, when he had heard them, he was unshakably sure. It was on an evening of the winter holidays, the Portuguese festival of *Menin'*[21] *Jesus.* Christ was born again in a hundred mangers on a hundred tiny altars; there were cake and wine; songs went shouting by to the accompaniment of mandolins and tramping feet. The wind blew cold under a clear sky. In all the houses there were lights; even in Boaz Negro's shop a lamp was lit just now, for a man had been in for a pair of boots which Boaz had patched. The man had gone out again. Boaz was thinking of blowing out the light. It meant nothing to him.

He leaned forward, judging the position of the lamp-chimney

18. integument (ĭn•tĕg′yə•mənt): covering.

19. travail (trăv′āl): strenuous physical or mental labor, especially that involving pain or suffering.

20. insidious (ĭn•sĭd′ē•əs): progressing gradually, but harmfully; treacherous.

21. *Menin':* a shortened form of the word *menino,* meaning "child or baby."

by the heat on his face, and puffed out his cheeks to blow. Then his cheeks collapsed suddenly, and he sat back again.

It was not odd that he had failed to hear the footfalls until they were actually within the door. A crowd of merrymakers was passing just then. Their songs and tramping almost shook the shop.

Boaz sat back. Beneath his passive exterior his nerves thrummed; his muscles had grown as hard as wood. Yes! Yes! But no. He had heard nothing; no more than a single step, a single foot-pressure on the planks within the door. Dear God! He could not tell!

Going through the pain of an enormous effort, he opened his lips.

"What can I do for you?"

"Well, I—I don't know. To tell the truth—"

The voice was unfamiliar, but it might be assumed. Boaz held himself. His face remained blank, interrogating, slightly helpless.

"I am a little deaf," he said. "Come nearer."

The footfalls came halfway across the intervening floor, and there appeared to hesitate. The voice, too, had a note of uncertainty.

"I was just looking around. I have a pair of—well, you mend shoes?"

Boaz nodded his head. It was not in response to the words, for they meant nothing. What he had heard was the footfalls on the floor.

Now he was sure. As has been said, for a moment at least after he had heard them he was unshakably sure. The congestion of his muscles had passed. He was at peace.

The voice became audible once more. Before the massive preoccupation of the blind man it became still less certain of itself.

"Well, I haven't got the shoes with me. I was—just looking around."

It was amazing to Boaz, this miraculous sensation of peace.

"Wait!" Then, bending his head as if listening to the winter wind: "It's cold tonight. You've left the door open. But wait!" Leaning down, his hand fell on a rope's end hanging by the chair. The gesture was one continuous, undeviating movement of the hand. No hesitation. No groping. How many hundreds, how many thousands of times, had his hand schooled itself in that gesture!

A single strong pull. With a little *bang* the front door had swung to and latched itself. Not only the front door. The other door, leading to the rear, had closed too, and latched itself with a little *bang*. And leaning forward from his chair, Boaz blew out the light.

There was not a sound in the shop. Outside, feet continued to go by, ringing on the frozen road; voices were lifted; the wind hustled about the corners of the wooden shell with a continuous, shrill note of whistling. All of this outside, as on another planet. Within the blackness of the shop the complete silence persisted.

Boaz listened. Sitting on the edge of his chair, half-crouching, his head, with its long, unkempt, white hair, bent slightly to one side, he concentrated upon this chambered silence the full powers of his senses. He hardly breathed. The other person in that room could not be breathing at all, it seemed.

No, there was not a breath, not the stirring of a sole on wood, not the infinitesimal rustle of any fabric. It was as if in this utter stoppage of sound, even the blood had ceased to flow in the veins and arteries of that man, who was like a rat caught in a trap.

It was appalling even to Boaz; even to the cat. Listening became more than a labor. He began to have to fight against a growing impulse to shout out loud, to leap, sprawl forward without aim in that unstirred darkness—do something. Sweat rolled down from behind his ears, into his shirt collar. He gripped the chair arms. To keep quiet he sank his teeth into his lower lip. He would not! He would not!

And of a sudden he heard before him, in the center of the room, an outburst of breath, an outrush from lungs in the extremity of pain, thick, laborious, fearful. A coughing up of dammed air.

Pushing himself from the arms of the chair, Boaz leaped.

His fingers, passing swiftly through the air, closed on something. It was a sheaf of hair, bristly and thick. It was a man's beard.

On the road outside, up and down the street for a hundred yards, merrymaking people turned to look at one another. With an abrupt cessation of laughter, of speech. Inquiringly. Even with an unconscious dilation of the pupils of their eyes.

"What was that?"

There had been a scream. There could be no doubt of that. A single, long-drawn note. Immensely high-pitched. Not as if it were human.

"God's sake! What was that? Where'd it come from?"

Those nearest said it came from the cobbler shop of Boaz Negro.

They went and tried the door. It was closed, even locked, as if for the night. There was no light behind the window shade. But Boaz would not have a light. They beat on the door. No answer.

But from where, then, had that prolonged, as if animal, note come?

They ran about, penetrating into the side lanes, interrogating, prying. Coming back at last, inevitably, to the neighborhood of Boaz Negro's shop.

The body lay on the floor at Boaz's feet, where it had tumbled down slowly after a moment from the spasmodic embrace of his arms—those ivory-colored arms which had beaten so long upon the bare iron surface of a last. Blows continuous and powerful. It seemed incredible. They were so weak now. They could not have lifted the hammer now.

But that beard! That bristly, thick, square beard of a stranger!

His hands remembered it. Standing with his shoulders fallen forward and his weak arms hanging down, Boaz began to shiver. The whole thing was incredible. What was on the floor there, upheld in the vast gulf of darkness, he could not see. Neither could he hear it, smell it. Nor (if he did not move his foot) could he feel it. What he did not hear, smell, or touch did not exist. It was not there.

But that beard! All the accumulated doubtings of those years fell down upon him. After all, the thing he had been so fearful of in his weak imaginings had happened. He had killed a stranger. He, Boaz Negro, had murdered an innocent man!

And all on account of that beard. His deep panic made him lightheaded. He began to confuse cause and effect. If it were not for that beard, it would have been that *cachorra*.

On this basis he began to reason with crazy directness. And to act. He went and pried open the door into the entry. From the shelf he took down his razor. A big heavy-heeled strop.[22] His hands began to hurry. And the mug, half full of soap. And water. It would have to be cold water. But after all, he thought (lightheadedly), at this time of night—

Outside, they were at the shop again. The crowd's habit is to forget a thing quickly, once it is out of sight and hearing. But there had been something about that solitary cry which continued to bother them, even in memory. Where had it been? Where had it come from? And those who had stood nearest the cobbler shop were heard again. They were certain now, dead certain. They could swear!

In the end they broke down the door.

22. strop: a strip of leather used for sharpening a razor.

If Boaz heard them he gave no sign. An absorption as complete as it was monstrous wrapped him. Kneeling in the glare of the lantern they had brought, as impervious[23] as his own shadow sprawling behind him, he continued to shave the dead man on the floor.

No one touched him. Their minds and imaginations were arrested by the gigantic proportions of the act. The unfathomable presumption of the act. As if throwing murder in their faces to the tune of a jig in a barbershop. It is a fact that none of them so much as thought of touching him. No less than all of them, together with all other men, shorn of their imaginations—that is to say, the expressionless and imperturbable creature of the Law—would be sufficient to touch that ghastly man.

On the other hand, they could not leave him alone. They could not go away. They watched. They saw the damp, lather-soaked beard of that victimized stranger falling away, stroke by stroke of the flashing, heavy razor. The dead denuded by the blind!

It was seen that Boaz was about to speak. It was something important he was about to utter; something, one would say, fatal. The words would not come all at once. They swelled his cheeks out. His razor was arrested. Lifting his face, he encircled the watchers with a gaze at once of imploration and of command. As if he could see them. As if he could read his answer in the expressions of their faces.

"Tell me one thing now. Is it that *cachorra?*"

For the first time those men in the room made sounds. They shuffled their feet. It was as if an uncontrollable impulse to ejaculation, laughter, derision, forbidden by the presence of death, had gone down into their boot soles.

"Manuel?" one of them said. "You mean *Manuel?*"

Boaz laid the razor down on the floor beside its work. He got up from his knees slowly, as if his joints hurt. He sat down in his chair, rested his hands on the arms, and once more encircled the company with his sightless gaze.

"Not Manuel. Manuel was a good boy. But tell me now, is it that *cachorra?*"

Here was something out of their calculations; something for them mentally to chew on. Mystification is a good thing sometimes. It gives the brain a fillip,[24] stirs memory, puts the gears of imagination

23. impervious (ĭm·pûr′vē·əs): unaffected; impenetrable.

24. fillip: stimulus or incentive. A sharp tap or fillip is made when a finger, pressed down by the thumb, is suddenly released or snapped outward.

in mesh. One man, an old, tobacco-chewing fellow, began to stare harder at the face on the floor. Something moved in his intellect.

"No, but look here now, by God—"

He had even stopped chewing. But he was forestalled by another.

"Say now, if it don't look like that fellow Wood, himself. The bank fellow—that was burned—remember? Himself."

"That *cachorra* was not burned. Not that Wood. You darned fool!"

Boaz spoke from his chair. They hardly knew his voice, emerging from its long silence; it was so didactic and arid.

"That *cachorra* was not burned. It was my boy that was burned. It was that *cachorra* called my boy upstairs. That *cachorra* killed my boy. That *cachorra* put his clothes on my boy, and he set my house on fire. I knew it all the time. Because when I heard those feet come out of my house and go away, I knew they were the feet of that *cachorra* from the bank. I did not know where he was going to. Something said to me—you better ask him where he is going to. But then I said, you are foolish. He had the money from the bank. I did not know. And then my house was on fire. No, it was not my boy that went away; it was that *cachorra* all the time. You darned fools! Did you think I was waiting for my own boy?

"Now I show you all," he said at the end. "And now I can get hanged."

No one ever touched Boaz Negro for that murder. For murder it was in the eye and letter of the Law. The Law in a small town is sometimes a curious creature; it is sometimes blind only in one eye.

Their minds and imaginations in that town were arrested by the romantic proportions of the act. Simply, no one took it up. I believe the man Wood was understood to have died of heart failure.

When they asked Boaz why he had not told what he knew as to the identity of that fugitive in the night, he seemed to find it hard to say exactly. How could a man of no education define for them his own but half-denied misgivings about the Law, his sense of oppression, constraint, and awe, of being on the defensive, even, in an abject way, his skepticism? About his wanting, come what might, to "keep clear of the Law"?

He did say this: "You would have laughed at me."

And this: "If I told folks it was Wood went away, then I say he would not dare come back again."

That was the last. Very shortly he began to refuse to talk about the thing at all. The act was completed. Like the creature of fable,[25] it had consumed itself. Out of that old man's consciousness it had departed. Amazingly. Like a dream dreamed out.

Slowly at first, in a makeshift, piece-at-a-time, poor man's way, Boaz commenced to rebuild his house. That "eyesore" vanished.

And slowly at first, like the miracle of a green shoot pressing out from the dead earth, that priceless and unquenchable exuberance of the man was seen returning. Unquenchable, after all.

25. **creature of fable:** an allusion to the phoenix, a legendary bird of Egyptian mythology. After living for five to six hundred years, the phoenix destroys itself in fire and rises again, renewed and youthful, to live through another long cycle.

Meaning

1. How does the first paragraph set the *tone* of the story—the author's attitude toward his subject and his characters? What is the tone?
2. How would you describe and characterize Boaz Negro? What is the meaning of the phrase "unquenchable exuberance"?
3. What is the point of view of the story? Through whose eyes do we see Mr. Wood?
4. What is the theme of the story?

Method

1. When a writer wants to introduce an important fact in a story, he usually mentions it early and usually quite casually. This is called a *plant.* Where do we first learn that Boaz Negro can recognize people by their footfalls?
2. How does Steele maintain suspense? Why does he have Negro repeatedly use the word *cachorra?*
3. The climax takes place during a Christmas festival. The writer uses this setting to account for the crowds in the street and for their presence in the shop. But he also intends it to be symbolic. How is the season symbolic of the subsequent change in Negro?
4. How are we prepared for the ending? Give some examples of foreshadowing in this story.

Language: Suffixes

"And those footfalls, upon which hinged, as it were, that *momentous* decade in his life, were gone." Anything that is *momentous* is full of importance. The suffix *-ous* means "full of" or "having." The word *moment* by itself may mean a short time or a particular period, such as a moment in history.

A *suffix* comes after the main part of a word and can change its meaning or function. Among the suffixes you should learn to recognize on sight as separate parts of words are *-less,* meaning "without"; *-ity,* meaning "state, condition, or quality of"; and *-ble,* meaning "capable of."

A knowledge of these four suffixes should help you in breaking down each of the following words from "Footfalls" and working out its meaning. Consult your dictionary to see if your analysis of each word is correct.

1. vigorous
2. aimless
3. laxity
4. unquenchable
5. adventurous
6. accessible
7. ruthless
8. infallibility
9. inscrutable

Write a sentence for each of these words.

Discussion and Composition

1. Is the ending of "Footfalls" a "trick ending"? Why or why not? Write a composition using the following topic sentence and giving reasons to support your point of view: The ending of "Footfalls" is (is not) completely justified by the clues Wilbur Daniel Steele gives in the story.

2. Outline the plot of a movie or television mystery or detective drama that you consider suspenseful. Compare its surprise conclusion with the ending of "Footfalls." Compare both stories for originality of theme, characterization, and realism of dialogue.

EDGAR ALLAN POE

(1809–1849)

Poet, short-story writer, editor, and critic, Edgar Allan Poe was a versatile genius, and the first great writer who grew up in the South. Born in Boston, Poe was the son of traveling actors. When he was two years old, his mother died, and Poe was taken in by a wealthy Virginia family named Allan. In 1826, he entered the University of Virginia, but left a year later when Mr. Allan refused to pay his gambling debts. Poe quarreled constantly with his foster father, who wanted Poe to follow a law career. In 1830, Poe received an appointment to West Point, but he was expelled within a year; Mr. Allan then discontinued his financial support of the young man.

Poe earned a meager living by editing and writing poetry and short stories. In 1835, he became editor of *The Southern Literary Messenger* and in the same year married his young cousin, Virginia Clemm. His wife became seriously ill and died at the age of twenty-four. Two years later, depressed and in debt, Poe died at an age when many writers are just beginning their careers.

"The Cask of Amontillado" (1846) is a horror story intended to produce a single emotional impact on the reader. It adheres to Poe's definition of plot as "that in which no part can be displaced without ruin to the whole."

---

*THE CASK OF AMONTILLADO**

The thousand injuries of Fortunato I had borne as I best could, but when he ventured upon insult, I vowed revenge. You, who so well know the nature of my soul, will not suppose, however, that I gave utterance to a threat. *At length* I would be avenged; this was a point definitely settled—but the very definitiveness with which it was resolved precluded the idea of risk. I must not only punish, but punish with impunity. A wrong is unredressed when retribution overtakes its

* **Amontillado:** sherry wine made near Montilla, a Spanish town.

redresser. It is equally unredressed when the avenger fails to make himself felt as such to him who has done the wrong.

It must be understood that neither by word nor deed had I given Fortunato cause to doubt my good will. I continued, as was my wont,[1] to smile in his face, and he did not perceive that my smile *now* was at the thought of his immolation.[2]

He had a weak point—this Fortunato—although in other regards he was a man to be respected and even feared. He prided himself on his connoisseurship[3] in wine. Few Italians have the true virtuoso spirit. For the most part their enthusiasm is adopted to suit the time and opportunity—to practice imposture upon the British and Austrian *millionaires.* In painting and gemmary[4] Fortunato, like his countrymen, was a quack, but in the matter of old wines he was sincere. In this respect I did not differ from him materially;—I was skillful in the Italian vintages myself and bought largely whenever I could.

It was about dusk, one evening during the supreme madness of the carnival season, that I encountered my friend. He accosted me with excessive warmth, for he had been drinking much. The man wore motley.[5] He had on a tight-fitting parti-striped dress, and his head was surmounted by the conical cap and bells. I was so pleased to see him that I thought I should never have done wringing his hand.

I said to him—"My dear Fortunato, you are luckily met. How remarkably well you are looking today! But I have received a pipe[6] of what passes for Amontillado, and I have my doubts."

"How?" said he, "Amontillado? A pipe? Impossible! And in the middle of the carnival!"

"I have my doubts," I replied; "and I was silly enough to pay the full Amontillado price without consulting you in the matter. You were not to be found, and I was fearful of losing a bargain."

"Amontillado!"

"I have my doubts."

"Amontillado!"

"And I must satisfy them."

1. **wont** (wônt): habit.
2. **immolation** (ĭm′ə•lā′•shən): being killed or sacrificed.
3. **connoisseurship** (kŏn′ə•sûr′shĭp): the ability to make competent judgments, based on thorough knowledge, in matters of art or taste.
4. **gemmary** (jĕm′•rē): knowledge of gems.
5. **motley** (mŏt′lē): a multicolored garment, especially that of a jester.
6. **pipe:** a large cask.

"Amontillado!"

"As you are engaged, I am on my way to Luchesi. If any one has a critical turn, it is he. He will tell me–"

"Luchesi cannot tell Amontillado from Sherry."

"And yet some fools will have it that his taste is a match for your own."

"Come, let us go."

"Whither?"

"To your vaults."

"My friend, no; I will not impose upon your good nature. I perceive you have an engagement. Luchesi–"

"I have no engagement;–come."

"My friend, no. It is not the engagement, but the severe cold with which I perceive you are afflicted. The vaults are insufferably damp. They are encrusted with niter."[7]

"Let us go, nevertheless. The cold is merely nothing. Amontillado! You have been imposed upon. And as for Luchesi, he cannot distinguish Sherry from Amontillado."

Thus speaking, Fortunato possessed himself of my arm; and putting on a mask of black silk, and drawing a *roquelaure*[8] closely about my person, I suffered him to hurry me to my palazzo.[9]

There were no attendants at home; they had absconded to make merry in honor of the time. I had told them that I should not return until the morning, and had given them explicit orders not to stir from the house. These orders were sufficient, I well knew, to insure their immediate disappearance, one and all, as soon as my back was turned.

I took from their sconces[10] two flambeaux,[11] and giving one to Fortunato, bowed him through several suites of rooms to the archway that led into the vaults. I passed down a long and winding staircase, requesting him to be cautious as he followed. We came at length to the foot of the descent, and stood together on the damp ground of the catacombs of the Montresors.

The gait of my friend was unsteady, and the bells upon his cap jingled as he strode.

7. **niter** (nī′tər): potassium nitrate; a salt deposit which forms on the damp walls of caves.

8. **roquelaure** (rok′ə•lôr): *French,* a knee-length cloak.

9. **palazzo** (pä•lot′zō): a palace or elegant town house in Italy.

10. **sconces** (skŏn′sez): wall brackets for holding candles or other lights.

11. **flambeaux** (flăm′bōz): burning torches.

"The pipe?" said he.

"It is farther on," said I; "but observe the white web-work which gleams from these cavern walls."

He turned toward me, and looked into my eyes with two filmy orbs that distilled the rheum[12] of intoxication.

"Niter?" he asked, at length.

"Niter," I replied. "How long have you had that cough?"

"Ugh! ugh! ugh!—ugh! ugh! ugh!—ugh! ugh! ugh!—ugh! ugh! ugh!—ugh! ugh! ugh!"

My poor friend found it impossible to reply for many minutes.

"It is nothing," he said at last.

"Come," I said with decision, "we will go back; your health is precious. You are rich, respected, admired, beloved; you are happy, as once I was. You are a man to be missed. For me it is no matter. We will go back; you will be ill, and I cannot be responsible. Besides, there is Luchesi—"

"Enough," he said; "the cough is a mere nothing: it will not kill me. I shall not die of a cough."

"True—true," I replied; "and, indeed, I had no intention of alarming you unnecessarily—but you should use all proper caution. A draft of this Médoc[13] will defend us from the damps."

Here I knocked off the neck of a bottle which I drew from a long row of its fellows that lay upon the mold.

"Drink," I said, presenting him the wine.

He raised it to his lips with a leer. He paused and nodded to me familiarly, while his bells jingled.

"I drink," he said, "to the buried that repose around us."

"And I to your long life."

He again took my arm, and we proceeded.

"These vaults," he said, "are extensive."

"The Montresors," I replied, "were a great and numerous family."

"I forget your arms."[14]

"A huge human foot d'or,[15] in a field azure; the foot crushes a serpent rampant[16] whose fangs are imbedded in the heel."

12. **rheum** (ro͞om): a watery discharge from the eyes and nose.
13. **Médoc** (mā•dôk′): a red wine made in Médoc, France.
14. **arms:** hereditary insignia of a family.
15. **d'or** (dôr): *French,* of gold.
16. **rampant** (răm′pənt): in heraldry, this means rearing up in a threatening manner; the word also means unrestrained, wild, or unchecked.

"And the motto?"

Nemo me impune lacessit."[17]

"Good!" he said.

The wine sparkled in his eyes and the bells jingled. My own fancy grew warm with the Médoc. We had passed through walls of piled bones, with casks and puncheons[18] intermingling, into the inmost recesses of the catacombs. I paused again, and this time I made bold to seize Fortunato by an arm above the elbow.

"The niter!" I said; "see, it increases. It hangs like moss upon the vaults. We are below the river's bed. The drops of moisture trickle among the bones. Come, we will go back before it is too late. Your cough—"

"It is nothing," he said; "let us go on. But first, another draft of Médoc."

I broke and reached him a flagon[19] of De Graves.[20] He emptied it at a breath. His eyes flashed with a fierce light. He laughed and threw the bottle upward with a gesticulation I did not understand.

I looked at him in surprise. He repeated the movement—a grotesque one. "You do not comprehend?" he said.

"Not I," I replied.

"Then you are not of the brotherhood."

"How?"

"You are not of the masons."[21]

"Yes, yes," I said; "yes, yes."

"You? Impossible! A mason?"

"A mason," I replied.

"A sign," he said.

"It is this," I answered, producing a trowel from beneath the folds of my *roquelaure.*

"You jest," he exclaimed, recoiling a few paces. "But let us proceed to the Amontillado."

"Be it so," I said, replacing the tool beneath the cloak and again offering him my arm. He leaned upon it heavily. We continued our

17. Nemo me impune lacessit (nē'mō mē im•pū'nē la•kes'sit): *Latin,* No one injures me and escapes punishment.

18. puncheons (pŭn'chənz): large casks for liquor.

19. flagon (flăg'ən): a large, bulging, short-necked bottle.

20. De Graves (gravz; gräv): a white or red wine produced in a district near Bordeaux, France.

21. masons: that is, Freemasons, members of a widespread secret fraternal society; the word also means bricklayers.

route in search of the Amontillado. We passed through a range of low arches, descended, passed on, and descending again, arrived at a deep crypt, in which the foulness of the air caused our flambeaux rather to glow than flame.

At the most remote end of the crypt there appeared another, less spacious. Its walls had been lined with human remains, piled to the vault overhead, in the fashion of the great catacombs of Paris. Three sides of this interior crypt were still ornamented in this manner. From the fourth the bones had been thrown down, and lay promiscuously upon the earth, forming at one point a mound of some size. Within the wall thus exposed by the displacing of the bones, we perceived a still interior crypt or recess, in depth about four feet, in width three, in height six, or seven. It seemed to have been constructed for no especial use within itself, but formed merely the interval between two of the colossal supports of the roof of the catacombs, and was backed by one of the circumscribing walls of solid granite.

It was in vain that Fortunato, uplifting his dull torch, endeavored to pry into the depths of the recess. Its termination the feeble light did not enable us to see.

"Proceed," I said; "herein is the Amontillado. As for Luchesi—"

"He is an ignoramus," interrupted my friend, as he stepped unsteadily forward, while I followed immediately at his heels. In an instant he had reached the extremity of the niche, and finding his progress arrested by the rock, stood stupidly bewildered. A moment more and I had fettered[22] him to the granite. In its surface were two iron staples,[23] distant from each other about two feet, horizontally. From one of these depended[24] a short chain, from the other a padlock. Throwing the links about his waist, it was but the work of a few seconds to secure it. He was too much astounded to resist. Withdrawing the key, I stepped back from the recess.

"Pass your hand," I said, "over the wall; you cannot help feeling the niter. Indeed it is *very* damp. Once more let me *implore* you to return. No? Then I must positively leave you. But I must first render you all the little attentions in my power."

"The Amontillado!" ejaculated my friend, not yet recovered from his astonishment.

22. fettered (fĕt′ərd): chained.
23. staples: *here,* U-shaped metal loops with pointed ends to be driven into a surface, used to secure a bolt or lock.
24. depended: hung.

"True," I replied: "the Amontillado."

As I said these words I busied myself among the pile of bones of which I have before spoken. Throwing them aside, I soon uncovered a quantity of building-stone and mortar. With these materials and with the aid of my trowel, I began vigorously to wall up the entrance of the niche.

I had scarcely laid the first tier of the masonry when I discovered that the intoxication of Fortunato had in a great measure worn off. The earliest indication I had of this was a low moaning cry from the depth of the recess. It was *not* the cry of a drunken man. There was then a long and obstinate silence. I laid the second tier, and the third, and the fourth; and then I heard the furious vibrations of the chain. The noise lasted for several minutes, during which, that I might hearken to it with the more satisfaction, I ceased my labors and sat down upon the bones. When at last the clanking subsided, I resumed the trowel, and finished without interruption the fifth, the sixth, and the seventh tier. The wall was now nearly upon a level with my breast. I again paused, and holding the flambeaux over the mason-work, threw a few feeble rays upon the figure within.

A succession of loud and shrill screams, bursting suddenly from the throat of the chained form, seemed to thrust me violently back. For a brief moment I hesitated—I trembled. Unsheathing my rapier,[25] I began to grope with it about the recess; but the thought of an instant reassured me. I placed my hand upon the solid fabric of the catacombs, and felt satisfied. I reapproached the wall. I replied to the yells of him who clamored. I re-echoed—I aided—I surpassed them in volume and in strength. I did this, and the clamorer grew still.

It was now midnight, and my task was drawing to a close. I had completed the eighth, the ninth, and the tenth tier. I had finished a portion of the last and the eleventh; there remained but a single stone to be fitted and plastered in. I struggled with its weight; I placed it partially in its destined position. But now there came from out the niche a low laugh that erected the hairs upon my head. It was succeeded by a sad voice, which I had difficulty in recognizing as that of the noble Fortunato. The voice said—

"Ha! ha! ha!—he! he! he!—a very good joke indeed—an excellent jest. We will have many a rich laugh about it at the palazzo—he! he! he!—over our wine—he! he! he!"

"The Amontillado!" I said.

25. rapier (rā′pē•ər): a straight, two-edged sword with a narrow, pointed blade.

"He! he! he!—he! he! he!—yes, the Amontillado. But is it not getting late? Will not they be awaiting us at the palazzo, the Lady Fortunato and the rest? Let us be gone."

"Yes," I said, "let us be gone."

"For the love of God, Montresor!"

"Yes," I said, "for the love of God!"

But to these words I hearkened in vain for a reply. I grew impatient. I called aloud—

"Fortunato!"

No answer. I called again:

"Fortunato!"

No answer still. I thrust a torch through the remaining aperture and let it fall within. There came forth in return only a jingling of the bells. My heart grew sick—on account of the dampness of the catacombs. I hastened to make an end of my labor. I forced the last stone into its position; I plastered it up. Against the new masonry I re-erected the old rampart of bones. For the half of a century no mortal has disturbed them. *In pace requiescat!*[26]

26. **In pace requiescat!** (in pə'kə•rek'wē•es'kat; in pə'chə rek'wē•es'chat): *Latin,* May he rest in peace.

Meaning

1. Poe quickly reveals Montresor to be a man with extraordinary powers of deception and manipulation. Cite some examples of Montresor's clever use of psychology.
2. Irony pervades "The Cask of Amontillado" and is carefully built into the structure of the story itself—into its setting, dialogue, and choice of characters. The story's setting is an example of *irony of situation* because a carnival is a place for merriment and shouts of laughter, not for intricate plans of murder and cries of terror.

   Montresor hails his friend with the deceptive words, "My dear Fortunato, you are luckily met." This is just one example of Poe's use of *irony of expression,* which means that a character's speech conveys a meaning opposite to what he is thinking. Cite other examples of Montresor's ironic manner of speech.
3. What in the story shows that the murder of Fortunato was premeditated?

4. Consider that Montresor is narrating the story a half-century after he has committed the crime. What has been the effect of the murder on him?

Method

1. When do you first suspect that Montresor is insane? What details cause you to be certain that he will kill Fortunato?
2. How does the setting contribute to the story? Could you change the setting without changing the atmosphere and mood of the story? If so, suggest a different setting.
3. Poe believed that every word in a story should contribute to a single emotional effect. Why do you think he carefully described the luring of Fortunato into a trap and the details of the murder itself, but only casually mentioned the motive for the crime in the first sentence?

Language: Prefixes

A *prefix* placed in front of the root of a word can change its meaning. For example, the word *impunity* is based on the Latin word *poena,* meaning "punishment or pain." The addition of the prefix *im-*, meaning "not," changes the meaning to "not punishable."

When Montresor says, "I must not only punish, but punish *with impunity,*" his intent is to punish with safety so that there will be no danger in, or penalty for, his act. In a sense, the perfect crime may be said to be one committed with impunity.

The prefix *im-* can also mean "in, on, or without." Add this prefix to the words *posture* and *pose.* How does it change their meanings? (Both of these words are derived from the Latin verb *ponere,* meaning "to place or put.")

Another common prefix is *re-*, meaning "back or again." Check your dictionary to see how this prefix affects the meaning of the following words taken from the first paragraph of "The Cask of Amontillado": *resolved, redresser, retribution,* and *revenge.*

Discussion and Composition

1. Write an essay in which you compare the skillful arrangements made by Poe, the author, and Montresor, the revenger, to achieve a preconceived effect or goal. Begin with a statement of the objectives of each man, and then use the following order to present a point-by-point comparison: **a.** the reasons for their choice of setting, **b.** the incidents that build toward the climactic moment, and **c.** the final outcome.

2. Write a different concluding paragraph for "The Cask of Amontillado." Find a way to save Fortunato. Try to maintain Poe's style as you rewrite the end of the story.

HONORÉ DE BALZAC
(1799–1850)

All levels of society in France during his own time were the subject of Honoré de Balzac's writing. He organized most of his fiction, almost one hundred separate novels and short stories, into a series that he called *La Comedie humaine* (*The Human Comedy*).

Balzac was born in Tours, France, the son of a government worker. He studied law in Paris but gave up his legal career for writing in 1819. Unwise in business and a lover of luxury, Balzac was constantly in debt. Although he was a creative genius, he was also a painstaking editor of his own work. He typically wrote and rewrote his fiction for more than ten hours a day.

Because he was more interested in recording the realistic details of human experience than in developing romantic plots, Balzac's writing was significant in the evolution of fiction as an art. It influenced many other authors. Historians of literature generally give him the title, "Father of the Modern Novel."

A PASSION IN THE DESERT

"The whole show is dreadful," she cried, coming out of the menagerie of M. Martin. She had just been looking at that daring speculator[1] "working with his hyena"—to speak in the style of the program.

"By what means," she continued, "can he have tamed these animals to such a point as to be certain of their affection for—"

"What seems to you a problem," said I, interrupting, "is really quite natural."

"Oh!" she cried, letting an incredulous smile wander over her lips.

"You think that beasts are wholly without passions?" I asked her. "Quite the reverse; we can communicate to them all the vices arising in our own state of civilization."

1. **speculator:** one who takes chances.

She looked at me with an air of astonishment.

"Nevertheless," I continued. "the first time I saw M. Martin, I admit, like you, I did give vent to an exclamation of surprise. I found myself next to an old soldier with the right leg amputated, who had come in with me. His face had struck me. He had one of those intrepid heads, stamped with the seal of warfare, and on which the battles of Napoleon are written. Besides, he had that frank good-humored expression which always impresses me favorably. He was without doubt one of those troopers who are surprised at nothing, who find matter for laughter in the contortions of a dying comrade, who bury or plunder him quite lightheartedly, who stand intrepidly in the way of bullets; in fact, one of those men who waste no time in deliberation, and would not hesitate to make friends with the devil himself. After looking very attentively at the proprietor of the menagerie getting out of his box, my companion pursed up his lips with an air of mockery and contempt, with that peculiar and expressive twist which superior people assume to show they are not taken in. Then when I was expatiating on the courage of M. Martin, he smiled, shook his head knowingly, and said, 'Well known.'

" 'How "well known"?' I said. 'If you would only explain to me the mystery I should be vastly obliged.'

"After a few minutes, during which we made acquaintance, we went to dine at the first restaurateur's whose shop caught our eye. At dessert a bottle of champagne completely refreshed and brightened up the memories of this odd old soldier. He told me his story, and I said he had every reason to exclaim, 'Well known.' "

When she got home, she teased me to that extent and made so many promises that I consented to communicate to her the old soldier's confidences. Next day she received the following episode of an epic which one might call "The Frenchman in Egypt."

During the expedition in Upper Egypt under General Desaix, a Provençal soldier fell into the hands of the Mangrabins and was taken by these Arabs into the desert beyond the falls of the Nile.

In order to place a sufficient distance between themselves and the French army, the Mangrabins made forced marches and only rested during the night. They camped around a well overshadowed by palm trees under which they had previously concealed a store of provisions. Not surmising that the notion of flight would occur to their prisoner, they contented themselves with binding his hands, and after eating a few dates and giving provender to their horses, went to sleep.

When the brave Provençal saw that his enemies were no longer watching him, he made use of his teeth to steal a scimitar, fixed the blade between his knees, and cut the cords which prevented using his hands; in a moment he was free. He at once seized a rifle and dagger; then, taking the precautions of providing himself with a sack of dried dates, oats, and powder and shot, and of fastening a scimitar to his waist, he leaped onto a horse, and spurred on vigorously in the direction where he thought to find the French army. So impatient was he to see a bivouac[2] again that he pressed on the already tired courser at such speed that its flanks were lacerated with his spurs, and at last the poor animal died, leaving the Frenchman alone in the desert. After walking some time in the sand with all the courage of an escaped convict, the soldier was obliged to stop, as the day had already ended. In spite of the beauty of an Oriental sky at night, he felt he had not strength enough to go on. Fortunately he had been able to find a small hill, on the summit of which a few palm trees shot up into the air; it was their verdure[3] seen from afar which had brought hope and consolation to his heart. His fatigue was so great that he lay down upon a rock of granite, capriciously cut out like a camp bed; there he fell asleep without taking any precaution to defend himself while he slept. He had made the sacrifice of his life. His last thought was one of regret. He repented having left the Mangrabins, whose nomad life seemed to smile on him now that he was afar from them and without help. He was awakened by the sun, whose pitiless rays fell with all their force on the granite and produced an intolerable heat—for he had had the stupidity to place himself inversely to the shadow thrown by the verdant majestic heads of the palm trees. He looked at the solitary trees and shuddered—they reminded him of the graceful shafts crowned with foliage which characterize the Saracen[4] columns in the cathedral of Arles.

But when, after counting the palm trees, he cast his eye around him, the most horrible despair was infused into his soul. Before him stretched an ocean without limit. The dark sand of the desert spread farther than sight could reach in every direction, and glittered like steel struck with a bright light. It might have been a sea of looking glass, or lakes melted together in a mirror. A fiery vapor carried up in streaks made a perpetual whirlwind over the quivering land. The sky

2. **bivouac** (bĭv′o͞o•ăk): camp without tents.
3. **verdure** (vûr′jər): greenness.
4. **Saracen** (săr′ə•sən): Arab.

was lit with an Oriental splendor of insupportable purity, leaving nought for the imagination to desire. Heaven and earth were on fire.

The silence was awful in its wild and terrible majesty. Infinity, immensity, closed in upon the soul from every side. Not a cloud in the sky, not a breath in the air, not a flaw on the bosom of the sand, ever moving in diminutive waves; the horizon ended as at sea on a clear day, with one line of light, definite as the cut of a sword.

The Provençal threw his arms around the trunk of one of the palm trees as though it were the body of a friend, and then, in the shelter of the thin straight shadow that the palm cast upon the granite, he wept. Then, sitting down, he remained as he was, contemplating with profound sadness the implacable scene, which was all he had to look upon. He cried aloud, to measure the solitude. His voice, lost in the hollows of the hill, sounded faintly, and aroused no echo—the echo was in his own heart. The Provençal was twenty-two years old; he loaded his carbine.

"There'll be time enough," he said to himself, laying on the ground the weapon which alone could bring him deliverance.

Looking by turns at the black expanse and the blue expanse, the soldier dreamed of France: he smelled with delight the gutters of Paris; he remembered the towns through which he had passed, the faces of his fellow soldiers, the most minute details of his life. His southern fancy soon showed him the stones of his beloved Provence, in the play of the heat which waved over the spread sheet of the desert. Fearing the danger of this cruel mirage, he went down the opposite side of the hill to that by which he had come up the day before. The remains of a rug showed that this place of refuge had at one time been inhabited; at a short distance he saw some palm trees full of dates. Then the instinct which binds us to life awoke again in his heart. He hoped to live long enough to await the passing of some Arabs, or perhaps he might hear the sound of cannon; for at this time Bonaparte was traversing Egypt.

This thought gave him new life. The palm tree seemed to bend with the weight of the ripe fruit. He shook some of it down. When he tasted this unhoped-for manna,[5] he felt sure that the palms had been cultivated by a former inhabitant—the savory, fresh meat of the dates was proof of the care of his predecessor. He passed suddenly from dark despair to an almost insane joy. He went up again to the top of the hill, and spent the rest of the day in cutting down one of

5. manna: food miraculously provided.

the sterile palm trees which the night before had served him for shelter. A vague memory made him think of the animals of the desert; and in case they might come to drink at the spring, visible from the base of the rocks but lost farther down, he resolved to guard himself from their visits by placing a barrier at the entrance of his hermitage.

In spite of his diligence, and the strength which the fear of being devoured asleep gave him, he was unable to cut the palm in pieces, though he succeeded in cutting it down. At eventide the king of the desert fell; the sound of its fall resounded far and wide, like a sign in the solitude. The soldier shuddered as though he had heard some voice predicting woe.

But like an heir who does not long bewail a deceased parent, he tore off from this beautiful tree the tall broad green leaves which are its poetic adornment, and used them to mend the mat on which he was to sleep.

Fatigued by the heat and his work, he fell asleep under the red curtains of his wet cave.

In the middle of the night his sleep was troubled by an extraordinary noise; he sat up, and the deep silence around him allowed him to distinguish the alternative accents of a respiration whose savage energy could not belong to a human creature.

A profound terror, increased still further by the darkness, the silence, and his waking images, froze his heart within him. He almost felt his hair stand on end, when by straining his eyes to their utmost he perceived through the shadows two faint yellow lights. At first he attributed these lights to the reflection of his own pupils, but soon the vivid brilliance of the night aided him gradually to distinguish the objects around him in the cave, and he beheld a huge animal lying but two steps from him. Was it a lion, a tiger, or a crocodile?

The Provençal was not educated enough to know under what species his enemy ought to be classed; but his fright was all the greater, as his ignorance led him to imagine all terrors at once. He endured a cruel torture, noting every variation of the breathing close to him without daring to make the slightest movement. An odor, pungent like that of a fox, but more penetrating—profounder, so to speak—filled the cave, and when the Provençal became sensible of this, his terror reached its height, for he could not longer doubt the proximity of a terrible companion, whose royal dwelling served him for shelter.

Presently the reflection of the moon, descending on the horizon, lit up the den, rendering gradually visible and resplendent the spotted skin of a panther.[6]

This lion of Egypt slept, curled up like a big dog, the peaceful possessor of a sumptuous niche at the gate of a hotel; its eyes opened for a moment and closed again; its face was turned toward the man. A thousand confused thoughts passed through the Frenchman's mind; first he thought of killing it with a bullet from his gun, but he saw there was not enough distance between them for him to take proper aim—the shot would miss the mark. And if it were to wake!—the thought made his limbs rigid. He listened to his own heart beating in the midst of the silence, and cursed the too violent pulsations which the flow of blood brought on, fearing to disturb that sleep which allowed him time to think of some means of escape.

Twice he placed his hand on his scimitar, intending to cut off the head of his enemy; but the difficulty of cutting stiff, short hair compelled him to abandon this daring project. To miss would be to die for *certain,* he thought; he preferred the chances of fair fight, and made up his mind to wait till morning. The morning did not leave him long to wait.

He could now examine the panther at ease; its muzzle was smeared with blood.

"She's had a good dinner," he thought, without troubling himself as to whether her feast might have been on human flesh. "She won't be hungry when she gets up."

It was a female. The fur on her belly and flanks was glistening white; many small marks like velvet formed beautiful bracelets round her feet; her sinuous tail was also white, ending with black rings; the overpart of her dress, yellow like unburnished gold, very lissome and soft, had the characteristic blotches in the form of rosettes which distinguish the panther from every other feline species.

This tranquil and formidable hostess snored in an attitude as graceful as that of a cat lying on a cushion. Her bloodstained paws, nervous and well armed, were stretched out before her face, which rested upon them, and from which radiated her straight, slender whiskers, like threads of silver.

If she had been like that in a cage, the Provençal would doubt-

6. panther: leopard. In the United States, only black leopards, on whom the characteristic spots are very faint, are called panthers.

less have admired the grace of the animal, and the vigorous contrasts of vivid color which gave her robe an imperial splendor; but just then his sight was troubled by her sinister appearance.

The presence of the panther, even asleep, could not fail to produce the effect which the magnetic eyes of the serpent are said to have on the nightingale.

For a moment the courage of the soldier began to fail before this danger, though no doubt it would have risen at the mouth of a cannon charged with shell. Nevertheless, a bold thought brought daylight into his soul and sealed up the source of the cold sweat which sprang forth on his brow. Like men driven to bay who defy death and offer their bodies to the smiter, so he, seeing in this merely a tragic episode, resolved to play his part with honor to the last.

"The day before yesterday the Arabs would have killed me perhaps," he said; so considering himself as good as dead already, he waited bravely, with excited curiosity, his enemy's awakening.

When the sun appeared, the panther suddenly opened her eyes; then she put out her paws with energy, as if to stretch them and get rid of cramp. At last she yawned, showing the formidable apparatus of her teeth and pointed tongue, rough as a file.

"A regular *petite maîtresse,*"[7] thought the Frenchman, seeing her roll herself about so softly and coquettishly.[8] She licked off the blood which stained her paws and muzzle, and scratched her head with reiterated gestures full of prettiness. "All right, make a little toilette," the Frenchman said to himself, beginning to recover his gaiety with his courage; "we'll say good morning to each other presently," and he seized the small, short dagger which he had taken from the Mangrabins. At this moment the panther turned her head toward the man and looked at him fixedly without moving.

The rigidity of her metallic eyes and their insupportable luster made him shudder, especially when the animal walked toward him. But he looked at her caressingly, staring into her eyes in order to magnetize her, and let her come quite close to him; then with a movement both gentle and amorous, as though he were caressing the most beautiful of women, he passed his hand over her whole body, from the head to the tail, scratching the flexible vertebrae which divided the panther's yellow back. The animal waved her tail voluptuously, and her eyes grew gentle; and when for the third time the

7. petite maîtresse (pə•tēt′ me•tres): *French,* little mistress.
8. coquettishly (kō kĕt′ĭsh•lē): flirtatiously.

Frenchman accomplished this interesting flattery, she gave forth one of those purrings by which our cats express their pleasure; but this murmur issued from a throat so powerful and so deep that it resounded through the cave like the last vibrations of an organ in a church. The man, understanding the importance of his caresses, redoubled them in such a way as to surprise and stupefy his imperious courtesan. When he felt sure of having extinguished the ferocity of his capricious companion, whose hunger had so fortunately been satisfied the day before, he got up to go out of the cave; the panther let him go out, but when he had reached the summit of the hill she sprang with the lightness of a sparrow hopping from twig to twig, and rubbed herself against his legs, putting up her back after the manner of all the race of cats. Then, regarding her guest with eyes whose glare had softened a little, she gave vent to that wild cry which naturalists compare to the grating of a saw.

"She is exacting," said the Frenchman, smilingly.

He was bold enough to play with her ears; he caressed her belly and scratched her head as hard as he could.

When he saw that he was successful, he tickled her skull with the point of his dagger, watching for the right moment to kill her, but the hardness of her bones made him tremble for his success.

The sultana of the desert showed herself gracious to her slave; she lifted her head, stretched out her neck, and manifested her delight by the tranquillity of her attitude. It suddenly occurred to the soldier that to kill this savage princess with one blow he must poignard her in the throat.

He raised the blade, when the panther, satisfied no doubt, laid herself gracefully at his feet, and cast up at him glances in which, in spite of their natural fierceness, was mingled confusedly a kind of good will. The poor Provençal ate his dates, leaning against one of the palm trees, and casting his eyes alternately on the desert in quest of some liberator and on his terrible companion to watch her uncertain clemency.

The panther looked at the place where the date stones fell, and every time that he threw one down her eyes expressed an incredible mistrust.

She examined the man with an almost commercial prudence. However, this examination was favorable to him, for when he had finished his meager meal she licked his boots with her powerful rough tongue, brushing off with marvelous skill the dust gathered in the creases.

"Ah, but when she's really hungry!" thought the Frenchman. In spite of the shudder this thought caused him, the soldier began to measure curiously the proportions of the panther, certainly one of the most splendid specimens of its race. She was three feet high and four feet long without counting her tail; this powerful weapon, rounded like a cudgel, was nearly three feet long. The head, large as that of a lioness, was distinguished by a rare expression of refinement. The cold cruelty of a tiger was dominant, it was true, but there was also a vague resemblance to the face of a sensual woman. Indeed the face of this solitary queen had something of the gaiety of a drunken Nero:[9] she had satiated herself with blood, and she wanted to play.

The soldier attempted to see whether he might walk up and down, and the panther left him free, contenting herself with following him with her eyes, less like a faithful dog than a big Angora cat, observing everything and every movement of her master.

When he looked around, he saw, by the spring, the remains of his horse; the panther had dragged the carcass all that way; about two-thirds of it had been devoured already. The sight reassured him.

It was easy to explain the panther's absence, and the respect she had had for him while he slept. The first piece of good luck emboldened him to tempt the future, and he conceived the wild hope of continuing on good terms with the panther during the entire day, neglecting no means of taming her and remaining in her good graces.

He returned to her, and had the unspeakable joy of seeing her wag her tail with an almost imperceptible movement at his approach. He sat down then, without fear, by her side, and they began to play together; he took her paws and muzzle, pulled her ears, rolled her over on her back, stroked her warm, delicate flanks. She let him do whatever he liked, and when he began to stroke the hair on her feet she drew her claws in carefully.

The man, keeping the dagger in one hand, thought to plunge it into the belly of the too-confiding panther, but he was afraid that he would be immediately strangled in her last conclusive struggle; besides, he felt in his heart a sort of remorse which bid him respect a creature that had done him no harm. He seemed to have found a friend, in a boundless desert; half unconsciously he thought of his first sweetheart, whom he had nicknamed "Mignonne"[10] by way of con-

9. **Nero:** cruel emperor of Rome (54–68 A.D.).
10. **Mignonne:** French name meaning "delicate" or "dainty."

trast, because she was so atrociously jealous that all the time of their love he was in fear of the knife with which she had always threatened him.

This memory of his early days suggested to him the idea of making the young panther answer to this name, now that he began to admire with less terror her swiftness, suppleness, and softness. Toward the end of the day he had familiarized himself with his perilous position; he now almost liked the painfulness of it. At last his companion got into the habit of looking up at him whenever he cried in a falsetto[11] voice, "Mignonne."

At the setting of the sun Mignonne gave, several times running, a profound melancholy cry. "She's been well brought up," said the lighthearted soldier; "she says her prayers." But his mental joke only occurred to him when he noticed what a pacific attitude his companion remained in. "Come, *ma petite blonde,* I'll let you go to bed first," he said to her, counting on the activity of his own legs to run away as quickly as possible, directly she was asleep, and seek another shelter for the night.

The soldier waited with impatience the hour of his flight, and when it had arrived he walked vigorously in the direction of the Nile; but hardly had he made a quarter of a league in the sand when he heard the panther bounding after him, crying with that sawlike cry more dreadful even than the sound of her leaping.

"Ah!" he said, "then she's taken a fancy to me; she has never met anyone before, and it is really quite flattering to have her first love." That instant the man fell into one of those movable quicksands so terrible to travelers and from which it is impossible to save oneself. Feeling himself caught, he gave a shriek of alarm; the panther seized him with her teeth by the collar, and, springing vigorously backward, drew him as if by magic out of the whirling sand.

"Ah, Mignonne!" cried the soldier, caressing her enthusiastically; "we're bound together for life and death—but no jokes, mind!" and he retraced his steps.

From that time the desert seemed inhabited. It contained a being to whom the man could talk, and whose ferocity was rendered gentle by him, though he could not explain to himself the reason for their strange friendship. Great as was the soldier's desire to stay upon guard, he slept.

11. falsetto (fôl•sĕt′ō): artificially high.

On awakening he could not find Mignonne; he mounted the hill, and in the distance saw her springing toward him after the habit of these animals, who cannot run on account of the extreme flexibility of the vertebral column. Mignonne arrived, her jaws covered with blood; she received the wonted caress of her companion, showing with much purring how happy it made her. Her eyes, full of languor, turned still more gently than the day before toward the Provençal who talked to her as one would to a tame animal.

"Ah! Mademoiselle, you are a nice girl, aren't you? Just look at that! So we like to be made much of, don't we? Aren't you ashamed of yourself? So you have been eating some Arab or other, have you? That doesn't matter. They're animals just the same as you are; but don't you take to eating Frenchmen, or I shan't like you any longer."

She played like a dog with its master, letting herself be rolled over, knocked about, and stroked, alternately; sometimes she herself would provoke the soldier, putting up her paw with a soliciting gesture.

Some days passed in this manner. This companionship permitted the Provençal to appreciate the sublime beauty of the desert; now that he had a living thing to think about, alternations of fear and quiet, and plenty to eat, his mind became filled with contrast and his life began to be diversified.

Solitude revealed to him all her secrets, and enveloped him in her delights. He discovered in the rising and setting of the sun sights unknown to the world. He knew what it was to tremble when he heard over his head the hiss of a bird's wing, so rarely did they pass, or when he saw the clouds, changing and many-colored travelers, melt one into another. He studied in the night time the effect of the moon upon the ocean of sand, where the simoom[12] made waves swift of movement and rapid in their change. He lived the life of the Eastern day, marveling at its wonderful pomp; then, having reveled in the sight of a hurricane over the plain where the whirling sands made red, dry mists and death-bearing clouds, he would welcome the night with joy, for then fell the healthful freshness of the stars, and he listened to imaginary music in the skies. Then solitude taught him to unroll the treasures of dreams. He passed whole hours in remembering mere nothings, and comparing his present life with his past.

At last he grew passionately fond of the panther; for some sort of affection was a necessity.

12. simoon (sī•mo͞om′): strong, hot wind.

Whether it was that his will, powerfully projected, had modified the character of his companion, or whether, because she found abundant food in her predatory excursions in the desert, she respected the man's life, he began to fear for it no longer, seeing her so well tamed.

He devoted the greater part of his time to sleep, but he was obliged to watch like a spider in its web that the moment of his deliverance might not escape him, if anyone should pass the line marked by the horizon. He had sacrificed his shirt to make a flag, which he hung at the top of a palm tree whose foliage he had torn off. Taught by necessity, he found the means of keeping it spread out by fastening it with little sticks; for the wind might not be blowing at the moment when the passing traveler was looking through the desert.

It was during the long hours, when he had abandoned hope, that he amused himself with the panther. He had come to learn the different inflections of her voice, the expressions of her eyes; he had studied the capricious patterns of all the rosettes which marked the gold of her robe. Mignonne was not even angry when he took hold of the tuft at the end of her tail to count her rings, those graceful ornaments which glittered in the sun like jewelry. It gave him pleasure to contemplate the supple, fine outlines of her form, the whiteness of her belly, the graceful pose of her head. But it was especially when she was playing that he felt most pleasure in looking at her. The agility and youthful lightness of her movements were a continual surprise to him. He wondered at the supple way in which she jumped and climbed, washed herself and arranged her fur, crouched down and prepared to spring. However rapid her spring might be, however slippery the stone she was on, she would always stop short at the word "Mignonne."

One day, in a bright midday sun, an enormous bird coursed through the air. The man left his panther to look at this new guest; but after waiting a moment the deserted sultana growled deeply.

"My goodness! I do believe she's jealous," he cried, seeing her eyes become hard again; "the soul of Virginie[13] has passed into her body; that's certain."

The eagle disappeared into the air, while the soldier admired the curved contour of the panther.

But there was such youth and grace in her form! She was

13. Virginie: young girl, beloved of Paul, in French tale of *Paul et Virginie.*

beautiful as a woman! The blond fur of her robe mingled well with the delicate tints of faint white which marked her flanks.

The profuse light cast down by the sun made this living gold, these russet markings, to burn in a way to give them indefinable attraction.

The man and the panther looked at one another with a look full of meaning. The coquette quivered when she felt her friend stroke her head. Her eyes flashed like lightning—then she shut them tightly.

"She has a soul," he said, looking at the stillness of this queen of the sands, golden like them, white like them, solitary and burning like them.

"Well," she said, "I have read your plea in favor of beasts; but how did two so well adapted to understand each other end?"

"Ah, well! You see, they ended as all great passions do end—by a misunderstanding. For some reason *one* suspects the other of treason; they don't come to an explanation through pride, and quarrel and part from sheer obstinacy."

"Yet sometimes at the best moments a single word or a look is enough—but anyhow go on with your story."

"It's horribly difficult, but you will understand, after what the old villain told me over his champagne.

"He said—'I don't know if I hurt her, but she turned round, as if enraged, and with her sharp teeth caught hold of my leg—gently, I daresay; but I, thinking she would devour me, plunged my dagger into her throat. She rolled over, giving a cry that froze my heart; and I saw her dying, still looking at me without anger. I would have given all the world—my cross[14] even, which I had not then—to have brought her to life again. It was as though I had murdered a real person; and the soldiers who had seen my flag, and were come to my assistance, found me in tears.'

" 'Well sir,' he said, after a moment of silence, 'since then I have been in war in Germany, in Spain, in Russia, in France; I've certainly carried my carcass about a good deal, but never have I seen anything like the desert. Ah! yes, it is very beautiful!'

" 'What did you feel there?' I asked him.

" 'Oh! that can't be described, young man. Besides, I do not always regret my palm trees and my panther. I should have to be very

14. cross: military decoration.

melancholy for that. In the desert, you see, there is everything, and nothing.'

"'Yes, but explain—'

"'Well,' he said, with an impatient gesture, 'it is God without mankind.'"

Meaning

1. At the beginning of the story, the old soldier, not impressed by the courage of the animal trainer, says, "Well known." What does he mean by this comment?
2. Why did the soldier not kill the panther when he first saw it?
3. Why did the soldier change his mind about running away from the panther?
4. How did his companionship with the panther change the soldier's life?

Method

1. "A Passion in the Desert" is an example of a *frame story*. The story of the young soldier and the panther is placed within the framework of another story. What function does the "outer story" serve? How does the author make the transition between the outer story and the inner story?
2. How does the narrator characterize the "old soldier"? Do you think that the character of the soldier changed as he grew older? Give reasons for your answer.
3. The beauty and terror of the desert are presented in counterpoint to the beauty and terror of the animal. How does the author show the soldier's change of heart towards both his savage surroundings and his savage companion?
4. How does the author convey the soldier's fantasy of the panther as a woman who is in love with him? What is ironic about the man's relationship to the animal, and its outcome?

Language: Context Clues to Meaning

As you read "A Passion in the Desert," you probably encountered some words that were unfamiliar to you. You can often understand the general meaning of a word because of its *context,* the part of the sentence or paragraph that occurs before and after it.

Using context clues, try to define each of the italicized words below. Check your definition with a dictionary.

1. "Not *surmising* that the notion of flight would occur to their prisoner, they contented themselves with binding his hands . . ."
2. ". . . he made use of his teeth to steal a *scimitar,* fixed the blade between his knees, and cut the cords which prevented using his hands . . ."
3. ". . . he remained as he was, *contemplating* with profound sadness the *implacable* scene . . ."
4. ". . . the overpart of her dress, yellow like *unburnished* gold, very *lissome* and soft . . ."
5. "The poor Provencal ate his dates . . . casting his eyes alternately on the desert in quest of some *liberator* and on his terrible companion to watch her uncertain *clemency.*"
6. ". . . because she found abundant food in her *predatory* excursions in the desert, she respected the man's life . . ."
7. "The *agility* and youthful lightness of her movements were a continual surprise to him."
8. ". . . I do not always regret my palm trees and my panther. I should have to be very *melancholy* for that."

Discussion and Composition

1. What animal do you consider to be most beautiful? Describe the physical appearance of any animal you have had as a pet or observed in the wild or in a zoo.

2. To what extent do you agree or disagree with the idea that animals have many of the same feelings that people have? Choose one of the following statements and write an essay in which you give reasons why you do or do not support it.

Some people believe that it is cruel to take wild animals from their native habitats and confine them in zoos.

Thousands of people every year protest the killing of baby harp seals and other animals for their fur.

The killing of whales has been banned by many nations.

3. Each step of "A Passion in the Desert" increases suspense, building to the climax. Discuss how the author creates tension by giving information gradually to the reader, and causes the reader to identify and sympathize first with the soldier, and then with the panther.

EUDORA WELTY
(born 1909)

The fiction of Eudora Welty is noted for its imaginative characterizations and its skillful use of Southern dialect. She writes with humor and compassion about the kind of small-town men and women she has known all her life, but her stories have themes that can be applied to all people. She explores the mystery of the personality and the need for people to understand themselves and others.

Born in Jackson, Mississippi, Miss Welty attended Mississippi State College for Women, the University of Wisconsin, and Columbia University. After working in the advertising and newspaper fields she became a publicity agent for the Works Progress Administration (WPA). During the Depression, she traveled throughout Mississippi taking pictures, writing articles, and meeting the people she would later bring to life in her stories. Her first story, "Death of a Travelling Salesman," was published in 1936, the same year that her photographs of Mississippians were first exhibited in New York.

Miss Welty is considered perhaps the most distinguished Southern writer living today.

WHY I LIVE AT THE P.O.

I was getting along fine with Mama, Papa-Daddy, and Uncle Rondo until my sister Stella-Rondo just separated from her husband and came back home again. Mr. Whitaker! Of course I went with Mr. Whitaker first, when he first appeared here in China Grove, taking "Pose Yourself" photos and Stella-Rondo broke us up. Told him I was one-sided. Bigger on one side than the other, which is a deliberate, calculated falsehood: I'm the same. Stella-Rondo is exactly twelve months to the day younger than I am and for that reason she's spoiled.

She's always had anything in the world she wanted and then she'd throw it away. Papa-Daddy gave her this gorgeous Add-a-Pearl necklace when she was eight years old and she threw it away playing baseball when she was nine, with only two pearls.

So as soon as she got married and moved away from home the

first thing she did was separate! From Mr. Whitaker! This photographer with the popeyes she said she trusted. Came home from one of those towns up in Illinois and to our complete surprise brought this child of two.

Mama said she like to made her drop dead for a second. "Here you had this marvelous blonde child and never so much as wrote your mother a word about it," says Mama. "I'm thoroughly ashamed of you." But of course she wasn't.

Stella-Rondo just calmly takes off this *hat,* I wish you could see it. She says, "Why, Mama, Shirley-T.'s adopted, I can prove it."

"How?" says Mama, but all I says was, "H'm!" There I was over the hot stove, trying to stretch two chickens over five people and a completely unexpected child into the bargain, without one moment's notice.

"What do you mean—'H'm!'?" says Stella-Rondo, and Mama says, "I heard that, Sister."

I said that oh, I didn't mean a thing, only that whoever Shirley-T. was, she was the spit-image of Papa-Daddy if he'd cut off his beard, which of course he'd never do in the world. Papa-Daddy's Mama's papa and sulks.

Stella-Rondo got furious! She said, "Sister, I don't need to tell you you got a lot of nerve and always did have and I'll thank you to make no future reference to my adopted child whatsoever."

"Very well," I said. "Very well, very well. Of course I noticed at once she looks like Mr. Whitaker's side too. That frown. She looks like a cross between Mr. Whitaker and Papa-Daddy."

"Well, all I can say is she isn't."

"She looks exactly like Shirley Temple to me," says Mama, but Shirley-T. just ran away from her.

So the first thing Stella-Rondo did at the table was turn Papa-Daddy against me.

"Papa-Daddy," she says. He was trying to cut up his meat. "Papa-Daddy!" I was taken completely by surprise. Papa-Daddy is about a million years old and's got this long-long beard. "Papa-Daddy, Sister says she fails to understand why you don't cut off your beard."

So Papa-Daddy l-a-y-s down his knife and fork! He's real rich. Mama says he is, he says he isn't. So he says, "Have I heard correctly? You don't understand why I don't cut off my beard?"

"Why," I says, "Papa-Daddy, of course I understand, I did not say any such of a thing, the idea!"

He says, "Hussy!"

I says, "Papa-Daddy, you know I wouldn't any more want you to cut off your beard than the man in the moon. It was the farthest thing from my mind! Stella-Rondo sat there and made that up while she was eating breast of chicken."

But he says, "So the postmistress fails to understand why I don't cut off my beard. Which job I got you through my influence with the government. 'Bird's nest'—is that what you call it?"

Not that it isn't the next to smallest P.O. in the entire state of Mississippi.

I says, "Oh, Papa-Daddy," I says, "I didn't say any such of a thing, I never dreamed it was a bird's nest, I have always been grateful though this is the next to smallest P.O. in the state of Mississippi, and I do not enjoy being referred to as a hussy by my own grandfather."

But Stella-Rondo says, "Yes, you did say it too. Anybody in the world could of heard you, that had ears."

"Stop right there," says Mama, looking at *me*.

So I pulled my napkin straight back through the napkin ring and left the table.

As soon as I was out of the room Mama says, "Call her back, or she'll starve to death," but Papa-Daddy says, "This is the beard I started growing on the Coast when I was fifteen years old." He would of gone on till nightfall if Shirley-T. hadn't lost the Milky Way she ate in Cairo.[1]

So Papa-Daddy says, "I am going out and lie in the hammock, and you can all sit here and remember my words: I'll never cut off my beard as long as I live, even one inch, and I don't appreciate it in you at all." Passed right by me in the hall and went straight out and got in the hammock.

It would be a holiday. It wasn't five minutes before Uncle Rondo suddenly appeared in the hall in one of Stella-Rondo's flesh-colored kimonos,[2] all cut on the bias,[3] like something Mr. Whitaker probably thought was gorgeous.

"Uncle Rondo!" I says. "I didn't know who that was! Where are you going?"

"Sister," he says, "get out of my way, I'm poisoned."

"If you're poisoned stay away from Papa-Daddy," I says. "Keep out of the hammock. Papa-Daddy will certainly beat you on the

1. **Cairo** (kâr′ō): a city in southwestern Illinois.
2. **kimonos** (kə•mō′nəs): a loose robe tied with a wide sash worn in Japan.
3. **cut on the bias:** cut diagonally across, usually to insure a smooth fit.

head if you come within forty miles of him. He thinks I deliberately said he ought to cut off his beard after he got me the P.O., and I've told him and told him and told him, and he acts like he just don't hear me. Papa-Daddy must of gone stone deaf."

"He picked a fine day to do it then," says Uncle Rondo, and before you could say "Jack Robinson" flew out in the yard.

What he'd really done, he'd drunk another bottle of that prescription. He does it every single Fourth of July as sure as shooting, and it's horribly expensive. Then he falls over in the hammock and snores. So he insisted on zigzagging right on out to the hammock, looking like a half-wit.

Papa-Daddy woke up with this horrible yell and right there without moving an inch he tried to turn Uncle Rondo against me. I heard every word he said. Oh, he told Uncle Rondo I didn't learn to read till I was eight years old and he didn't see how in the world I ever got the mail put up at the P.O., much less read it all, and he said if Uncle Rondo could only fathom the lengths he had gone to to get me that job! And he said on the other hand he thought Stella-Rondo had a brilliant mind and deserved credit for getting out of town. All the time he was just lying there swinging as pretty as you please and looping out his beard, and poor Uncle Rondo was *pleading* with him to slow down the hammock, it was making him as dizzy as a witch to watch it. But that's what Papa-Daddy likes about a hammock. So Uncle Rondo was too dizzy to get turned against me for the time being. He's Mama's only brother and is a good case of a one-track mind. Ask anybody. A certified pharmacist.

Just then I heard Stella-Rondo raising the upstairs window. While she was married she got this peculiar idea that it's cooler with the windows shut and locked. So she has to raise the window before she can make a soul hear her outdoors.

So she raises the window and says, "*Oh!*" You would have thought she was mortally wounded.

Uncle Rondo and Papa-Daddy didn't even look up, but kept right on with what they were doing. I had to laugh.

I flew up the stairs and threw the door open! I says, "What in the wide world's the matter, Stella-Rondo? You mortally wounded?"

"No," she says, "I am not mortally wounded but I wish you would do me the favor of looking out that window there and telling me what you see."

So I shade my eyes and look out the window.

"I see the front yard," I says.

"Don't you see any human beings?" she says.

"I see Uncle Rondo trying to run Papa-Daddy out of the hammock," I says. "Nothing more. Naturally, it's so suffocating-hot in the house, with all the windows shut and locked, everybody who cares to stay in their right mind will have to go out and get in the hammock before the Fourth of July is over."

"Don't you notice anything different about Uncle Rondo?" asks Stella-Rondo.

"Why, no, except he's got on some terrible-looking flesh-colored contraption I wouldn't be found dead in, is all I can see," I says.

"Never mind, you won't be found dead in it, because it happens to be part of my trousseau, and Mr. Whitaker took several dozen photographs of me in it," says Stella-Rondo. "What on earth could Uncle Rondo *mean* by wearing part of my trousseau out in the broad open daylight without saying so much as 'Kiss my foot,' *knowing* I only got home this morning after my separation and hung my negligee up on the bathroom door, just as nervous as I could be?"

"I'm sure I don't know, and what do you expect me to do about it?" I says. "Jump out the window?"

"No, I expect nothing of the kind. I simply declare that Uncle Rondo looks like a fool in it, that's all," she says. "It makes me sick to my stomach."

"Well, he looks as good as he can," I says. "As good as anybody in reason could." I stood up for Uncle Rondo, please remember. And I said to Stella-Rondo, "I think I would do well not to criticize so freely if I were you and came home with a two-year-old child I had never said a word about, and no explanation whatever about my separation."

"I asked you the instant I entered this house not to refer one more time to my adopted child, and you gave me your word of honor you would not," was all Stella-Rondo would say, and started pulling out every one of her eyebrows with some cheap Kress[4] tweezers.

So I merely slammed the door behind me and went down and made some green-tomato pickle. Somebody had to do it. Of course Mama had turned both the servants loose; she always said no earthly power could hold one anyway on the Fourth of July, so she wouldn't

4. Kress: refers to S. H. Kress, a chain of five-and-ten-cent stores.

even try. It turned out that Jaypan fell in the lake and came within a very narrow limit of drowning.

So Mama trots in. Lifts up the lid and says, "H'm! Not very good for your Uncle Rondo in his precarious condition, I must say. Or poor little adopted Shirley-T. Shame on you!"

That made me tired. I says, "Well, Stella-Rondo had better thank her lucky stars it was her instead of me came trotting in with that very peculiar-looking child. Now if it had been me that trotted in from Illinois and brought a peculiar-looking child of two, I shudder to think of the reception I'd of got, much less controlled the diet of an entire family."

"But you must remember, Sister, that you were never married to Mr. Whitaker in the first place and didn't go up to Illinois to live," says Mama, shaking a spoon in my face. "If you had I would of been just as overjoyed to see you and your little adopted girl as I was to see Stella-Rondo, when you wound up with your separation and came on back home."

"You would not," I says.

"Don't contradict me, I would," says Mama.

But I said she couldn't convince me though she talked till she was blue in the face. Then I said, "Besides, you know as well as I do that that child is not adopted."

"She most certainly is adopted," says Mama, stiff as a poker.

I says, "Why, Mama, Stella-Rondo had her just as sure as anything in this world, and just too stuck up to admit it."

"Why, Sister," said Mama. "Here I thought we were going to have a pleasant Fourth of July, and you start right out not believing a word your own baby sister tells you!"

"Just like Cousin Annie Flo. Went to her grave denying the facts of life," I remind Mama.

"I told you if you ever mentioned Annie Flo's name I'd slap your face," says Mama, and slaps my face.

"All right, you wait and see," I says.

"I," says Mama, "*I* prefer to take my children's word for anything when it's humanly possible." You ought to see Mama, she weighs two hundred pounds and has real tiny feet.

Just then something perfectly horrible occurred to me.

"Mama," I says, "can that child talk?" I simply had to whisper! "Mama, I wonder if that child can be—you know—in any way? Do you realize," I says, "that she hasn't spoken one single, solitary word to a human being up to this minute? This is the way she looks," I says, and I looked like this.

Well, Mama and I just stood there and stared at each other. It was horrible!

"I remember well that Joe Whitaker frequently drank like a fish," says Mama. "I believed to my soul he drank *chemicals*." And without another word she marches to the foot of the stairs and calls Stella-Rondo.

"Stella-Rondo? O-o-o-o-o! Stella-Rondo!"

"What?" says Stella-Rondo from upstairs. Not even the grace to get up off the bed.

"Can that child of yours talk?" asks Mama.

Stella-Rondo says, "Can she what?"

"Talk! Talk!" says Mama. "Burdyburdyburdyburdy!"

So Stella-Rondo yells back, "Who says she can't talk?"

"Sister says so," says Mama.

"You didn't have to tell me, I know whose word of honor don't mean a thing in this house," says Stella-Rondo.

And in a minute the loudest Yankee voice I ever heard in my life yells out, "OE'm Pop-OE the Sailor-r-r-r Ma-a-an!" And then somebody jumps up and down in the upstairs hall. In another second the house would of fallen down.

"Not only talks, she can tap-dance!" calls Stella-Rondo. "Which is more than some people I won't name can do."

"Why, the little precious darling thing!" Mama says, so surprised. "Just as smart as she can be!" Starts talking baby talk right there. Then she turns on me. "Sister, you ought to be thoroughly ashamed! Run upstairs this instant and apologize to Stella-Rondo and Shirley-T."

"Apologize for what?" I says. "I merely wondered if the child was normal, that's all. Now that she's proved she is, why, I have nothing further to say."

But Mama just turned on her heel and flew out, furious. She ran right upstairs and hugged the baby. She believed it was adopted. Stella-Rondo hadn't done a thing but turn her against me from upstairs while I stood there helpless over the hot stove. So that made Mama, Papa-Daddy and the baby all on Stella-Rondo's side.

Next, Uncle Rondo.

I must say that Uncle Rondo has been marvelous to me at various times in the past and I was completely unprepared to be made to jump out of my skin, the way it turned out. Once Stella-Rondo did something perfectly horrible to him—broke a chain letter from Flanders Field—and he took the radio back he had given her and gave it to me. Stella-Rondo was furious! For six months we all had to call her Stella instead of Stella-Rondo, or she wouldn't answer. I always thought Uncle Rondo had all the brains of the entire family. Another time he sent me to Mammoth Cave,[5] with all expenses paid.

But this would be the day he was drinking that prescription, the Fourth of July.

So at supper Stella-Rondo speaks up and says she thinks Uncle Rondo ought to try to eat a little something. So finally Uncle Rondo said he would try a little cold biscuits and ketchup, but that was all. So *she* brought it to him.

"Do you think it wise to disport[6] with ketchup in Stella-Rondo's flesh-colored kimono?" I says. Trying to be considerate! If Stella-Rondo couldn't watch out for her trousseau, somebody had to.

"Any objections?" asks Uncle Rondo, just about to pour out all the ketchup.

"Don't mind what she says, Uncle Rondo," says Stella-Rondo. "Sister has been devoting this solid afternoon to sneering out my bedroom window at the way you look."

"What's that?" says Uncle Rondo. Uncle Rondo has got the most terrible temper in the world. Anything is liable to make him tear the house down if it comes at the wrong time.

So Stella-Rondo says, "Sister says, 'Uncle Rondo certainly does look like a fool in that pink kimono!' "

Do you remember who it was really said that?

Uncle Rondo spills out all the ketchup and jumps out of his chair and tears off the kimono and throws it down on the dirty floor and puts his foot on it. It had to be sent all the way to Jackson to the cleaners and repleated.

"So that's your opinion of your Uncle Rondo, is it?" he says. "I look like a fool, do I? Well, that's the last straw. A whole day in this house with nothing to do, and then to hear you come out with a remark like that behind my back!"

"I didn't say any such of a thing, Uncle Rondo," I says, "and I'm not saying who did, either. Why, I think you look all right. Just

5. Mammoth Cave: a national park in west central Kentucky, comprising a series of underground limestone caverns.
6. disport: frolic about.

try to take care of yourself and not talk and eat at the same time," I says. "I think you better go lie down."

"Lie down my foot," says Uncle Rondo. I ought to of known by that he was fixing to do something perfectly horrible.

So he didn't do anything that night in the precarious state he was in—just played casino with Mama and Stella-Rondo and Shirley-T. and gave Shirley-T. a nickel with a head on both sides. It tickled her nearly to death, and she called him "Papa." But at 6:30 A.M. the next morning, he threw a whole five-cent package of some unsold one-inch firecrackers from the store as hard as he could into my bedroom and they every one went off. Not one bad one in the string. Anybody else, there'd be one that wouldn't go off.

Well, I'm just terribly susceptible to noise of any kind, the doctor has always told me I was the most sensitive person he had ever seen in his whole life, and I was simply prostrated. I couldn't eat! People tell me they heard it as far as the cemetery, and old Aunt Jep Patterson, that had been holding her own so good, thought it was Judgment Day and she was going to meet her whole family. It's usually so quiet here.

And I'll tell you it didn't take me any longer than a minute to make up my mind what to do. There I was with the whole entire house on Stella-Rondo's side and turned against me. If I have anything at all I have pride.

So I just decided I'd go straight down to the P.O. There's plenty of room there in the back, I says to myself.

Well! I made no bones about letting the family catch on to what I was up to. I didn't try to conceal it.

The first thing they knew, I marched in where they were all playing Old Maid and pulled the electric oscillating fan out by the plug, and everything got real hot. Next I snatched the pillow I'd done the needlepoint on right off the davenport from behind Papa-Daddy. He went "Ugh!" I beat Stella-Rondo up the stairs and finally found my charm bracelet in her bureau drawer under a picture of Nelson Eddy.[7]

"So that's the way the land lies," says Uncle Rondo. There he was, piecing[8] on the ham. "Well, Sister, I'll be glad to donate my army cot if you got any place to set it up, providing you'll leave right

7. Nelson Eddy (1901–1967): American movie star of the late 1930s, famous for his singing roles.

8. piecing: *dialect,* having a snack, eating between meals.

this minute and let me get some peace." Uncle Rondo was in France.

"Thank you kindly for the cot and 'peace' is hardly the word I would select if I had to resort to firecrackers at 6:30 A.M. in a young girl's bedroom," I says back to him. "And as to where I intend to go, you seem to forget my position as postmistress of China Grove, Mississippi," I says, "I've always got the P.O."

Well, that made them all sit up and take notice.

I went out front and started digging up some four-o'clocks[9] to plant around the P.O.

"Ah-ah-ah!" says Mama, raising the window. "Those happen to be my four-o'clocks. Everything planted in that star is mine. I've never known you to make anything grow in your life."

"Very well," I says. "But I take the fern. Even you, Mama, can't stand there and deny that I'm the one watered that fern. And I happen to know where I can send in a box top and get a packet of one thousand mixed seeds, no two the same kind, free."

"Oh, where?" Mama wants to know.

But I says, "Too late. You 'tend to your house, and I'll 'tend to mine. You hear things like that all the time if you know how to listen to the radio. Perfectly marvelous offers. Get anything you want free."

So I hope to tell you I marched in and got that radio, and they could of all bit a nail in two, especially Stella-Rondo, that it used to belong to, and she well knew she couldn't get it back, I'd sue for it like a shot. And I very politely took the sewing-machine motor I helped pay the most on to give Mama for Christmas back in 1929, and a good big calendar, with the first-aid remedies on it. The thermometer and the Hawaiian ukulele certainly were rightfully mine, and I stood on the stepladder and got all my watermelon-rind preserves and every fruit and vegetable I'd put up, every jar. Then I began to pull the tacks out of the bluebird wall vases on the archway to the dining room.

"Who told you you could have those, Miss Priss?"[10] says Mama, fanning as hard as she could.

"I bought 'em and I'll keep track of 'em," I says. "I'll tack 'em up one on each side the post office window, and you can see 'em when you come to ask me for your mail, if you're so dead to see 'em."

"Not I! I'll never darken the door to that post office again if I

9. four-o'clock: a common garden herb with yellow, red, or white blossoms, so called because it blooms from late afternoon until early morning.

10. Miss Priss: A priss is a person who acts, dresses, or speaks in an overly precise manner.

live to be a hundred," Mama says. "Ungrateful child! After all the money we spent on you at the Normal."[11]

"Me either," says Stella-Rondo. "You can just let my mail lie there and *rot*, for all I care. I'll never come and relieve you of a single, solitary piece."

"I should worry," I says. "And who you think's going to sit down and write you all those big fat letters and postcards, by the way? Mr. Whitaker? Just because he was the only man ever dropped down in China Grove and you got him—unfairly—is he going to sit down and write you a lengthy correspondence after you came home giving no rhyme nor reason whatsoever for your separation and no explanation for the presence of that child? I may not have your brilliant mind, but I fail to see it."

So Mama says, "Sister, I've told you a thousand times that Stella-Rondo simply got homesick, and this child is far too big to be hers," and she says, "Now, why don't you all just sit down and play casino?"

Then Shirley-T. sticks out her tongue at me in this perfectly horrible way. She has no more manners than the man in the moon. I told her she was going to cross her eyes like that some day and they'd stick.

"It's too late to stop me now," I says. "You should have tried that yesterday. I'm going to the P.O. and the only way you can possibly see me is to visit me there."

So Papa-Daddy says, "You'll never catch me setting foot in that post office, even if I should take a notion into my head to write a letter some place." He says, "I won't have you reachin' out of that little old window with a pair of shears and cuttin' off any beard of mine. I'm too smart for you!"

"We all are," says Stella-Rondo.

But I said, "If you're so smart, where's Mr. Whitaker?"

So then Uncle Rondo says, "I'll thank you from now on to stop reading all the orders I get on postcards and telling everybody in China Grove what you think is the matter with them," but I says, "I draw my own conclusions and will continue in the future to draw them." I says, "If people want to write their inmost secrets on penny postcards, there's nothing in the wide world you can do about it, Uncle Rondo."

11. Normal: normal school, a type of state-supported institution which prepares high school graduates to become teachers, largely for the elementary grades. [From French *école normale.*]

"And if you think we'll ever *write* another postcard you're sadly mistaken," says Mama.

"Cutting off your nose to spite your face then," I says. "But if you're all determined to have no more to do with the U.S. mail, think of this: What will Stella-Rondo do now, if she wants to tell Mr. Whitaker to come after her?"

"Wah!" says Stella-Rondo. I knew she'd cry. She had a conniption fit right there in the kitchen.

"It will be interesting to see how long she holds out," I says. "And now—I am leaving."

"Good-by," says Uncle Rondo.

"Oh, I declare," says Mama, "to think that a family of mine should quarrel on the Fourth of July, or the day after, over Stella-Rondo leaving old Mr. Whitaker and having the sweetest little adopted child! It looks like we'd all be glad!"

"Wah!" says Stella-Rondo, and has a fresh conniption fit.

"*He* left *her*—you mark my words," I says. "That's Mr. Whitaker. I know Mr. Whitaker. After all, I knew him first. I said from the beginning he'd up and leave her. I foretold every single thing that's happened."

"Where did he go?" asks Mama.

"Probably to the North Pole, if he knows what's good for him," I says.

But Stella-Rondo just bawled and wouldn't say another word. She flew to her room and slammed the door.

"Now look what you've gone and done, Sister," says Mama. "You go apologize."

"I haven't got time, I'm leaving," I says.

"Well, what are you waiting around for?" asks Uncle Rondo.

So I just picked up the kitchen clock and marched off, without saying "Kiss my foot" or anything, and never did tell Stella-Rondo good-by.

There was a Negro girl going along on a little wagon right in front.

I says, "Come help me haul these things down the hill, I'm going to live in the post office."

Took her nine trips in her express wagon. Uncle Rondo came out on the porch and threw her a nickel.

And that's the last I've laid eyes on any of my family or my family laid eyes on me for five solid days and nights. Stella-Rondo may be telling the most horrible tales in the world about Mr. Whitaker, but I haven't heard them. As I tell everybody, I draw my own conclusions.

But oh, I like it here. It's ideal, as I've been saying. You see, I've got everything cater-cornered,[12] the way I like it. Hear the radio? All the war news. Radio, sewing machine, book ends, ironing board, and that great big piano lamp—peace, that's what I like. Butter bean[13] vines planted all along the front where the strings are.

Of course, there's not much mail. My family are naturally the main people in China Grove, and if they prefer to vanish from the face of the earth, for all the mail they get or the mail they write, why, I'm not going to open my mouth. Some of the folks here in town are taking up for me and some turned against me. I know which is which. There are always people who will quit buying stamps just to get on the right side of Papa-Daddy.

But here I am, and here I'll stay. I want the world to know I'm happy.

And if Stella-Rondo should come to me this minute, on bended knees, and *attempt* to explain the incidents of her life with Mr. Whitaker, I'd simply put my fingers in both my ears and refuse to listen.

12. **cater-cornered:** diagonal; also catty-cornered and kitty-cornered.
13. **butter bean:** in the southern United States, the lima bean.

Meaning

1. Judging from the narrator's words in the first three paragraphs, what has caused the friction between the two sisters? Is Sister right in claiming that Stella-Rondo starts all the trouble? Why or why not?
2. What do the things Sister takes to the P.O. reveal about her?

Method

1. A *dramatic monologue* is a speech by one person who reveals his or her character in the process of narrating the story. Eudora Welty uses this technique in "Why I Live at the P.O.," having Sister reveal herself through her own words as she tells her story to the reader. What kind of person does Sister reveal herself to be?
2. The humor in this story lies not only in the peculiarities of the individual characters, but also in the behavior of the family as a

whole. Miss Welty gently *satirizes,* or ridicules, some of the habits of the rural Southern family. A *satire* uses wit and irony to expose and indirectly attack an action, point of view, custom, or character that the author does not like. Give some examples of customs, attitudes, and characters that are the objects of Miss Welty's satire in this story.

3. One way an author creates humor in a story is by using *hyperbole,* an exaggerated statement, as when Sister says, "She's always had anything in the world she wanted, and then she'd throw it away." And "Papa-Daddy is about a million years old." Find some other examples of hyperbole in the story.

Language: A Story Told in the Vernacular

A person unfamiliar with the *vernacular* or common language that Sister speaks may be confused by a statement such as "I made no bones about letting the family catch on to what I was up to." These expressions are an integral part of Sister's everyday vocabulary. To have Sister deliver her monologue in a more formal language would be inconsistent with her background.

Vernacular comes from the Latin word *vernaculus,* meaning domestic or native. When Latin was the universal language of scholars, the word vernacular was used to designate the changes that occurred in the vocabulary and pronunciation of "classical" Latin.

Today, vernacular refers to the slang words, colloquial expressions, and nonstandard usages that characterize the native speech of the people of a specific area.

Change the following statements from the story into logical, straightforward, and grammatically correct English:

1. "Mama said she like to made her drop dead for a second."
2. "I did not say any such of a thing, the idea!"
3. "Anybody in the world could of heard you, that had ears."

Discussion and Composition

Ask members of an older generation to give you examples of slang expressions that were popular years ago. Which of these slang expressions are still being used by you and your friends today? Make a list of ten slang words that you and your friends use. Include definitions. Study the list of slang expressions from another generation and your own generation. What generalizations about slang can you make, based on the two lists?

ARTHUR C. CLARKE
(born 1917)

Writing and scientific talents combine in Arthur Charles Clarke, several of whose science fiction concepts have become reality. Most famous perhaps for his collaboration with Stanley Kubrick in making the film *2001: A Space Odyssey*, Clarke, in 1945, predicted a system of earth satellites that would improve radio and television communication. His detailed plan for manned space stations powered by solar energy is credited with helping to lay the groundwork for today's radio, telephone, and television communication by means of satellite.

Clarke was born in Minehead, England. Interested in science even as a child, at thirteen he mapped the moon using a telescope he had constructed from a cardboard tube and an old lens. Clarke became an auditor for the British Civil Service and participated in the activities of the British Interplanetary Society. In 1941, he joined the Royal Air Force, where he was a flight lieutenant and radar instructor. While in the service, Clarke wrote his first science fiction stories and articles on electronics. After the war, Clarke entered King's College in London and graduated in 1948 with top honors in mathematics and physics. In 1951, he left his job as an editor of a scientific journal so that he would have more time for writing fiction.

Clarke has written more than forty volumes of fiction and nonfiction with subjects ranging from astronomy to space travel and underwater exploration. Making his home in Sri Lanka (Ceylon), Clarke, who has been called the "colossus of science fiction," finds time for a second career of skindiving and underwater photography.

HISTORY LESSON

No one could remember when the tribe had begun its long journey. The land of great rolling plains that had been its first home was now no more than a half-forgotten dream.

For many years Shann and his people had been fleeing through a country of low hills and sparkling lakes, and now the mountains lay ahead. This summer they must cross them to the southern lands. There was little time to lose. The white terror that had come down from the poles, grinding continents to dust and freezing the very air before it, was less than a day's march behind.

Shann wondered if the glaciers could climb the mountains ahead, and within his heart he dared to kindle a little flame of hope. This might prove a barrier against which even the remorseless ice would batter in vain. In the southern lands of which the legends spoke, his people might find refuge at last.

It took weeks to discover a pass through which the tribe and the animals could travel. When midsummer came, they had camped in a lonely valley where the air was thin and the stars shone with a brilliance no one had ever seen before.

The summer was waning when Shann took his two sons and went ahead to explore the way. For three days they climbed, and for three nights slept as best they could on the freezing rocks, and on the fourth morning there was nothing ahead but a gentle rise to a cairn[1] of gray stones built by other travelers, centuries ago.

Shann felt himself trembling, and not with cold, as they walked toward the little pyramid of stones. His sons had fallen behind. No one spoke, for too much was at stake. In a little while they would know if all their hopes had been betrayed.

To east and west, the wall of mountains curved away as if embracing the land beneath. Below lay endless miles of undulating[2] plain, with a great river swinging across it in tremendous loops. It was a fertile land; one in which the tribe could raise crops knowing that there would be no need to flee before the harvest came.

Then Shann lifted his eyes to the south, and saw the doom of all his hopes. For there at the edge of the world glimmered that deadly light he had seen so often to the north—the glint of ice below the horizon.

There was no way forward. Through all the years of flight, the glaciers from the south had been advancing to meet them. Soon they would be crushed beneath the moving walls of ice. . . .

Southern glaciers did not reach the mountains until a generation later. In that last summer the sons of Shann carried the sacred treasures of the tribe to the lonely cairn overlooking the plain. The ice

1. **cairn** (kârn): heap in the shape of a cone, built as a landmark or monument.
2. **undulating** (ŭn′jo͞o·lāt′ĭng): wavy.

that had once gleamed below the horizon was now almost at their feet. By spring it would be splintering against the mountain walls.

No one understood the treasures now. They were from a past too distant for the understanding of any man alive. Their origins were lost in the mists that surrounded the Golden Age, and how they had come at last into the possession of this wandering tribe was a story that now would never be told. For it was the story of a civilization that had passed beyond recall.

Once, all these pitiful relics had been treasured for some good reason, and now they had become sacred though their meaning had long been lost. The print in the old books had faded centuries ago though much of the lettering was still visible—if there had been any to read it. But many generations had passed since anyone had had a use for a set of seven-figure logarithms, an atlas of the world, and the score of Sibelius' Seventh Symphony printed, according to the flyleaf, by H. K. Chu and Sons, at the City of Pekin in the year A.D. 2371.

The old books were placed reverently in the little crypt that had been made to receive them. There followed a motley[3] collection of fragments—gold and platinum coins, a broken telephoto lens, a watch, a cold-light lamp, a microphone, the cutter from an electric razor, some midget radio tubes, the flotsam that had been left behind when the great tide of civilization had ebbed forever.

All these treasures were carefully stowed away in their resting place. Then came three more relics, the most sacred of all because the least understood.

The first was a strangely shaped piece of metal, showing the coloration of intense heat. It was, in its way, the most pathetic of all these symbols from the past, for it told of man's greatest achievement and of the future he might have known. The mahogany stand on which it was mounted bore a silver plate with the inscription.

Auxiliary Igniter from Starboard Jet
Spaceship *Morning Star*
Earth-Moon, A.D. 1985

Next followed another miracle of the ancient science—a sphere of transparent plastic with strangely shaped pieces of metal imbedded in it. At its center was a tiny capsule of synthetic radioelement, surrounded by the converting screens that shifted its radiation far

3. **motley** (mŏt′lē): varied; miscellaneous.

down the spectrum. As long as the material remained active, the sphere would be a tiny radio transmitter, broadcasting power in all directions. Only a few of these spheres had ever been made. They had been designed as perpetual beacons to mark the orbits of the asteroids. But man had never reached the asteroids and the beacons had never been used.

Last of all was a flat, circular tin, wide in comparison with its depth. It was heavily sealed, and rattled when shaken. The tribal lore predicted that disaster would follow if it was ever opened, and no one knew that it held one of the great works of art of nearly a thousand years before.

The work was finished. The two men rolled the stones back into place and slowly began to descend the mountainside. Even to the last, man had given some thought to the future and had tried to preserve something for posterity.

That winter the great waves of ice began their first assault on the mountains, attacking from north and south. The foothills were overwhelmed in the first onslaught, and the glaciers ground them into dust. But the mountains stood firm, and when the summer came the ice retreated for a while.

So, winter after winter, the battle continued, and the roar of the avalanches, the grinding of rock and the explosions of splintering ice filled the air with tumult. No war of man's had been fiercer than this, and even man's battles had not quite engulfed the globe as this had done.

At last the tidal waves of ice began to subside and to creep slowly down the flanks of the mountains they had never quite subdued. The valleys and passes were still firmly in their grip. It was stalemate. The glaciers had met their match, but their defeat was too late to be of any use to man.

So the centuries passed, and presently there happened something that must occur once at least in the history of every world in the Universe, no matter how remote and lonely it may be.

The ship from Venus came five thousand years too late, but its crew knew nothing of this. While still many millions of miles away, the telescopes had seen the great shroud of ice that made Earth the most brilliant object in the sky next to the sun itself.

Here and there the dazzling sheet was marred by black specks that revealed the presence of almost buried mountains. That was all. The rolling oceans, the plains and forests, the deserts and lakes—all that had been the world of man was sealed beneath the ice, perhaps forever.

The ship closed in to Earth and established an orbit less than a thousand miles away. For five days it circled the planet, while cameras recorded all that was left to see and a hundred instruments gathered information that would give the Venusian scientists many years of work.

An actual landing was not intended. There seemed little purpose in it. But on the sixth day the picture changed. A panoramic monitor, driven to the limit of its amplification, detected the dying radiation of the five-thousand-year-old-beacon. Through all the centuries, it had been sending out its signals with ever-failing strength as its radioactive heart steadily weakened.

The monitor locked on the beacon frequency. In the control room, a bell clamored for attention. A little later, the Venusian ship broke free from its orbit and slanted down toward Earth, toward a range of mountains that still towered proudly above the ice, and to a cairn of gray stones that the years had scarcely touched. . . .

The great disk of the sun blazed fiercely in a sky no longer veiled with mist, for the clouds that had once hidden Venus had now completely gone. Whatever force had caused the change in the sun's radiation had doomed one civilization, but had given birth to another. Less than five thousand years before, the half-savage people of Venus had seen sun and stars for the first time. Just as the science of Earth had begun with astronomy, so had that of Venus, and on the warm, rich world that man had never seen progress had been incredibly rapid.

Perhaps the Venusians had been lucky. They never knew the Dark Age that held man enchained for a thousand years. They missed the long detour into chemistry and mechanics but came at once to the more fundamental laws of radiation physics. In the time that man had taken to progress from the Pyramids to the rocket-propelled spaceship, the Venusians had passed from the discovery of agriculture to antigravity itself—the ultimate secret that man had never learned.

The warm ocean that still bore most of the young planet's life rolled its breakers languidly against the sandy shore. So new was this continent that the very sands were coarse and gritty. There had not yet been time enough for the sea to wear them smooth.

The scientists lay half in the water, their beautiful reptilian bodies gleaming in the sunlight. The greatest minds of Venus had gathered on this shore from all the islands of the planet. What they were going to hear they did not know, except that it concerned the Third World and the mysterious race that had peopled it before the coming of the ice.

The Historian was standing on the land, for the instruments he wished to use had no love of water. By his side was a large machine which attracted many curious glances from his colleagues. It was clearly concerned with optics, for a lens system projected from it toward a screen of white material a dozen yards away.

The Historian began to speak. Briefly he recapitulated what little had been discovered concerning the Third Planet and its people.

He mentioned the centuries of fruitless research that had failed to interpret a single word of the writings of Earth. The planet had been inhabited by a race of great technical ability. That, at least, was proved by the few pieces of machinery that had been found in the cairn upon the mountain.

"We do not know why so advanced a civilization came to an end," he observed. "Almost certainly, it had sufficient knowledge to survive an Ice Age. There must have been some other factor of which we know nothing. Possibly disease or racial degeneration may have been responsible. It has even been suggested that the tribal conflicts endemic[4] to our own species in prehistoric times may have continued on the Third Planet after the coming of technology.

"Some philosophers maintain that knowledge of machinery does not necessarily imply a high degree of civilization, and it is theoretically possible to have wars in a society possessing mechanical power, flight, and even radio. Such a conception is alien to our thoughts, but we must admit its possibility. It would certainly account for the downfall of the lost race.

"It has always been assumed that we should never know anything of the physical form of the creatures who lived on Planet Three. For centuries our artists have been depicting scenes from the history of the dead world, peopling it with all manner of fantastic beings. Most of these creations have resembled us more or less closely, though it has often been pointed out that because *we* are reptiles it does not follow that all intelligent life must necessarily be reptilian.

"We now know the answer to one of the most baffling problems of history. At last, after hundreds of years of research, we have discovered the exact form and nature of the ruling life on the Third Planet."

4. **endemic** (ĕn•dĕm′ĭk): found regularly in a particular group or place.

There was a murmur of astonishment from the assembled scientists. Some were so taken aback that they disappeared for a while into the comfort of the ocean, as all Venusians were apt to do in moments of stress. The Historian waited until his colleagues re-emerged into the element they so disliked. He himself was quite comfortable, thanks to the tiny sprays that were continually playing over his body. With their help he could live on land for many hours before having to return to the ocean.

The excitement slowly subsided and the lecturer continued:

"One of the most puzzling of the objects found on Planet Three was a flat metal container holding a great length of transparent plastic material, perforated at the edges and wound tightly into a spool. This transparent tape at first seemed quite featureless, but an examination with the new subelectronic microscope has shown that this is not the case. Along the surface of the material, invisible to our eyes but perfectly clear under the correct radiation, are literally thousands of tiny pictures. It is believed that they were imprinted on the material by some chemical means, and have faded with the passage of time.

"These pictures apparently form a record of life as it was on the Third Planet at the height of its civilization. They are not independent. Consecutive pictures are almost identical, differing only in the detail of movement. The purpose of such a record is obvious. It is only necessary to project the scenes in rapid succession to give an illusion of continuous movement. We have made a machine to do this, and I have here an exact reproduction of the picture sequence.

"The scenes you are now going to witness take us back many thousands of years, to the great days of our sister planet. They show a complex civilization, many of whose activities we can only dimly understand. Life seems to have been very violent and energetic, and much that you will see is quite baffling.

"It is clear that the Third Planet was inhabited by a number of different species, none of them reptilian. That is a blow to our pride, but the conclusion is inescapable. The dominant type of life appears to have been a two-armed biped. It walked upright and covered its body with some flexible material, possibly for protection against the cold, since even before the Ice Age the planet was at a much lower temperature than our own world. But I will not try your patience any further. You will now see the record of which I have been speaking."

A brilliant light flashed from the projector. There was a gentle whirring, and on the screen appeared hundreds of strange beings moving rather jerkily to and fro. The picture expanded to embrace one of the creatures, and the scientists could see that the Historian's description had been correct.

The creature possessed two eyes, set rather close together, but the other facial adornments were a little obscure. There was a large orifice in the lower portion of the head that was continually opening and closing. Possibly it had something to do with the creature's breathing.

The scientists watched spellbound as the strange being became involved in a series of fantastic adventures. There was an incredibly violent conflict with another, slightly different creature. It seemed certain that they must both be killed, but when it was all over neither seemed any the worse.

Then came a furious drive over miles of country in a four-wheeled mechanical device which was capable of extraordinary feats of locomotion. The ride ended in a city packed with other vehicles moving in all directions at breath-taking speeds. No one was surprised to see two of the machines meet head-on with devastating results.

After that, events became even more complicated. It was now quite obvious that it would take many years of research to analyze and understand all that was happening. It was also clear that the record was a work of art, somewhat stylized, rather than an exact reproduction of life as it actually had been on the Third Planet.

Most of the scientists felt themselves completely dazed when the sequence of pictures came to an end. There was a final flurry of motion, in which the creature that had been the center of interest became involved in some tremendous but incomprehensible catastrophe. The picture contracted to a circle, centered on the creature's head.

The last scene of all was an expanded view of its face, obviously expressing some powerful emotion. But whether it was rage, grief, defiance, resignation or some other feeling could not be guessed. The picture vanished. For a moment some lettering appeared on the screen, then it was all over.

For several minutes there was complete silence, save for the lapping of the waves upon the sand. The scientists were too stunned to speak. The fleeting glimpse of Earth's civilization had had a shattering effect on their minds. Then little groups began to start talking together, first in whispers and then more and more loudly as the implications of what they had seen became clearer. Presently the Historian called for attention and addressed the meeting again.

"We are now planning," he said, "a vast program of research to extract all available knowledge from this record. Thousands of copies are being made for distribution to all workers. You will appreciate the problems involved. The psychologists in particular have an immense task confronting them.

"But I do not doubt that we shall succeed. In another generation, who can say what we may not have learned of this wonderful race? Before we leave, let us look again at our remote cousins, whose wisdom may have surpassed our own but of whom so little has survived."

Once more the final picture flashed on the screen, motionless this time, for the projector had been stopped. With something like awe, the scientists gazed at the still figure from the past, while in turn the little biped stared back at them with its characteristic expression of arrogant bad temper.

For the rest of time it would symbolize the human race. The psychologists of Venus would analyze its actions and watch its every movement until they could reconstruct its mind. Thousands of books would be written about it. Intricate philosophies would be contrived to account for its behavior.

But all this labor, all this research, would be utterly in vain. Perhaps the proud and lonely figure on the screen was smiling sardonically at the scientists who were starting on their age-long fruitless quest.

Its secret would be safe as long as the Universe endured, for no one now would ever read the lost language of Earth. Millions of times in the ages to come those last few words would flash across the screen, and none could ever guess their meaning:

A Walt Disney Production.

Meaning

1. "History Lesson" falls naturally into three parts. What is the setting (place and time) of each part?
2. In the first part of this story, why do Shann and his sons climb the mountain?
3. What is the immediate cause for the destruction of the Third World? What other causes are implied?

4. What relics, left behind by Shann's people, prove valuable to the Venusians? What is ironic about the relics?
5. What conclusions about Earth people do the Venusians draw from the film they view?

Method

1. What is the significance of the title? How is the title related to the theme of the story?
2. Why do you think the author did not include dialogue in the story? What is the purpose of the one long speech?
3. Arthur Clarke is a master at heightening suspense by withholding information from the reader. Give some examples of this technique in "History Lesson."
4. One reason why "History Lesson" is so powerful is that it sounds as if it could be true. What scientific details in the story make it seem authentic?

Language: Using Vivid Verbs

There is little action on the part of the characters in "History Lesson." Yet the story moves along swiftly and keeps you interested. Strong, specific verbs can do much to give forward movement to a story. Notice, for example, the verbs Arthur Clarke uses to describe the advance of the ice.

1. "For there at the edge of the world *glimmered* the deadly light . . ."
2. "By spring it would be *splintering* against the mountain walls."
3. "The foothills were *overwhelmed* in the first onslaught, and the glaciers *ground* them into dust."

Find other examples of vivid action words in "History Lesson."

Discussion and Composition

1. Science fiction is often a prophecy and a warning. How does Arthur Clarke's vision of the future relate to problems that you see in the world today? Discuss other science fiction stories and films that you know. Compare their authors' ideas about the future of humanity with Arthur Clarke's. In this story, would you say that Arthur Clarke is basically optimistic or pessimistic?

2. The objects found in the cairn served as a "time capsule" telling the Venusians as much as they would ever know about the Third World. Why were the thirteen objects found in the cairn of little value as information to the Venusians? List thirteen objects that you would place in a time capsule to tell inhabitants of other worlds about civilization on earth. Give at least one reason why you would include each item you choose for the capsule.

3. Do some research on general conditions (size and distance from the sun, for example) of one of the planets in our solar system. Assume that some form of intelligent life would be possible there. Describe the inhabitants of the planet you have selected. Tell as much about their living conditions, customs, and ideas as you can draw from your imagination.

4. Arthur Clarke writes, ". . . presently there happened something that must occur once at least in the history of every world in the Universe, no matter how remote and lonely it may be." To what does he refer? Do you agree with him? Why or why not?

JAMES JOYCE
(1882–1941)

The short stories of James Joyce often seem to have little plot. There is almost no dramatic action in "Araby," for instance, which is part of his short story collection, *Dubliners* (1914). One of Joyce's contributions to the development of the short story was his idea that the story should build toward a moment of clear vision, truth, or self-discovery, which he called "epiphany."

One of the most influential and controversial writers of the twentieth century, James Joyce was born in Dublin, Ireland, the oldest son of a large family that sank deep into poverty as he grew up. He attended a Catholic grammar school on scholarship and graduated from University College in Dublin in 1902. Joyce left Dublin soon after his mother died in 1903, and spent the rest of his life in Paris, Zurich, and Trieste, supporting himself by teaching languages and writing.

Joyce's most important books are *A Portrait of the Artist as a Young Man* (1916), *Ulysses* (1922), and *Finnegans Wake* (1939). Almost all of his writing deals with Dublin and contains elements of his own life, which was often wild and sometimes sad. Although he suffered from eye disease and was sometimes blind, he was always committed to excellence and originality in his writing. Several of his works are considered masterpieces because of his sensitive portrayal of human nature and his brilliant use of language with many levels of meaning. He is credited with developing the stream-of-consciousness technique, which takes the reader inside the mind of a character to experience a free flow of ideas and sensations. Joyce pointed out new and exciting directions to writers who have followed him.

ARABY

North Richmond Street, being blind,[1] was a quiet street except at the hour when the Christian Brothers' School set the boys free. An uninhabited house of two storeys stood at the blind end, detached

1. **blind:** dead-end.

from its neighbours in a square ground. The other houses of the street, conscious of decent lives within them, gazed at one another with brown imperturbable faces.

The former tenant of our house, a priest, had died in the back drawing-room. Air, musty from having been long enclosed, hung in all the rooms, and the waste room behind the kitchen was littered with old useless papers. Among these I found a few paper-covered books, the pages of which were curled and damp: *The Abbot,* by Walter Scott, *The Devout Communicant* and *The Memoirs of Vidocq.* I liked the last best because its leaves were yellow. The wild garden behind the house contained a central apple-tree and a few straggling bushes under one of which I found the late tenant's rusty bicycle-pump. He had been a very charitable priest; in his will he had left all his money to institutions and the furniture of his house to his sister.

When the short days of winter came dusk fell before we had well eaten our dinners. When we met in the street the houses had grown sombre. The space of sky above us was the colour of ever-changing violet and towards it the lamps of the street lifted their feeble lanterns. The cold air stung us and we played till our bodies glowed. Our shouts echoed in the silent street. The career of our play brought us through the dark muddy lanes behind the houses where we ran the gantlet of the rough tribes from the cottages, to the back doors of the dark dripping gardens where odours arose from the ashpits, to the dark odorous stables where a coachman smoothed and combed the horse or shook music from the buckled harness. When we returned to the street light from the kitchen windows had filled the areas. If my uncle was seen turning the corner we hid in the shadow until we had seen him safely housed. Or if Mangan's sister came out on the doorstep to call her brother in to his tea we watched her from our shadow peer up and down the street. We waited to see whether she would remain or go in and, if she remained, we left our shadow and walked up to Mangan's steps resignedly. She was waiting for us, her figure defined by the light from the half-opened door. Her brother always teased her before he obeyed and I stood by the railings looking at her. Her dress swung as she moved her body and the soft rope of her hair tossed from side to side.

Every morning I lay on the floor in the front parlour watching her door. The blind was pulled down to within an inch of the sash so that I could not be seen. When she came out on the doorstep my heart leaped. I ran to the hall, seized my books and followed her. I kept her brown figure always in my eye and, when we came near the point at which our ways diverged, I quickened my pace and passed her. This happened morning after morning. I had never spoken to her, except for a few casual words, and yet her name was like a summons to all my foolish blood.

Her image accompanied me even in places the most hostile to romance. On Saturday evenings when my aunt went marketing I had to go to carry some of the parcels. We walked through the flaring streets, jostled by drunken men and bargaining women, amid the curses of labourers, the shrill litanies[2] of shop-boys who stood on guard by the barrels of pigs' cheeks, the nasal chanting of street-singers, who sang a *come-all-you* about O'Donovan Rossa,[3] or a ballad about the troubles in our native land. These noises converged in a single sensation of life for me: I imagined that I bore my chalice safely through a throng of foes. Her name sprang to my lips at moments in strange prayers and praises which I myself did not understand. My eyes were often full of tears (I could not tell why) and at times a flood from my heart seemed to pour itself out into my bosom. I thought little of the future. I did not know whether I would ever speak to her or not or, if I spoke to her, how I could tell her of my confused adoration. But my body was like a harp and her words and gestures were like fingers running upon the wires.

One evening I went into the back drawing-room in which the priest had died. It was a dark rainy evening and there was no sound in the house. Through one of the broken panes I heard the rain impinge upon the earth, the fine incessant needles of water playing in the sodden beds. Some distant lamp or lighted window gleamed below me. I was thankful that I could see so little. All my senses seemed to desire to veil themselves and, feeling that I was about to slip from them, I pressed the palms of my hands together until they trembled, murmuring: *O love! O love!* many times.

At last she spoke to me. When she addressed the first words to me I was so confused that I did not know what to answer. She asked me was I going to *Araby*. I forget whether I answered yes or no. It would be a splendid bazaar, she said; she would love to go.

—And why can't you? I asked.

While she spoke she turned a silver bracelet round and round

2. litanies (lĭt′n•ēs): prayers in which a priest and congregation alternate with recitation and response.

3. come-all-you . . . Rossa: a ballad about an Irish hero.

her wrist. She could not go, she said, because there would be a retreat[4] that week in her convent. Her brother and two other boys were fighting for their caps and I was alone at the railings. She held one of the spikes, bowing her head towards me. The light from the lamp opposite our door caught the white curve of her neck, lit up her hair that rested there and, falling, lit up the hand upon the railing. It fell over one side of her dress and caught the white border of a petticoat, just visible as she stood at ease.

—It's well for you, she said.

—If I go, I said, I will bring you something.

What innumerable follies laid waste my waking and sleeping thoughts after that evening! I wished to annihilate the tedious intervening days. I chafed against the work of school. At night in my bedroom and by day in the classroom her image came between me and the page I strove to read. The syllables of the word *Araby* were called to me through the silence in which my soul luxuriated and cast an Eastern enchantment over me. I asked for leave to go to the bazaar on Saturday night. My aunt was surprised and hoped it was not some Freemason[5] affair. I answered few questions in class. I watched my master's face pass from amiability to sternness; he hoped I was not beginning to idle. I could not call my wandering thoughts together. I had hardly any patience with the serious work of life which, now that it stood between me and my desire, seemed to me child's play, ugly monotonous child's play.

On Saturday morning I reminded my uncle that I wished to go to the bazaar in the evening. He was fussing at the hallstand, looking for the hat-brush, and answered me curtly:

—Yes, boy, I know.

As he was in the hall I could not go into the front parlour and lie at the window. I left the house in bad humour and walked slowly towards the school. The air was pitilessly raw and already my heart misgave me.

When I came home to dinner my uncle had not yet been home. Still it was early. I sat staring at the clock for some time and, when its ticking began to irritate me, I left the room. I mounted the staircase and gained the upper part of the house. The high cold empty gloomy rooms liberated me and I went from room to room singing. From the

4. **retreat:** a period of prayer and contemplation.
5. **Freemason:** secret society considered anti-Catholic in Ireland.

front window I saw my companions playing below in the street. Their cries reached me weakened and indistinct and, leaning my forehead against the cool glass, I looked over at the dark house where she lived. I may have stood there for an hour, seeing nothing but the brown-clad figure cast by my imagination, touched discreetly by the lamplight at the curved neck, at the hand upon the railings and at the border below the dress.

When I came downstairs again I found Mrs Mercer sitting at the fire. She was an old garrulous woman, a pawnbroker's widow, who collected used stamps for some pious purpose. I had to endure the gossip of the tea-table. The meal was prolonged beyond an hour and still my uncle did not come. Mrs Mercer stood up to go: she was sorry she couldn't wait any longer, but it was after eight o'clock and she did not like to be out late, as the night air was bad for her. When she had gone I began to walk up and down the room, clenching my fists. My aunt said:

–I'm afraid you may put off your bazaar for this night of Our Lord.

At nine o'clock I heard my uncle's latchkey in the halldoor. I heard him talking to himself and heard the hallstand rocking when it had received the weight of his overcoat. I could interpret these signs. When he was midway through his dinner I asked him to give me the money to go to the bazaar. He had forgotten.

–The people are in bed and after their first sleep now, he said.

I did not smile. My aunt said to him energetically:

–Can't you give him the money and let him go? You've kept him late enough as it is.

My uncle said he was very sorry he had forgotten. He said he believed in the old saying: *All work and no play makes Jack a dull boy.* He asked me where I was going and, when I had told him a second time he asked me did I know *The Arab's Farewell to his Steed.* When I left the kitchen he was about to recite the opening lines of the piece to my aunt.

I held a florin[6] tightly in my hand as I strode down Buckingham Street towards the station. The sight of the streets thronged with buyers and glaring with gas recalled to me the purpose of my journey. I took my seat in a third-class carriage of a deserted train. After an intolerable delay the train moved out of the station slowly. It crept

6. florin: a silver coin equal to two shillings, or 1/10 of a pound, about $.20 in U.S. money.

onward among ruinous houses and over the twinkling river. At Westland Row Station a crowd of people pressed to the carriage doors; but the porters moved them back, saying that it was a special train for the bazaar. I remained alone in the bare carriage. In a few minutes the train drew up beside an improvised wooden platform. I passed out on to the road and saw by the lighted dial of a clock that it was ten minutes to ten. In front of me was a large building which displayed the magical name.

I could not find any sixpenny entrance and, fearing that the bazaar would be closed, I passed in quickly through a turnstile, handing a shilling to a weary-looking man. I found myself in a big hall girdled at half its height by a gallery. Nearly all the stalls were closed and the greater part of the hall was in darkness. I recognised a silence like that which pervades a church after a service. I walked into the centre of the bazaar timidly. A few people were gathered about the stalls which were still open. Before a curtain, over which the words *Café Chantant* were written in coloured lamps, two men were counting money on a salver[7]. I listened to the fall of the coins.

Remembering with difficulty why I had come I went over to one of the stalls and examined porcelain vases and flowered tea-sets. At the door of the stall a young lady was talking and laughing with two young gentlemen. I remarked their English accents and listened vaguely to their conversation.

—O, I never said such a thing!

—O, but you did!

—O, but I didn't!

—Didn't she say that?

—Yes. I heard her.

—O, there's a . . . fib!

Observing me the young lady came over and asked me did I wish to buy anything. The tone of her voice was not encouraging; she seemed to have spoken to me out of a sense of duty. I looked humbly at the great jars that stood like eastern guards at either side of the dark entrance to the stall and murmured:

—No, thank you.

The young lady changed the position of one of the vases and went back to the two young men. They began to talk of the same subject. Once or twice the young lady glanced at me over her shoulder.

7. salver (săl′vər): tray.

I lingered before her stall, though I knew my stay was useless, to make my interest in her wares seem the more real. Then I turned away slowly and walked down the middle of the bazaar. I allowed the two pennies to fall against the sixpence in my pocket. I heard a voice call from one end of the gallery that the light was out. The upper part of the hall was now completely dark.

Gazing up into the darkness I saw myself as a creature driven and derided by vanity; and my eyes burned with anguish and anger.

Meaning

1. What kind of person is the boy in "Araby"? What evidence can you find that he has a romantic view of life? How can you tell that the narrator is telling a story about his youth?
2. Why is Mangan's sister unable to go to the bazaar? Why does the boy want to go there?
3. There is little dramatic action in "Araby." It is typical of Joyce's stories in which a character arrives at an *epiphany*, a time when the character discovers an important truth that changes his or her view of life. What discovery about himself does the boy make at the bazaar?
4. Describe the boy's uncle. Why do you think the aunt at first seems to disapprove of the bazaar, but later urges her husband to let the boy go?

Method

1. What is the function of the first two paragraphs in the story?
2. What does the bazaar symbolize? What does the old priest symbolize?
3. *Images* are word pictures and impressions that appeal to our senses. Images of darkness and light pervade "Araby" and help to convey mood and atmosphere. Explain the significance of the following images:

   a. "The career of our play brought us through the *dark muddy lanes behind the houses* . . . to the *back doors of the dark dripping gardens* . . . "

   b. "*The light from the lamp* opposite our door *caught the white curve of her neck, lit up her hair that rested there and, falling, lit up the hand* upon the railing."

   c. "I heard a voice call from one end of the gallery that *the light was out.* The upper part of the hall was now *completely dark.*"

Language: Poetic Prose Style

Joyce describes his style in *Dubliners,* from which "Araby" is taken, as one of "scrupulous meanness," that is, flat and unadorned with figures of speech. Although the stories in *Dubliners,* in general, are much less metaphoric and rhythmical than Joyce's novels, "Araby" contains several elements that are seen more often in poetry than in prose.

In addition to similes and metaphors, Joyce uses a figure of speech called *personification,* that is, he gives human or animal characteristics to inanimate objects and ideas. "Towards it the lamps of the street lifted their feeble lanterns." He also uses the poetic techniques of alliteration and assonance. *Alliteration* is the repetition of initial consonants, as, for example, in the following sentence: "Our *s*houts echoed in the *s*ilent *s*treet." *Assonance* is the repetition of internal vowel sounds in words that occur close to one another in a sentence, for example, "Her dress swung as she moved her b*o*dy and the s*o*ft rope *o*f her hair t*o*ssed fr*o*m side to side." Find other examples of personification, alliteration, and assonance in "Araby."

Discussion and Composition

1. Do you think that "Araby" describes a typical adolescent experience? In a composition, tell why or why not. Support each reason with examples or incidents.

2. Write about an incident that helped you grow up. It could be a time when you lost some illusions, gained new responsibilities, or did something on your own. In your first sentence, tell how the incident made you feel.

GORDON WOODWARD

(born 1921)

A self-educated native of Canada, Gordon Woodward was born in Regina, in the western province of Saskatchewan. Because his family could not afford to send him to high school, Woodward taught himself by reading widely on his own.

Writing articles and short stories for magazines primarily in the evening and on weekends, Woodward has supported himself with a variety of jobs, including those of laborer, foreman, sales clerk, and civil servant. He has also written a novel about British Columbia, radio scripts, and a television documentary. He lives in Vancouver, which provides the setting for "Escape to the City." This story was chosen for Marth Foley's collection of *The Best American Short Stories of 1957.*

ESCAPE TO THE CITY

It was almost three o'clock when I arrived in the city that afternoon.

It was that day in late September when I had started out early in the morning while the thick white mist lay close to the ground and I could see the willow bushes down by the river poking up through the filmy blanket beneath the bridge where Clifford and I had always gone fishing; the dew that morning clustered in thick glistening drops on the handlebars of my bike as I wheeled it quietly down from the porch so as not to wake up Jeannie and Father, who would not even know I was gone until they got up and found that note I had left on the kitchen table saying I had gone to the city to visit Clifford.

And I knew Father would be angry, because he hadn't even written to Clifford since that day over two months before when they had argued about Clifford going into the business because he was seventeen and through high school. Clifford had refused; instead he had answered an ad in the newspaper for a position as an apprentice in a chemical firm in the city and then had drawn all of his money out of the local bank (which had been seven dollars and nineteen cents) and had climbed on the bus with no one there to even say good-by to him; and I hadn't seen him since that day.

I was beginning to get tired. I'd ridden over fifty-three miles since I had turned off by Galloway's Dairy on the outskirts of Abbotsford that morning and then had headed down the highway through the smell of trees and rotting leaves and the sun throwing bright patches of early sunlight across the fields. I pulled over to the curb and took out the letter I had received from Clifford and looked at the house number again; it was in the next block, so I rode close to the curb with my bike wheels crunching over the dried leaves in the gutter until I came to it.

It was one of those big old houses which line the streets in the west end of Vancouver;[1] it was better looked after than most of them and was painted a bright cream-and-brown color. I got off my bike and wheeled it through the gate; then I untied the parcel on the carrier and went up the steps and rang the doorbell.

After a minute a lady came to the door; she was not very old but had gray hair and glasses. "Does Clifford Barton live here, ma'am?" I said.

"Yes, he does," she said. "But he's not in right now."

"Well, I'm his brother," I said.

"Oh, I see." She seemed as though she didn't know what to say.

"I just came in from Abbotsford where we live," I said. I pointed to my blue CCM lying at the bottom of the steps. "I rode in on my bike," I said.

"That's a long way to ride," she said.

"It certainly is," I said. She still didn't move; and I knew she was stalling for some reason. "I haven't seen Clifford for a couple of months," I said.

"That's quite a coincidence, you coming," she said, "because he was telling me just yesterday about all his brothers at home."

"Oh, there must be some mistake, ma'am," I said. "He doesn't have any other brothers except me . . . only a sister." Then all at once I realized that she had been trying to find out if I really *was* Clifford's brother; and she knew I knew it.

"I'm sorry," she said, and she smiled. "I have to be careful." She opened the door wider. "Would you like to go up to his room? He should be home about six."

1. Vancouver (văn•kōō′vər): a city and port in southern British Columbia, Canada.

I followed her into the hallway, and she closed the door and then led me up two flights of winding, carpeted stairs to a room on the top floor; she opened the door and let me go in first, and then stood in the doorway a moment. "Are you hungry?" she said.

"No thanks," I said. "I had a hamburger and a milkshake at a place on the highway."

She looked at me for a minute with a kind of warm smile on her face. "You don't look much like Clifford," she said.

"I guess just about everybody tells us that," I said.

"You're the youngest, are you?" she said.

"I'm fifteen," I said. "Just turned fifteen."

"Well, if there's anything you want you just come downstairs," she said. She started to close the door and then she came back again. "The bathroom is right across the hall," she said. She closed the door and I could hear her footsteps going down the stairs.

I sat down on the edge of the bed and looked around at the small room; it was very clean and bright. There was linoleum on the floor, and the wallpaper had white flowers all over it. In one corner there was a small cupboard, and below it a table covered with oilcloth with a small electric hot plate and a kettle sitting on it; there were also two white wooden chairs. In the opposite corner there was a closet with a door on it; and the bed on which I was sitting was covered with a bright homemade quilt.

I looked at the two windows that opened out above the porch on the front of the house; there were small birds twittering and chirping on the roof outside. The leaves on the maple trees along the sidewalk on the opposite side of the street were yellow and soft brown and yet-bright green, suddenly fluttering one by one to the ground with a frail and brittle scraping sound, as though made of balsa wood.

My legs and my backside felt stiff and sore, and I lay back on the bed and looked up at the ceiling, just gazing blankly, the way I had been lying in my own bed in Abbotsford and looking up at the ceiling that morning Clifford had come into the room all dressed and wearing his pale-blue shirt and the maroon tie I had given him for his birthday, when I hadn't even known he was going anywhere until that moment he said, "I'm going, Pat. Take care of yourself. I'll write," and then was gone.

Not even waiting to say good-by to Father (who wouldn't have answered pleasantly anyway), but just walking out through the door and down to the bus stop and getting on that bus with his battered suitcase in which were all his clothes and that small Wedgwood[2] vase which had belonged to Mother, and the sum of seven dollars and nineteen cents in his pocket, and heading for the city where he didn't know anyone; so that when I had finally struggled awake that morning and had put on my clothes and jumped on my bike and raced down to the bus stop I had been just in time to see the bus pulling away and had pedaled hard to get alongside and catch just one glimpse of his face and have him see me so that he would know that I at least had wanted to say good-by; and yet I hadn't been fast enough. It had been almost two months before that letter had come and I had even known where he was living in the city.

There was a cool breeze coming through the open window and I pulled the corner of the quilt up over me and put my head on the pillow, and then I must have fallen sound asleep, because all at once I felt someone shaking me by the shoulder and calling my name. "Pat! Wake up!" Then a slight pause and another shake. "Pat!"

I slowly opened my eyes and saw Clifford standing by the bed grinning at me, the room looking a little darker and shadier than it had been, so that I knew I had slept quite a while. "Am I ever surprised to see you!" he said. "You could have knocked me over when the landlady told me you were here!"

I struggled to come fully awake. "Hi, Clifford!" I said.

"When did you get here?" he said.

"About three o'clock."

"I was expecting you to write," he said, "but I didn't think you'd be able to come in. How did you ever find that place? Did you come in on the bus?"

"I came on my bike," I said. "Didn't you see my CCM out front?"

"I guess I saw it," he said. "But it never struck me it was yours. Did you ride all the way?"

"Sure," I said. I went to get up and felt the stiffness in my thighs. "But I'm a little stiff now," I said. "I'm not used to riding that far."

"You must be starved," he said. "Wait till I have a wash and we'll go and get something to eat." He took off his jacket and hung it in the closet. "Tell me what's been going on," he said.

"I brought you a fish I caught yesterday by the bridge," I said.

2. **Wedgwood** (wĕj′wo͝od): a fine chinaware of superior quality, characterized by a tinted clay background and small white cameo reliefs, usually of a classical and minutely detailed design; first produced by Josiah Wedgwood (1730–1795), an English potter and inventor.

"A spring. He put up a good fight." I walked over to the table and started to take it out of the paper bag. "And I swiped a jar of Jeannie's raspberry jam," I said. "Jeannie doesn't make very good jam anyway." We both laughed.

Clifford took a towel and some soap and went across the hall to the bathroom, and I could hear him running water in the basin; then after a few minutes he came back drying his neck with the towel. He had taken his glasses off; he always looked different without his glasses, as though his eyes had shrunk. "Holy Moses!" he said. "Was I ever surprised when I came in and found you here!" He put his glasses back on and slipped his tie over his head and tightened it and put his jacket on. Then he went over to the cupboard and took down a small bowl and took some money out of it and then put the bowl back in the cupboard. "Come on, kid," he said. "Let's get some food before you collapse from hunger."

We went downstairs and he knocked on the landlady's door and asked her if it would be all right for me to put my bike in the basement, and she said it would, so we went around to the side door and put the bike away; then we went down the front sidewalk and out through the gate. The sun was blood-orange and low in the sky and as we walked down the tree-shaded street it threw long shadows down the sidewalk in front of us; our feet crunched on the dried leaves which had fallen on the cement.

"How do you like it, Clifford?" I said.

"You mean Vancouver?" he said. "Or my job?"

"Everything," I said. "Being in Vancouver . . . and having your job . . . and living here . . . you know what I mean."

"I like it fine," he said. "I guess I'm pretty lucky." He went along looking at his feet for a minute. "You should see the building I work in, Pat!" he said. "It covers a whole city block."

"I guess it must be a pretty big company," I said.

"Yes," he said. "They're really big . . . they ship all over the world."

"I guess they must have an awful lot of money," I said.

We came to a corner and turned down toward the harbor. There was a sparkling-white freighter heading out toward The Narrows, and the deep glow of evening sunlight rolled across the windows in the wheelhouse like bright liquid fire.

"Do they pay you pretty good money?" I said.

He didn't say anything. We turned another corner and went down the street a little way and turned into a café. The place smelled of cigarette smoke and frying food the way Gerry's Hamburger Bar in Abbotsford smelled on Saturday night when all the gang hung around listening to the jukebox. There were no vacant booths, so we sat down at the counter in the bucket-shaped wooden stool-seats. The waitress came, and I ordered some veal cutlets and mashed potatoes and a glass of milk and a piece of cherry pie. Clifford ordered a cup of coffee and some doughnuts. She gave us each a glass of water and went away along the counter.

"Aren't you going to eat?" I said.

"I'm not hungry," he said. "Down at work we're always eating doughnuts or cookies or candy or some other stuff . . . it ruins a guy's appetite."

"Yes," I said. "I guess it does."

The waitress brought my veal cutlets and I started to eat. I hadn't realized until then just how hungry I really was, and I was enjoying it. Then I happened to look in the big mirror behind the counter, and I saw Clifford watching me closely. "Are you *sure* you aren't going to eat something, Clifford?" I said.

"I'm not the least hungry," he said. "Really I'm not. What made you ask that?"

"Nothing," I said.

I finished my dinner and we got up and Clifford took the check and went over to the cashier and put a two-dollar bill on the counter as though he couldn't understand how he happened to have such a small bill in his pocket. She rang up one dollar and ten cents and gave him ninety cents and we went outside and turned up Granville Street.

"Feel better?" Clifford said.

"Boy, do I ever!" I said. "That was really good!"

It was beginning to get dark; the streetlights were all on and the neon signs flashed red and green and yellow. There were a lot of people crowding up and down the sidewalk and we had to keep dodging first to one side and then the other. It was hard to think that out in Abbotsford at that moment there would be only a few neon signs shining in the whole town, and the only places which would even be open would be Gerry's Hamburger Bar and Watson's Drug-store. I dodged around a couple of old ladies and came up beside Clifford again.

"What do you do at night, Clifford?" I said. "I mean what do you do for fun?"

"Oh, I have lots to do," he said. "I have to study, you know. And every Tuesday night I go to a show."

"Why Tuesday?" I said.

"No reason," he said. "I just started going on Tuesday when I first came here. That's the day I get paid: Tuesday."

"Don't you ever go to parties?" I said. "Or anything like that?"

"I could go to lots if I wanted to," he said, "but I don't usually have time."

"I guess a guy kind of grows out of parties after a while, anyway," I said.

"Yeah," he said. "You get tired of them."

We kept walking down the street. The crowd wasn't quite so thick where we were then and we didn't have to dodge so much. We came to the intersection and had to stop for a traffic light.

"What would you like to do now, Pat?" Clifford said. "Would you like to just walk around or what?" The light changed and we crossed over and when we got to the opposite curb he said, "If I'd brought more money with me we could have gone to a show. I never carry any more money with me than I need. I keep it all in a bowl on the shelf back at the room."

"Why don't you put it in the bank?" I said.

"I can't be bothered with banks," he said. "Maybe later on when I get better organized."

"Anyway," I said, "this is Friday night, and Tuesday night is when you go to the show."

"That's right," he said. "It is." He didn't say anything for several minutes, and then he said, "Do they still have the shows two nights a week at home?"

"Yes," I said. "But they're talking about making it every night because of all those construction workers coming into town from that camp on the meridian road. It will sure liven the town up," I said.

"It seems like a year since I left," he said. He stopped to look at some cigarette lighters in a window we were passing.

"Clifford," I said. "Haven't you got some friend here in Vancouver you go to shows with, or somebody you just chum around with?" He didn't answer; instead he leaned forward a little and looked closer at the lighters. I knew the minute it was out of my mouth that I'd said the wrong thing, because Clifford didn't make very many friends; he was hard to get to know, but when he did make a friend he was really loyal, as though he expected the friendship to go on as long as he was alive.

Maybe that was why he had felt the way he had that morning when they had told him that his friend Tink Martin had been shot in the stomach while cleaning a shotgun. Clifford had ridden thirteen miles to the hospital in Sardis where they had taken Tink and then had sat there until they came out and told him that Tink had died without ever regaining consciousness. He had turned around and ridden all the way back and then had sat in the corner of the living room and stared at the wall, not even crying, and that was what made it so terrible, just sitting there in the corner while Jeannie and Father had nagged at him to eat something until he finally had and then had been sick right away (perhaps it was because Tink had been shot in the stomach) and then had gone back and sat in the corner again. I'd never forgotten the lost look on his face then. We started walking again.

"I guess there are more important things in the world than just having a lot of friends everywhere," I said.

We turned a corner and started along another street. Not far ahead we could see the courthouse with its trimming of little white lights; it looked like a fairy palace. After a minute Clifford said, "When do you have to go back, Pat?"

"Tomorrow," I said. "I guess I should head back tomorrow morning."

"It's too bad you couldn't have stayed longer," he said. "If you'd been here Sunday I could have showed you around the city. I don't work Sunday."

"I really think I should go back," I said.

"Yeah," he said. He took out a pack of gum and gave me a stick and then took one himself and put the pack back in his pocket. "Does Father know you came?" he said.

"Yes," I said. "I left before they were up, but I left a note and told them."

"He'd be angry when he found out," he said.

"I don't care," I said. "Let him get mad."

We came to another intersection and looking over to our right we could see the harbor and beyond that the mountains on the north shore. The sun had gone down and the whole sky was covered with blood-orange and pink and yellow and purple; it made the mountains look shadowy purple, almost black. There was a dotted line of lights climbing up the side of one of the mountains and I knew it was the mountain chair lift. "You know what I'd like to do now?" I said.

"What's that, Pat?" he said.

"I'd just like to go back to your place," I said. "Maybe we could look at some magazines or something."

"Okay," he said.

We started walking faster. We passed a little bakery and Clifford went in and I saw the woman take four little chocolate cream things out of the window and put them in a cardboard box and then Clifford paid her and came out carrying the box. "I thought you'd like these," he said. "They're really good . . . I've had them before."

"They looked really good in the window," I said.

We walked back to the house and went upstairs and put on the small drop-cord light. Clifford took the kettle and went into the bathroom and put some water in it and then came back and closed the door. "I'll make some tea," he said. "Would you like some tea?"

"Yes, I would," I said. I sat down on the edge of the bed. My legs really felt stiff and I ran my hands up and down my thighs and watched Clifford. He turned the hot plate on and then got down the teapot and started putting tea bags in it. "How's Father?" he said suddenly. "And Jeannie?"

"They're okay," I said. "I guess."

He didn't say anything else but he seemed to be taking an awful long time to put the tea in the pot, so I said, "Father never mentions you. I guess he's still mad."

"Yeah, I guess so," he said. He walked over to the corner and took down a couple of scribblers from a small shelf. "Like to see some of the stuff I'm studying?" he said.

"Sure," I said.

He opened one of the notebooks and there were some drawings in colored pencil and some handwritten notes and a lot of loose typewritten sheets. "This is what they call biochemistry," he said. "I have to study this before I take my exams."

"When are your exams?" I said.

"Oh, not for a long time yet," he said. "Not until I finish my apprenticeship. But it doesn't hurt to get started ahead of time." He put the book down on the bed and went over to make the tea. I flipped some of the pages. "I guess you get a pretty good salary," I said.

"I don't get very much right now," he said. "You see, I'm only an apprentice and that means they're teaching me. It's like going to school in a way, except that I get paid."

"How much?" I said.

"I get eleven dollars a week right now," he said. "But next year I get fourteen; and I also get a week's holiday with pay next summer."

He poured some boiling water into the teapot and put the lid on it and then turned the hot plate off. I just kept looking around at the room; it was clean and bright and neat, but there wasn't very much homeyness about it. There was a stack of magazines on a chair in the corner and a few pocket novels on the shelf by the bed and a calendar from some produce company on the door of the closet and mother's Wedgwood vase sitting up on top of the cupboard, but there was no radio and there were no lamps or cushions. The window was still open and there was a cool breeze floating in, and when I looked out I could see the soft-orange squares of lighted windows in the houses across the street.

"A year is a long time," I said.

He brought two cups over and put them on the table and then got a bowl of sugar out of the cupboard and a small can of milk and some teaspoons and put them all on the table. "It's too bad you haven't got a radio, Clifford," I said.

"I've never been much of a guy for listening to the radio, anyway," he said. "You know that." He poured out some tea and put the pot back and then opened up the box with the chocolate cream pastries in it. "Dig in," he said. "They're good. You'll like them."

I picked one up and took a bite out of it; they were really good. I'd never tasted anything like that in Abbotsford. Clifford took one and ate it and then started drinking his tea. "Finish them up, Pat," he said.

"You have another one," I said.

"Not for me," he said. "I can't eat much of that stuff. It makes me sick. Besides, I can get them any time I want." He watched me eat them with a little smile on his pale face. "Do you like them?" he said.

"They're super!" I said. "What do you call them?"

"I don't know," he said. "They've probably got some European name." He picked up his cup and took a drink and I noticed that every time he did the steam fogged his glasses and he had to wait a couple of minutes before they cleared again. "What are you going to do now that you've quit school, Pat?" he said.

"I don't know," I said. "I can go to work in Abbotsford. I can even work for Father in the store."

"Is there any kind of work you want to do?" he said. "Anything in particular?"

"No," I said. "I haven't made up my mind yet."

We finished our tea and then Clifford went and washed the cups out and dried them and put them back in the cupboard. We just sat around for a while and then we both decided we were tired so we went to bed and put the light out. I was lying on the outside of the bed and I could see out of the window without moving.

There were a lot of bright-lighted windows and street lights, and car lights sliding down the street; but they all seemed as though they had nothing at all to do with Clifford and me lying there in the darkened room; then away in the distance against the dark night sky I could see the bright amber-pointed lights of the Lions Gate Bridge curving through the darkness across The Narrows.

I must have been just dozing off when Clifford spoke. "Pat?" he said. "Are you asleep?"

"Not yet," I said.

"Pat, why do you suppose Father got so angry with me?" he said. "I only wanted to live my own life."

I didn't answer for a moment. I wanted to say that it was all because Father was such a bullheaded character; but I knew Clifford wouldn't believe that about anybody, let alone Father. He'd just say there was some reason beneath that. "I don't know, Clifford," I said. "Maybe he just wanted to have his own way."

He didn't say anything for several minutes, and I thought he must have gone to sleep; then all of a sudden he said, "So you think he really hates me, Pat?"

"I don't think so, Clifford," I said. "Maybe you just don't see things the same way, that's all. It'll work out okay." I waited for quite a while but there was no sound, so I reached over in the darkness and put my hand on his shoulder; he didn't move.

The next morning Clifford woke me up. "Pat! It's half-past seven," he said. "I've got to leave pretty soon. Pat?"

I sat up and opened my eyes; there was bright sunlight pouring through the window and brushing across the cups on the table like liquid amber. Clifford was already dressed and sitting at the table drinking a cup of tea. "I thought I'd let you sleep for a while," he said. "You looked tired."

"I'm okay," I said. I got up and put on my clothes and went across the hall and had a wash and then came back and sat down at the table. "That toast sure does smell good," I said.

"I'm sorry I haven't got more than just toast for your breakfast," he said. "But the fact is that I forgot to get any bacon yesterday."

"That's okay," I said.

He got up and started to make some toast on the hot plate, but I went over and took the bread from him. "I'll do that," I said. "You drink your tea."

He went and sat down again and took a sip of his tea, then he looked out of the window. "You've got a nice day for your trip back," he said.

"Yeah," I said. "It should be okay." I turned the piece of bread over on the wire mesh on top of the electric plate. "What time do you have to leave for work?" I said.

"I usually leave about fifteen to eight," he said. "It takes me about fifteen minutes to walk." He drank the rest of his tea and washed the cup out and then came back and dried it on the dishtowel and put it back in the cupboard. "Don't bother with those dishes before you go, Pat," he said. "I'll clean them up when I come home."

"I can do them," I said. I took the toast over to the table and put some butter on it and then poured some tea into a cup. "It won't hurt me to do a few dishes," I said.

"Well, I guess I'd better go," he said. He walked over and opened the door and stood there a minute with his hand on the doorknob. "I guess you'll come in again sometime when you get a chance," he said. "I don't mean right away, but. . . ."

"Sure, I'll be in again, Clifford," I said.

He was still standing there with his hand on the doorknob as though he wanted to say something but didn't know just how to say it. "Well, anyway," he said, "watch yourself on the highway. And give my best to Abbotsford when you get back. So long!"

"So long, Clifford," I said. "And thanks for everything."

He closed the door and I could hear him going down the stairs; then I got up and went to the window and watched him go out through the gate and start along the street. He was walking very fast and he had his head down; he didn't look back.

I went back to the table and ate the rest of my toast and drank the tea and then I went back to the window. The bright morning sunlight sparkled and shimmered over the harbor and the windows in the buildings on the distant north shore. I kept thinking about Clifford and when he would come home again that night and there would be no one in the room and he would sit down all alone and eat his supper and then wash the plate and the cup and put them back in the cupboard and then maybe go for a walk or else do some of his studying until it was time to go to bed.

I went over to the cupboard and took down the bowl I had seen him taking money from and looked inside. There were some receipts for his room rent every week, each one made out for five dollars and signed by the landlady; and there was one quarter, a nickel, and two pennies. I put the bowl back and sat down on the edge of the bed again. I kept remembering the way he had watched me when I was eating in the café, and the way he had put the two-dollar bill on the counter so casually, and the chocolate cream pastries he had bought me on the way home; for a minute I thought I was going to bawl.

After a while I got up and went downstairs and asked the landlady if I could use her phone to call home and told her I would see that she got paid in a few days. Then I called the long distance operator and asked for Abbotsford 723 and waited until the buzzing and clicking stopped and I heard the receiver being lifted on the other end fifty-some miles away. "Hello?"

"Hello," I said. "Jeannie? This is Pat."

"Patrick Barton!" she said. "Where are you?"

"I'm in Vancouver," I said. "Where did you think I was, Siberia?"

"You don't need to think you're being smart," she said. "You're going to get into plenty of trouble when Father sees you! You'd better get right back here this very minute!"

"I'll just go outside and get in my jet," I said. "I should be there by the time you get out to the back porch." That's the only way I can hold my own with Jeannie.

"I'm not fooling, either," she said.

"Neither am I," I said. "Is Father there?"

"No," she said. "He's gone down to open the store. He's been absolutely *sick* worrying about you!"

"Well, tell him I'm staying here!" I said. "Did you get that? I'm staying here with Clifford!"

"You're what?" she said.

"I'm staying here," I said. "I'm going to get a job here in the city. Don't you understand English?"

"Now look, Mister Man," she said. "Just because Clifford gets too big for his boots is no reason for you to think you can just do what you want! Don't either of you ever think of Father. . . ."

"Oh, shut up!" I said. "This call is costing money. Are you going to tell him or not?"

"Of course I'm going to tell him," she said. "And he is going to be as mad as. . . ."

"Then he'll just have to be mad!" I said, and hung up.

I went back upstairs and washed the dishes and put them away in the cupboard; then I looked in the want ads in the paper and I saw an ad for a delivery boy so I went downstairs and phoned the number and the man took my name and told me to come Monday morning and I would have first call for the job. Then I got my bike out of the basement and went for a ride down by the docks.

About four o'clock I came back and put the bike away and went down to the shopping district. I still had sixty-five cents I'd been going to use for hamburgers and stuff on the way home, so I bought some butter and some tomatoes and some jam tarts and took them all back to the room. Then I cut some salmon steaks and fried them in butter and put them on a plate and slid it under the hot plate, and after I'd done that I cut up some of the tomatoes and put the kettle on and then set the table.

I kept going over to the window and watching for Clifford, and then all at once I saw him coming down the street. He had a newspaper in one hand and he was walking more slowly than usual and he still had his head down. I waited until I saw him turn in at the gate and then I put everything on the table and poured some boiling water in the teapot and put the lid on it and then I sat down and waited for the sound of his footsteps on the stairs.

Meaning

1. Clifford's life in the city is actually quite different from the impression he tries to convey to his brother. What problems in Clifford's life are revealed by his answers to Pat's questions?
2. What is the conflict between Clifford and his father?
3. What was Clifford escaping from? What did he find in the city?

Method

1. Very often a character's feelings are indicated by physical movement rather than by a direct statement of the author, as in the following:

   a. "He was walking very fast and he had his head down; he didn't look back."

   b. "I kept going over to the window and watching for Clifford . . ."

   What does each physical action tell you about the emotional state of the character? Try substituting a direct statement to indicate this emotional feeling. How does the direct statement compare with the indirect?

2. A character's actions should be consistent with the personality given him or her by the author. How does the author prepare us to accept the decision that Pat makes at the end of the story?
3. What is the mood of the story? How has the mood changed at the end of the story?

Language: Style

Style, a writer's way of expressing thoughts in language, depends on such things as word choice, sentence construction, and the use of adjectives and adverbs. A writer adopts the style which is most appropriate for his or her material and audience. A story told from the first-person point of view, as is "Escape to the City," may have a style that is in keeping with the background and age of the speaker. Thus Woodward uses a simple vocabulary, one that a fifteen-year-old boy would have. In addition, Pat's sentences usually begin simply (subject + verb), as is appropriate for his level of learning. By skimming through the first words of each paragraph you can see that they generally begin with "It was," "And I knew," "I was," "I sat," "I finished." The word *and* is used frequently by the narrator to join verbs and to form compound sentences.

What probably would be the characteristics of an appropriate style for writing:

1. an account of a prizefight, a baseball, football, or basketball game?
2. a description of the funeral of a political, social, or religious leader?

Would the sentences be long or short? Why? Would the verbs be active or passive? Why? Would the writer be more likely to use long or short words? Why?

Discussion and Composition

1. Write a description of the ideal room for a high school student. Describe the size and shape of the room, the furniture, the accessories, the windows, and what they face. Try to help your reader *see* the room by using words and phrases which appeal to the senses. Help your reader understand the physical arrangement of the furnishings by describing the room from a clockwise or counterclockwise point of view, using such transitional words and phrases as *as you enter, to the left, in front of, across from, next to, in back of, opposite,* and *in the center.*

2. Near the beginning of "Escape to the City," you are told that Pat has just received a letter from Clifford. Write the letter that Clifford might have sent to Pat.

3. Clifford's ambition was to be a chemist. What kind of work do you think you would like to do when you finish school? Find out how you might prepare for the career you would like to have. Also try to find out how much the preparation will cost, if anything. Write a composition in which you tell about your vocational goals, explain why you are choosing that career, and describe the course of study, experience, and money you will need. In your composition, consider how you will obtain the funds that you will need.

FRANK O'CONNOR

(1903–1966)

The land and the people of Ireland are the subject of Frank O'Connor's fiction. Born Michael O'Donovan in Cork, Ireland, he was able to attend school only through the fourth grade, but he educated himself by reading widely while holding odd jobs to help support his family. His father was a laborer; his mother, a cleaning woman. He began writing short stories while still a child, and adopted the pseudonym Frank O'Connor.

As a youth, O'Connor spent a year in prison for his political support of the Irish Republican Army. He later worked as a professional librarian and directed the famous Abbey Theater in Dublin during the 1930s. Learning Gaelic as a child from his grandmother, he subsequently taught Gaelic and translated Gaelic literature into English. During the last twenty years of his life, O'Connor lived in the United States, where he taught creative writing at Northwestern University and at Harvard.

O'Connor wrote poetry, plays, and scholarly works, but his major contribution was to the short story. Asked what he believed to be the most important element of a story, he replied, "You have to have a theme, a story to tell. . . . A theme is something that is worth something to everybody." O'Connor recalls his childhood and adolescence in his autobiography, *An Only Child* (1961).

MY OEDIPUS COMPLEX

Father was in the army all through the war—the first war, I mean—so, up to the age of five, I never saw much of him, and what I saw did not worry me. Sometimes I woke and there was a big figure in khaki peering down at me in the candlelight. Sometimes in the early morning I heard the slamming of the front door and the clatter of nailed boots down the cobbles of the lane. These were Father's entrances and exits. Like Santa Claus he came and went mysteriously.

In fact, I rather liked his visits, though it was an uncomfortable squeeze between Mother and him when I got into the big bed in the early morning. He smoked, which gave him a pleasant musty smell, and shaved, an operation of astounding interest. Each time he left a trail of souvenirs—model tanks and Gurkha knives with handles made of bullet cases, and German helmets and cap badges and button-sticks, and all sorts of military equipment—carefully stowed away in a long box on the top of the wardrobe, in case they ever came in handy. There was a bit of the magpie about Father; he expected everything to come in handy. When his back was turned, Mother let me get a chair and rummage through his treasures. She didn't seem to think so highly of them as he did.

The war was the most peaceful period of my life. The window of my attic faced southeast. My mother had curtained it, but that had small effect. I always woke with the first light and, with all the responsibilities of the previous day melted, feeling myself rather like the sun, ready to illumine and rejoice. Life never seemed so simple and clear and full of possibilities as then. I put my feet out from under the clothes—I called them Mrs. Left and Mrs. Right—and invented dramatic situations for them in which they discussed the problems of the day. At least Mrs. Right did; she was very demonstrative, but I hadn't the same control of Mrs. Left, so she mostly contented herself with nodding agreement.

They discussed what Mother and I should do during the day, what Santa Claus should give a fellow for Christmas, and what steps should be taken to brighten the home. There was that little matter of the baby, for instance. Mother and I could never agree about that. Ours was the only house in the terrace without a new baby, and Mother said we couldn't afford one till Father came back from the war because they cost seventeen and six. That showed how simple she was. The Geneys up the road had a baby, and everyone knew they couldn't afford seventeen and six. It was probably a cheap baby, and Mother wanted something really good, but I felt she was too exclusive. The Geneys' baby would have done us fine.

Having settled my plans for the day, I got up, put a chair under the attic window, and lifted the frame high enough to stick out my head. The window overlooked the front gardens of the terrace behind ours, and beyond these it looked over a deep valley to the tall, red-brick houses terraced up the opposite hillside, which were all still in shadow, while those at our side of the valley were all lit up, though with long strange shadows that made them seem unfamiliar; rigid and painted.

After that I went into Mother's room and climbed into the big bed. She woke and I began to tell her of my schemes. By this time, though I never seem to have noticed it, I was petrified in my nightshirt, and I thawed as I talked until, the last frost melted, I fell asleep beside her and woke again only when I heard her below in the kitchen, making the breakfast.

After breakfast we went into town; heard Mass at St. Augustine's and said a prayer for Father, and did the shopping. If the afternoon was fine we either went for a walk in the country or a visit to Mother's great friend in the convent, Mother St. Dominic. Mother had them all praying for Father, and every night, going to bed, I asked God to send him back safe from the war to us. Little, indeed, did I know what I was praying for!

One morning, I got into the big bed, and there, sure enough, was Father in his usual Santa Claus manner, but later, instead of uniform, he put on his best blue suit, and Mother was as pleased as anything. I saw nothing to be pleased about, because, out of uniform, Father was altogether less interesting, but she only beamed, and explained that our prayers had been answered, and off we went to Mass to thank God for having brought Father safely home.

The irony of it! That very day when he came in to dinner he took off his boots and put on his slippers, donned the dirty old cap he wore about the house to save him from colds, crossed his legs, and began to talk gravely to Mother, who looked anxious. Naturally, I disliked her looking anxious, because it destroyed her good looks, so I interrupted him.

"Just a moment, Larry!" she said gently.

This was only what she said when we had boring visitors, so I attached no importance to it and went on talking.

"Do be quiet, Larry!" she said impatiently. "Don't you hear me talking to Daddy?"

This was the first time I had heard those ominous words, "talking to Daddy," and I couldn't help feeling that if this was how God answered prayers, he couldn't listen to them very attentively.

"Why are you talking to Daddy?" I asked with as great a show of indifference as I could muster.

"Because Daddy and I have business to discuss. Now, don't interrupt again!"

In the afternoon, at Mother's request, Father took me for a walk. This time we went into town instead of out to the country, and I thought at first, in my usual optimistic way, that it might be an improvement. It was nothing of the sort. Father and I had quite different notions of a walk in town. He had no proper interest in trams, ships, and horses, and the only thing that seemed to divert him was talking to fellows as old as himself. When I wanted to stop he simply went on, dragging me behind him by the hand; when he wanted to stop I had no alternative but to do the same. I noticed that it seemed to be a sign that he wanted to stop for a long time whenever he leaned against a wall. The second time I saw him do it I got wild. He seemed to be settling himself forever. I pulled him by the coat and trousers, but, unlike Mother who, if you were too persistent, got into a wax and said: "Larry, if you don't behave yourself, I'll give you a good slap," Father had an extraordinary capacity for amiable inattention. I sized him up and wondered would I cry, but he seemed to be too remote to be annoyed even by that. Really, it was like going for a walk with a mountain! He either ignored the wrenching and pummeling entirely, or else glanced down with a grin of amusement from his peak. I had never met anyone so absorbed in himself as he seemed.

At teatime, "talking to Daddy" began again, complicated this time by the fact that he had an evening paper, and every few minutes he put it down and told Mother something new out of it. I felt this was foul play. Man for man, I was prepared to compete with him any time for Mother's attention, but when he had it all made up for him by other people it left me no chance. Several times I tried to change the subject without success.

"You must be quiet while Daddy is reading, Larry," Mother said impatiently.

It was clear that she either genuinely liked talking to Father better than talking to me, or else that he had some terrible hold on her which made her afraid to admit the truth.

"Mummy," I said that night when she was tucking me up, "do you think if I prayed hard God would send Daddy back to the war?"

She seemed to think about that for a moment.

"No dear," she said with a smile. "I don't think he would."

"Why wouldn't he, Mummy?"

"Because there isn't a war any longer, dear."

"But Mummy, couldn't God make another war, if he liked?"

"He wouldn't like to, dear. It's not God who makes wars, but bad people."

"Oh!" I said.

I was disappointed about that. I began to think that God wasn't quite what he was cracked up to be.

Next morning I woke at my usual hour, feeling like a bottle of champagne. I put out my feet and invented a long conversation in which Mrs. Right talked of the trouble she had with her own father till she put him in the Home. I didn't quite know what the Home was but it sounded the right place for Father. Then I got my chair and stuck my head out of the attic window. Dawn was just breaking, with a guilty air that made me feel I had caught it in the act. My head bursting with stories and schemes, I stumbled in next door, and in the half-darkness scrambled into the big bed. There was no room at Mother's side so I had to get between her and Father. For the time being I had forgotten about him, and for several minutes I sat bolt upright, racking my brains to know what I could do with him. He was taking up more than his fair share of the bed, and I couldn't get comfortable, so I gave him several kicks that made him grunt and stretch. He made room all right, though. Mother waked and felt for me. I settled back comfortably in the warmth of the bed with my thumb in my mouth.

"Mummy!" I hummed, loudly and contentedly.

"Sssh! dear," she whispered. "Don't wake Daddy!"

This was a new development, which threatened to be even more serious than "talking to Daddy." Life without my early-morning conferences was unthinkable.

"Why!" I asked severely.

"Because poor Daddy is tired."

This seemed to me a quite inadequate reason, and I was sickened by the sentimentality of her "poor Daddy." I never liked that sort of gush; it always struck me as insincere.

"Oh!" I said lightly. Then in my most winning tone: "Do you know where I want to go with you today, Mummy?"

"No, dear," she sighed.

"I want to go down the Glen and fish for thornybacks with my new net, and then I want to go out to the Fox and Hounds, and—"

"Don't-wake-Daddy!" she hissed angrily, clapping her hand across my mouth.

But it was too late. He was awake, or nearly so. He grunted and reached for the matches. Then he stared incredulously at his watch.

"Like a cup of tea, dear?" asked Mother in a meek, hushed voice I had never heard her use before. It sounded almost as though she were afraid.

"Tea?" he exclaimed indignantly. "Do you know what the time is?"

"And after that I want to go up the Rathcooney Road," I said loudly, afraid I'd forget something in all those interruptions.

"Go to sleep at once, Larry!" she said sharply.

I began to snivel. I couldn't concentrate, the way that pair went on, and smothering my early-morning schemes was like burying a family from the cradle.

Father said nothing, but lit his pipe and sucked it, looking out into the shadows without minding Mother or me. I knew he was mad. Every time I made a remark Mother hushed me irritably. I was mortified. I felt it wasn't fair; there was even something sinister in it. Every time I had pointed out to her the waste of making two beds when we could both sleep in one, she had told me it was healthier like that, and now here was this man, this stranger, sleeping with her without the least regard for her health!

He got up early and made tea, but though he brought Mother a cup he brought none for me.

"Mummy," I shouted, "I want a cup of tea, too."

"Yes, dear," she said patiently. "You can drink from Mummy's saucer."

That settled it. Either Father or I would have to leave the house. I didn't want to drink from Mother's saucer; I wanted to be treated as an equal in my own home, so, just to spite her, I drank it all and left none for her. She took that quietly, too.

But that night when she was putting me to bed she said gently: "Larry, I want you to promise me something."

"What is it?" I asked.

"Not to come in and disturb poor Daddy in the morning. Promise?"

"Poor Daddy" again! I was becoming suspicious of everything involving that quite impossible man.

"Why?" I asked.

"Because poor Daddy is worried and tired and he doesn't sleep well."

"Why doesn't he, Mummy?"

"Well, you know, don't you, that while he was at the war Mummy got the pennies from the Post Office?"

"From Miss MacCarthy?"

"That's right. But now, you see, Miss MacCarthy hasn't any more pennies, so Daddy must go out and find us some. You know what would happen if he couldn't?"

"No," I said, "tell us."

"Well, I think we might have to go out and beg for them like the poor old woman on Fridays. We wouldn't like that, would we?"

"No," I agreed. "We wouldn't."

"So you'll promise not to come in and wake him?"

"Promise."

Mind you, I meant that. I knew pennies were a serious matter, and I was all against having to go out and beg like the old woman on Fridays. Mother laid out all my toys in a complete ring round the bed so that, whatever way I got out, I was bound to fall over one of them.

When I woke I remembered my promise all right. I got up and sat on the floor and played—for hours, it seemed to me. Then I got my chair and looked out the attic window for more hours. I wished it was time for Father to wake; I wished someone would make me a cup of tea. I didn't feel in the least like the sun; instead, I was bored and so very, very cold! I simply longed for the warmth and depth of the big featherbed.

At last I could stand it no longer. I went into the next room. As there was still no room at Mother's side I climbed over her and she woke with a start.

"Larry," she whispered, gripping my arm very tightly, "what did you promise?"

"But I did, Mummy," I wailed, caught in the very act. "I was quiet for ever so long."

"Oh, dear, and you're perished!" she said sadly, feeling me all over. "Now, if I let you stay will you promise not to talk?"

"But I want to talk, Mummy," I wailed.

"That has nothing to do with it," she said with a firmness that was new to me. "Daddy wants to sleep. Now, do you understand that?"

I understood it only too well. I wanted to talk, he wanted to sleep—whose house was it, anyway?

"Mummy," I said with equal firmness, "I think it would be healthier for Daddy to sleep in his own bed."

That seemed to stagger her, because she said nothing for a while.

"Now, once for all," she went on, "you're to be perfectly quiet or go back to your own bed. Which is it to be?"

The injustice of it got me down. I had convicted her out of her own mouth of inconsistency and unreasonableness, and she hadn't even attempted to reply. Full of spite, I gave Father a kick, which she didn't notice but which made him grunt and open his eyes in alarm.

"What time is it?" he asked in a panic-stricken voice, not looking at Mother but the door, as if he saw someone there.

"It's early yet," she replied soothingly. "It's only the child. Go to sleep again. . . . Now, Larry," she added, getting out of bed, "You've wakened Daddy and you must go back."

This time, for all her quiet air, I knew she meant it, and knew that my principal rights and privileges were as good as lost unless I asserted them at once. As she lifted me, I gave a screech, enough to wake the dead, not to mind Father. He groaned.

"That damn child! Doesn't he ever sleep?"

"It's only a habit, dear," she said quietly, though I could see she was vexed.

"Well, it's time he got out of it," shouted Father, beginning to heave in the bed. He suddenly gathered all the bedclothes about him, turned to the wall, and then looked back over his shoulder with nothing showing only two small, spiteful, dark eyes. The man looked very wicked.

To open the bedroom door, Mother had to let me down, and I broke free and dashed for the farthest corner, screeching. Father sat bolt upright in bed.

"Shut up, you little puppy!" he said in a choking voice.

I was so astonished that I stopped screeching. Never, never had anyone spoken to me in that tone before. I looked at him incredulously and saw his face convulsed with rage. It was only then that I fully realized how God had codded[1] me, listening to my prayers for the safe return of this monster.

"Shut up, you!" I bawled, beside myself.

"What's that you said?" shouted Father, making a wild leap out of bed.

"Mick, Mick!" cried Mother. "Don't you see the child isn't used to you?"

"I see he's better fed than taught," snarled Father, waving his arms wildly. "He wants his bottom smacked."

All his previous shouting was as nothing to these obscene words referring to my person. They really made my blood boil.

"Smack your own!" I screamed hysterically. "Smack your own! Shut up! Shut up!"

At this he lost his patience and let fly at me. He did it with the

1. **codded:** tricked.

lack of conviction you'd expect of a man under Mother's horrified eyes, and it ended up as a mere tap, but the sheer indignity of being struck at all by a stranger, a total stranger who had cajoled his way back from the war into our big bed as a result of my innocent intercession, made me completely dotty. I shrieked and shrieked, and danced in my bare feet, and Father, looking awkward and hairy in nothing but a short grey army shirt, glared down at me like a mountain out for murder. I think it must have been then that I realized he was jealous too. And there stood Mother in her nightdress, looking as if her heart was broken between us. I hoped she felt as she looked. It seemed to me that she deserved it all.

From that morning out my life was a hell. Father and I were enemies, open and avowed. We conducted a series of skirmishes against one another, he trying to steal my time with Mother and I his. When she was sitting on my bed, telling me a story, he took to looking for some pair of old boots which he alleged he had left behind him at the beginning of the war. While he talked to Mother I played loudly with my toys to show my total lack of concern. He created a terrible scene one evening when he came in from work and found me at his box, playing with his regimental badges, Gurkha knives and button-sticks. Mother got up and took the box from me.

"You mustn't play with Daddy's toys unless he lets you, Larry," she said severely. "Daddy doesn't play with yours."

For some reason Father looked at her as if she had struck him and then turned away with a scowl.

"Those are not toys," he growled, taking down the box again to see had I lifted anything. "Some of those curios are very rare and valuable."

But as time went on I saw more and more how he managed to alienate Mother and me. What made it worse was that I couldn't grasp his method or see what attraction he had for Mother. In every possible way he was less winning than I. He had a common accent and made noises at his tea. I thought for a while that it might be the newspapers she was interested in, so I made up bits of news of my own to read to her. Then I thought it might be the smoking, which I personally thought attractive, and took his pipes and went round the house dribbling into them till he caught me. I even made noises at my tea, but Mother only told me I was disgusting. It all seemed to hinge round that unhealthy habit of sleeping together, so I made a point of dropping into their bedroom and nosing round, talking to myself, so that they wouldn't know I was watching them, but they were never up to anything that I could see. In the end it beat me. It seemed to depend on being grownup and giving people rings, and I realized I'd have to wait.

But at the same time I wanted him to see that I was only waiting, not giving up the fight. One evening when he was being particularly obnoxious, chattering away well above my head, I let him have it.

"Mummy," I said, "do you know what I'm going to do when I grow up?"

"No, dear," she replied. "What?"

"I'm going to marry you," I said quietly.

Father gave a great guffaw out of him, but he didn't take me in. I knew it must only be pretense. And Mother, in spite of everything, was pleased. I felt she was probably relieved to know that one day Father's hold on her would be broken.

"Won't that be nice?" she said with a smile.

"It'll be very nice," I said confidently. "Because we're going to have lots and lots of babies."

"That's right, dear," she said placidly. "I think we'll have one soon, and then you'll have plenty of company."

I was no end pleased about that because it showed that in spite of the way she gave in to Father she still considered my wishes. Besides, it would put the Geneys in their place.

It didn't turn out like that, though. To begin with, she was very preoccupied—I supposed about where she would get the seventeen and six—and though Father took to staying out late in the evenings it did me no particular good. She stopped taking me for walks, became as touchy as blazes, and smacked me for nothing at all. Sometimes I wished I'd never mentioned the confounded baby—I seemed to have a genius for bringing calamity on myself.

And calamity it was! Sonny arrived in the most appalling hullabaloo—even that much he couldn't do without a fuss—and from the first moment I disliked him. He was a difficult child—so far as I was concerned he was always difficult—and demanded far too much attention. Mother was simply silly about him, and couldn't see when he was only showing off. As company he was worse than useless. He slept all day, and I had to go round the house on tiptoe to avoid waking him. It wasn't any longer a question of not waking Father. The slogan now was "Don't-wake-Sonny!" I couldn't understand why the child wouldn't sleep at the proper time, so whenever Mother's back was turned I woke him. Sometimes to keep him awake

I pinched him as well. Mother caught me at it one day and gave me a most unmerciful flaking.

One evening, when Father was coming in from work, I was playing trains in the front garden. I let on not to notice him; instead, I pretended to be talking to myself, and said in a loud voice: "If another bloody baby comes into this house, I'm going out."

Father stopped dead and looked at me over his shoulder.

"What's that you said?" he asked sternly.

"I was only talking to myself," I replied, trying to conceal my panic. "It's private."

He turned and went in without a word. Mind you, I intended it as a solemn warning, but its effect was quite different. Father started being quite nice to me. I could understand that, of course. Mother was quite sickening about Sonny. Even at mealtimes she'd get up and gawk at him in the cradle with an idiotic smile, and tell Father to do the same. He was always polite about it, but he looked so puzzled you could see he didn't know what she was talking about. He complained of the way Sonny cried at night, but she only got cross and said that Sonny never cried except when there was something up with him—which was a flaming lie, because Sonny never had anything up with him, and only cried for attention. It was really painful to see how simple-minded she was. Father wasn't attractive, but he had a fine intelligence. He saw through Sonny, and now he knew that I saw through him as well.

One night I woke with a start. There was someone beside me in the bed. For one wild moment I felt sure it must be Mother, having come to her senses and left Father for good, but then I heard Sonny in convulsions in the next room, and Mother saying: "There! There! There!" and I knew it wasn't she. It was Father. He was lying beside me, wide awake, breathing hard and apparently as mad as hell.

After a while it came to me what he was mad about. It was his turn now. After turning me out of the big bed, he had been turned out himself. Mother had no consideration now for anyone but that poisonous pup, Sonny. I couldn't help feeling sorry for Father. I had been through it all myself, and even at that age I was magnanimous.[2] I began to stroke him down and say: "There! There!" He wasn't exactly responsive.

"Aren't you asleep either?" he snarled.

"Ah, come on and put your arm around us, can't you?" I said,

2. **magnanimous** (măg-năn′ə-məs): generous and forgiving.

and he did, in a sort of way. Gingerly, I suppose, is how you'd describe it. He was very bony but better than nothing.

At Christmas he went out of his way to buy me a really nice model railway.

Meaning and Method

1. Explain the title of the story.
2. What is the conflict between Larry and his father?
3. How do Larry and his father become allies?
4. How are the relative sizes of father and son used humorously in this story?
5. Why does the author have Larry tell his story some time after the main events have happened? What is the advantage of learning about the boy through his own words and actions?
6. How does this story illustrate Frank O'Connor's idea about the most important element in a story (see biographical introduction)?

Discussion and Composition

1. Frank O'Connor has said that a short story "doesn't deal with problems; it doesn't have any solutions, it just states the human condition." Discuss how this applies to several stories you have read.

2. Try to recapture an early childhood memory in a short story. Write it from the point of view you would have had then.

MAY SARTON
(born 1912)

Poetry and novels are a good combination, May Sarton says. "Poetry comes in spurts, whereas, after the initial imaginative creation, a novel can and perhaps must be written day after day on a very regular schedule."

Born in Belgium, Miss Sarton came to the United States with her parents when she was two years old. Her father was a distinguished historian of science; her mother, an artist. When she was a senior in a Cambridge, Massachusetts, high school, she saw a play for the first time and decided to become an actress instead of going on to college. Over the next several years, she acted, directed, and founded her own actors' theater. In 1937, her acting company disbanded, and Miss Sarton's first book of poems, *Encounter in April,* was published. In addition to producing poetry and novels, she has written books for children and young people.

Miss Sarton has lectured extensively on poetry and has taught literature and creative writing at Wellesley College and Harvard University. Her autobiography, *I Knew a Phoenix* (1959), tells about her childhood, her education, and her theatrical and literary work. She lives in Maine.

THE RETURN OF CORPORAL GREENE

He didn't get home for Christmas. He waited six weeks at an embarkation point in southern France, without mail—and it was not until early in February that Corporal Ben Greene became Benjamin Greene, old Josiah Greene's grandson, Harvard '42, and found himself "like a dream walking,"[1] walking down Brattle Street in Cambridge, Massachusetts, on his way to Cousin Emily's. His family was in

1. **"like . . . walking":** a reference to a popular song of years ago, "Did You Ever See a Dream Walking?"

Miami—he would fly down in a day or so, but meanwhile it was good to have a couple of days to walk around the town on his own, just being himself, before getting involved in the high tension of a family reunion. He had dropped in on a couple of his old professors who remembered only vaguely who he was and congratulated him for having been in the war, or for being out of it, he didn't know which. He had not been a memorable student: had barely managed to pass the entrance examinations after being tutored for a year, and what he remembered most clearly of his college life was the time when he was turned down for the freshman football team and saw his hope of being a success at Harvard fade. Otherwise college had been a cram and a squeeze before exams and a lot of debutante parties and a lot of bull sessions and beer.

In his uniform with a modest row of ribbons and three battle stars, Ben Greene looked like thousands of other returned veterans and had about as much idea as they about what he wanted to do with himself. "What are you planning to do now, son?" That is what his father would ask.

After spending a half hour at the Coop buying some ties and wandering around the book department with an eye out for possible acquaintances, he thought suddenly of Cousin Emily. It was just about teatime. And now for the first time he had a feeling of excitement, of anticipation; he decided not to call her up. He would surprise her. He passed a florist with daffodils in the window and bought a dozen: Cousin Emily loved flowers.

"Like a dream walking," he murmured to himself again, pleased with the old tune, pleased with himself, pleased with the warm air, the water running in the gutters, even with the dirty snow. Cambridge was just the same as ever—shabby, endearing, homely old town.

His family had had to move into an apartment while he was away: his mother was not very well; it had been impossible to keep up the house without servants—so his father explained in a letter Ben read, sitting in a tent in the middle of a dank field in the Ardennes,[2] trying to dry some socks.

"What's the matter, Ben, bad news?" his buddy, an Italian from New York, asked.

"No, just my family had to move to another place."

2. Ardennes (är•dĕn′): a wooded plateau region that extends from southwest Belgium into northeast France.

How could Pietro understand the desolation of that sentence? Not to have a place where he could fix his thoughts, not to be able to imagine his father smoking his after-dinner pipe in the study, reading Plato in Greek, not to see his mother coming down the spiral staircase to dinner in her Fortuny dress which she had worn every evening for the last ten years—Ben got up and went out for a walk, angry with himself, with his family, with his wet boots, with the whole cockeyed world; angry with this grief that was petty enough beside the misery around him, but so acute that he had tears in his eyes, cursing as he brushed them off. It was a hopeless homesickness for something that was not there any more. What had they done with all his junk? Put it in storage somewhere? Damn it, couldn't they have waited one more year—just till he got home?

So it happened that after awhile when he thought of "home," he thought of Cousin Emily's. She was one of the innumerable family connections he had taken for granted before the war. He had called on her every three months or so while he was in college because his mother said, "Darling, be an angel and go and see Cousin Emily—it's so near where you are, and she would be so pleased to see you." So he went when he had nothing else to do. He liked the house. When he was a small boy he had spent a winter there while his parents were abroad: he had passionately loved the large polar bear spread out on the floor of the guest room, with its bright glassy eyes and terrifying red mouth and soft, curled-up ears. And then the cabinet of shells! On Sundays he was allowed to get the little key and open it and take out the chambered nautilus and all the others. Now that he had no home of his own, he thought of these things on the cold miserable nights in tents, and on the long joggling truck rides across Belgium and Germany to the Danube.

He found it a comfort to know that at midnight in Europe, which he figured must be four in Cambridge, Cousin Emily was surely sitting before the fire, hidden by the back of her chair, so you did not see her when you pushed open the front door, but saw only the buckled shoe on the footstool and perhaps the silver teapot. Over there, where nothing was the same for more than a few days, it had become of extreme importance to Ben to know absolutely that one thing was being done in the same hour, in the same surroundings, every single day.

Cousin Emily herself was obscured by these rites and objects. Or rather she, her character itself, was so interwoven with them that, in memory, she and the teapot had almost the same value. She was a gentle, shy spinster, discreetly well-off, whose charities were anonymous and whose life itself had a kind of anonymity. She read a great deal. She was a good listener. Her day had its inalterable pattern. She was devoted to her two old servants and to her nurse who lived upstairs in an apartment of her own. It was like Cousin Emily to have taken it for granted that one who had served the family so long should now be served in turn. And this she did with delicacy, humor, and tenderness. But her passion was reserved for the two spoiled fat Scotties, Richard and Tribulation, who padded up and down the stairs all day long and demanded constantly either to be let in or to be let out.

When, as an undergraduate, Ben made his duty calls, he was amazed to find himself talking to her rather intimately about his troubles and anxieties. She was soothing. She made him feel that perhaps simply living was enough, that one did not need to strain after the great prizes; she did not expect him to be more than himself, to be anything but himself. And now, far off, bewildered, often physically miserable, these afternoon conversations came back to him as precious. He began to write her long letters and to wait eagerly for her replies, full of the small details of her days, and of the escapades of Richard and Tribulation, sometimes containing a poem she copied out in her spidery writing from *The Atlantic Monthly,* or enclosing a newspaper clipping she thought might be of interest.

But of course he had not had any letters now for a long time. The embarkation center was limbo: from the time he left Germany in a boxcar his mail had been cut off, so Cousin Emily could have no idea that he had finally arrived.

From quite a distance he could see the faded yellow paint of her house and the big elm that shaded it in summer but now made a beautifully traced arc of branches against the sky. Now that he was so near it was hard to keep from running. But playing the childish game that it is bad luck to hurry toward anything you want badly, or to seem to want it, he forced himself to keep to a walk, looking down at the uneven brick pavement at his feet, and whistling the old tune he couldn't get out of his head, "Did you ever see a dream walking?"

At last he reached the two stone pillars at the drive and turned in, up the boardwalk, his feet making the familiar hollow sound, and the same loose board clattering back after him. Of course she would not be at the window, but he glanced up at the formidable façade[3] of lace curtains just on the chance. He didn't want to be seen. He wanted to push open the big front door without ringing, as he always did, and to hear Cousin Emily's shy, light voice call from the back of her chair:

"Who's that? Roger? Charles? Ben? Come in, dear." Anyone who pushed open the door was bound to be family and bound to be dear.

He ran up the steps and flung himself against the door. It did not give as he pushed and so jolted him a little. Strange, it seemed to be locked. In forty years, this door had never been locked before eleven o'clock at night. Well, he would ring. He pulled the stiff bell handle out hard and heard its plaintive tinkle inside.

The maids were awfully slow of course, they were so old—and probably deaf. He waited a moment and then pulled the bell again, hard. Again he heard the faint tinkle. Then he leaned down and slid the keyhole-guard back. Through the tiny aperture he could see the hall, the hall table piled with books as always, the corner of the stairway, and through the arch into the drawing room, Cousin Emily's chair. But there was no sign that anyone had heard.

Had she gone away? Standing there, impatient and unaccountably cross, Ben felt foolish with the flowers in his hands. It wasn't fair of Cousin Emily not to be there, when it was the one thing in the world he really wanted—to see her today, when he had come back alive and with daffodils in his hands; it just wasn't fair.

Ben looked around now to see if there was anyone he could ask. As he glanced up the drive to the barn he heard the creak of a wheelbarrow behind him.

"Foster!" Never had he been so glad to see anyone as the old gardener, grouch though he was, and though many a time he had driven young Ben off the flower beds when he was looking for a tennis ball.

The wheelbarrow grated to a stop. Foster wiped his hands on his pants and came up to greet him.

"Well, if it ain't Ben! Glad to see you. Glad you're back."

"Foster, where's Cousin Emily? I rang and rang and there's nobody in." In spite of himself, Ben's tone was angry and imperious.

3. **façade** (fə•säd′): the front or face of anything; especially a false front designed to convey a favorable or impressive effect to the person viewing it.

Foster screwed up his eyes a little the way he always did. "Guess you don't know then—guess you don't—" he said reluctantly.

"Don't know what?"

Foster made some calculations, interminable calculations. "Your cousin passed away a month ago. Yup, just a month ago tomorrow, she was taken. Pneumony."

Ben found it hard to realize. "But then—where are they all? Where's Nurse? Isn't *anyone* here?" If there were just someone to let him in, with his daffodils, safe and alive and back from the wars. Not to stand here any longer outside.

Foster looked off into the distance. "Well, I guess Nurse just couldn't manage to keep alive after that—she just faded away. Best thing for her—she was old."

They were all gone, then.

"Foster, haven't you got a key? I'd like to go in—" he tried to smile but couldn't quite make it.

"Sure." Foster was glad to be able to do something. "Here you are. That opens the front door. I'll be 'round back when you're ready to go."

For the first time in forty years a young Greene put a key in the lock and unlocked his way in to Cousin Emily's.

He stood with his back to the fireplace in the drawing room. On his left was Cousin Emily's blue velvet chair, on his right the bench, and on it last month's *Harper's* and *The Atlantic Monthly,* some copies of *Life,* and a *Christian Science Monitor.* On the little table was a box of chocolate-covered peppermints. He opened it, dusting off the cover, and ate one mechanically. Now that he was standing here where everything was the same, where nothing had changed, except that all the life was gone, he felt completely bewildered. It wasn't grief exactly—it was just that he didn't know now who he was or why he was here, or why indeed he was anywhere at all.

Well, he said to himself, I might as well put these in water. He pushed the swinging door into the pantry and took down a tall silver vase his cousin often used for flowers. He unwrapped the daffodils, so fresh and clean-looking with their frilled cups; then he turned on the tap, but nothing happened. Of course, the water was turned off. Stupid of him not to think of that. Well, the daffodils would just have to die then. Ben stood against the sink, blinded by tears, and retched like a child. Someone else would have to clean up the mess. He fled, leaving the door unlocked behind him, thrust the key into Foster's hands and said:

"Lock the door, Foster."

The night he arrived in Miami he shocked his family by making a scene. He shouted at his father:

"You might have told me—cabled—done something!"

And when his father said, "Ben, we had no idea—why, Cousin Emily had no idea how much she meant to you—" and when his mother added gently, "She just sat there in that old house—you never seemed to want to see her when you were in college—dear Cousin Emily, she never amounted to much, we always thought, just sitting in that old house with the dogs. . . ." Ben had almost screamed, "Don't say it again, Mother. You've said it twice. It's a great deal, more than any of you know, to sit in the same place at the same time and have people know you're there!"

They looked at him in astonishment. He was unstrung, of course. One must make allowances.

But Ben did not feel unstrung now. He went upstairs, flushed with triumph, as if in some curious way which he did not fully understand, he had come into his own.

Meaning

1. What was Cousin Emily's life like? Why had Ben found it so appealing during his early youth and subsequent college days?
2. The *immediate* cause of Ben's breakdown in Cousin Emily's kitchen is his learning of her death. What are the *underlying* causes?
3. What is the author saying about persons like Cousin Emily? What would you say is the theme of the story?

Method

1. One way to decide if an author has meant something to be symbolic is to think about what the object looks like and what it calls to mind. What or whom do you think the daffodils are meant to symbolize? Why?
2. A *motif* is a recurring image or detail that provides a meaningful pattern in a story. The line from the old song, "like a dream walking," repeated throughout the story provides such a motif. Notice where in the story this line is repeated. What function does it serve each time?
3. How does the author foreshadow the impact of Cousin Emily's death on Ben?

Language: Synonyms

Synonyms are words of similar meaning. For example, words such as *aged* and *antique* convey the same general idea. Each, however, has its specific application: aged means advanced in years and antique pertains to ancient times or to an earlier period. Thus we can correctly speak about "the aged woman" and "the antique furniture."

Appropriate synonyms for the word *aged* would be: elderly, old, along in years, advanced in life, venerable, patriarchal, hoary, gray-haired, and wrinkled. A standard reference book to consult for such a list of synonyms is Roget's *Thesaurus of the English Language.* A *thesaurus* (thə•sôr′əs) is a collection of synonyms and antonyms arranged in categories. Synonyms for *aged* and *antique* are found under the category "Time."

Consult a thesaurus to find synonyms for the following italicized words taken from "The Return of Corporal Greene."

1. ". . . sitting in a tent in the middle of a *dank* field in the Ardennes . . ."
2. "How could Pietro understand the *desolation* of that sentence?"
3. "Cousin Emily herself was *obscured* by these rites and objects."
4. And now, far off, *bewildered,* often physically miserable, these afternoon conversations came back to him as precious."
5. "In spite of himself, Ben's tone was angry and *imperious.*"

Discussion and Composition

1. "People like Cousin Emily make silent but important contributions to society." Write a character sketch of Cousin Emily or someone like her that you have known. Show how the above statement explains the significance of her or his life.

2. Psychologists have said that any change in a person's life, even a pleasant change, produces stress. They advise people to avoid having to cope with more than one important change at a time. What changes was Ben facing in his life? What changes in your life would you consider most upsetting?

3. In an essay, describe the town, city, and neighborhood that you live in. Tell what you like and don't like about them.

MURIEL SPARK
(born 1918)

The British writer Muriel Spark began her literary career as a poet and critic. In the past ten years, her fiction has become increasingly satirical, focusing on the ridiculous aspects of modern life. Her most well-known novel is *The Prime of Miss Jean Brodie* (1961).

Miss Spark was born in Edinburgh of an upper-middle-class family. After attending school in Edinburgh, she went to South Africa and lived in Rhodesia for several years. During World War II, she returned to England and worked in the political intelligence department of the Foreign Office.

In the 1950s Miss Spark worked part-time as an editor while writing poetry and critical biographies of literary figures. Since her conversion to Roman Catholicism in 1954, she has included supernatural elements and religious or ethical themes in many of her works.

THE TWINS

When Jennie was at school with me, she was one of those well-behaved and intelligent girls who were, and maybe still are, popular with everyone in Scottish schools. The popularity of boys and girls in English schools so far as I gather, goes by other, less easily definable qualities, and also by their prowess at games. However, it was not so with us, and although Jennie was not much use at hockey, she was good and quiet and clever, and we all liked her. She was rather nice-looking too, plump, dark-haired, clear, neat.

She married a Londoner, Simon Reeves. I heard from her occasionally. She was living in Essex, and once or twice, when she came to London, we met. But it was some years before I could pay my long-promised visit to them, and by the time I got round to it, her twins, Marjie and Jeff, were five years old.

They were noticeably beautiful children; dark, like Jennie, with a charming way of holding their heads. Jennie was, as she always had been, a sensible girl. She made nothing of their beauty, on which everyone felt compelled to remark. 'As long as they behave themselves—' said Jennie; and I thought what a pretty girl she was herself, and how little notice she took of her looks, and how much care she took with other people. I noticed that Jennie assumed that everyone else was inwardly as quiet, as peacefully inclined, as little prone to be perturbed, as herself. I found this very restful and was grateful to Jennie for it. Her husband resembled her in this; but otherwise, Simon was more positive. He was brisk, full of activity, as indeed was Jennie; the difference between them was that Jennie never appeared to be bustling, even at her busiest hours, while Simon always seemed to live in the act of doing something. They were a fine match. I supposed he had gained from Jennie, during their six years of marriage, a little of her sweet and self-denying nature for he was really considerate. Simon would stop mowing the lawn at once, if he caught sight of the old man next door asleep in a deck-chair, although his need to do something about the lawn was apparently intense. For Jennie's part, she had learned from Simon how to speak to men without embarrassment. This was something she had been unable to do at the age of eighteen. Jennie got from Simon an insight into the mentalities of a fair variety of people, because his friends were curiously mixed, socially and intellectually. And in a way, Simon bore within himself an integrated combination of all those people he brought to the house; he represented them, almost, and kept his balance at the same time. So that Jennie derived from Simon a knowledge of the world, without actually weathering the world. A happy couple. And then, of course, there were the twins.

I arrived on a Saturday afternoon, to spend a week. The lovely twins were put to bed at six, and I did not see them much on Sunday, as a neighbouring couple took them off for a day's picnicking with their own children. I spent most of Monday chatting with Jennie about old times and new times, while little Marjie and Jeff played in the garden. They were lively, full of noise and everything that goes with healthy children. And they were advanced for their years; both could read and write, taught by Jennie. She was sending them to school in September. They pronounced their words very clearly, and I was amused to notice some of Jennie's Scottish phraseology coming out of their English intonation.

Well, they went off to bed at six sharp that day: Simon came home shortly afterwards, and we dined in a pleasant hum-drum peace.

It wasn't until the Tuesday morning that I really got on close speaking terms with the twins. Jennie took the car to the village to fetch some groceries, and for an hour I played with them in the garden. Again, I was struck by their loveliness and intelligence, especially of the little girl. She was the sort of child who noticed everything. The boy was quicker with words, however; his vocabulary was exceptionally large.

Jennie returned, and after tea, I went indoors to write letters. I heard Jennie telling the children 'Go and play yourselves down the other end of the garden and don't make too much noise, mind.' She went to do something in the kitchen. After a while, there was a ring at the back door. The children scampered in from the garden, while Jennie answered the ring.

'Baker,' said the man.

'Oh, yes,' said Jennie: 'wait, I'll get my purse.'

I went on writing my letter, only half-hearing the sound of Jennie's small-change as she, presumably, paid the baker's man.

In a moment, Marjie was by my side.

'Hallo,' I said.

Marjie did not answer.

'Hallo, Marjie,' I said. 'Have you come to keep me company?'

'Listen,' said little Marjie in a whisper, looking over her shoulder. 'Listen.'

'Yes,' I said.

She looked over her shoulder again, as if afraid her mother might come in.

'Will you give me half-a-crown?[1] whispered Marjie, holding out her hand.

'Well,' I said, 'what do you want it for?'

'I want it,' said Marjie, looking furtively behind her again.

'Would your mummy want you to have it?' I said.

'Give me half-a-crown,' said Marjie.

'I'd rather not,' I said. 'But I'll tell you what, I'll buy you a—'

But Marjie had fled, out of the door, into the kitchen. 'She'd rather not,' I heard her say to someone.

Presently, Jennie came in, looking upset.

'Oh,' she said, 'I hope you didn't feel hurt. I only wanted to pay the baker, and I hadn't enough change. He hadn't any either; so just on the spur of the moment I sent Marjie for a loan of a half-a-crown

1. half-a-crown: a silver coin equal to 2½ shillings.

till tonight. But I shouldn't have done it. I *never* borrow anything as a rule.'

'Well, of course!' I said. 'Of course I'll lend you half-a-crown. I've got plenty of change. I didn't understand and I got the message all wrong; I thought she wanted it for herself and that you wouldn't like that.'

Jennie looked doubtful. I funked[2] explaining the whole of Marjie's act. It isn't easy to give evidence against a child of five.

'Oh, they never ask for money,' said Jennie. 'I would never allow them to ask anyone for anything. They never do *that.*'

'I'm sure they don't,' I said, floundering a bit.

Jennie was much too kind to point out that this was what I had just been suggesting. She was altogether too nice to let the incident make any difference during my stay. That night, Simon came home just after six. He had bought two elaborate spinning-tops for the twins. These tops had to be wound up, and they sang a tinny little tune while they spun.

'You'll ruin those children,' said Jennie.

Simon enjoyed himself that evening, playing with the tops.

'You'll break them before the children even see them,' said Jennie.

Simon put them away. But when one of his friends, a pilot from a nearby aerodrome, looked in later in the evening, Simon brought out the tops again; and the two men played delightedly with them, occasionally peering into the works and discussing what made the tops go; while Jennie and I made scornful comments.

Little Marjie and Jeff were highly pleased with the tops next morning, but by the afternoon they had tired of them and gone on to something more in the romping line. After dinner Simon produced a couple of small gadgets. They were the things that go inside musical cigarette-boxes, he explained, and he thought they would fit into the spinning-tops, so that the children could have a change of tune.

'When they get fed up with *Pop Goes the Weasel,*' he said, 'they can have *In and Out the Windows.*'

He got out one of the tops to take it apart and fit in the new tune. But when he had put the pieces together again, the top wouldn't sing at all. Jennie tried to help, but we couldn't get *In and Out the Windows.* So Simon patiently unpieced the top, put the gadgets aside, and said they would do for something else.

2. **funked:** avoided.

'That's Jeff's top,' said Jennie, in her precise way, looking at the pieces on the carpet. 'Jeff's is the red one, Marjie has the blue.'

Once more, Simon started piecing the toy together, with the old tune inside it, while Jennie and I went to make some tea.

'I'll bet it won't work now,' said Jennie with a giggle.

When we returned, Simon was reading and the top was gone.

'Did you fix it?' said Jennie.

'Yes,' he said absently, 'I've put it away.'

It rained the next morning and the twins were indoors.

'Why not play with your tops?' Jennie said.

'Your Daddy took one of them to pieces last night,' Jennie informed them, 'and put all the pieces back again.'

Jennie had the stoic[3] in her nature and did not believe in shielding her children from possible disappointment.

'He was hoping,' she added, 'to fit new tunes inside it. But it wouldn't work with the new tune. . . . But he's going to try again.'

They took this quite hopefully, and I didn't see much of them for some hours although, when the rain stopped and I went outside, I saw the small boy spinning his bright-red top on the hard concrete of the garage floor. About noon little Jeff came running into the kitchen where Jennie was baking. He was howling hard, his small face distorted with grief. He held in his arms the spare parts of his top.

'My top!' he sobbed. 'My top!'

'Goodness,' said Jennie, 'what did you do to it? Don't cry, poor wee pet.'

'I found it,' he said. 'I found my top all in pieces under the box behind Daddy's car.

'My top,' he wept. 'Daddy's broken my top.'

Marjie came in and looked on unmoved, hugging her blue top.

'But you were playing with the top this morning!' I said. 'Isn't yours the red one? You were spinning it.'

'I was playing with the blue one,' he wept. 'And then I found my own top all broken. Daddy broke it.'

Jennie sat them up to their dinner, and Jeff presently stopped crying.

Jennie was cheerful about it, although she said to me afterwards, 'I think Simon might have told me he couldn't put it together again.

3. stoic (stō′ĭk)**:** someone who accepts the events of life calmly. The stoics belonged to an ancient Greek school of philosophy which believed that people were governed by a rational fate.

But isn't it just like a man? They're that proud of themselves, men.'

As I have said, it isn't easy to give evidence against a child of five. And especially, to its mother.

Jennie tactfully put the pieces of the top back in the box behind the garage. They were still there, rusty and untouched, in a pile of other rusty things, seven years later, for I saw them. Jennie got skipping ropes for the twins that day and when they had gone to bed, she removed Marjie's top from the toy-cupboard, 'It'll only make wee Jeff cry to see it,' she said to me. 'We'll just forget about the tops.

'And I don't want Simon to find out that I found *him* out,' she giggled.

I don't think tops were ever mentioned again in the household. If they were, I am sure Jennie would change the subject. An affectionate couple; it was impossible not to feel kindly towards them; not so, towards the children.

I was abroad for some years after that, and heard sometimes from Jennie at first; later, we seldom wrote, and then not at all. I had been back in London for about a year when I met Jennie in Baker Street. She was excited about her children, now aged twelve, who had both won scholarships and were going off to boarding schools in the autumn.

'Come and see them while they've got their holidays,' she said. 'We often talk about you, Simon and I.' It was good to hear Jennie's kind voice again.

I went to stay for a few days in August. I felt sure the twins must have grown out of their peculiarities, and I was right. Jennie brought them to meet me at the station. They had grown rather quiet; both still extremely good-looking. These children possessed an unusual composure for their years. They were well-mannered as Jennie had been at their age, but without Jennie's shyness.

Simon was pruning something in the garden when we got to the house.

'Why, you haven't changed a bit,' he said. 'A bit thinner maybe. Nice to see you so flourishing.'

Jennie went to make tea. In these surroundings she seemed to have endured no change; and she had made no change in her ways in the seven years since my last visit.

The twins started chatting about their school life, and Simon asked me questions I could not answer about the size of the population of the places I had lived in abroad. When Jennie returned, Simon leapt off to wash.

'I'm sorry Simon said that,' said Jennie to me when he had gone. 'I don't think he should have said it, but you know how tactless men are?'

'Said what?' I asked.

'About you looking thin and ill,' said Jennie.

'Oh, I didn't take it *that* way!' I said.

'Didn't you?' said Jennie with an understanding smile. 'That was sweet of you.

'Thin and haggard indeed!' said Jennie as she poured out the tea, and the twins discreetly passed the sandwiches.

That night I sat up late talking to the couple. Jennie retained the former habit of making a tea-session at nine o'clock and I accompanied her to the kitchen. While she was talking, she packed a few biscuits neatly into a small green box.

'There's the kettle boiling,' said Jennie, going out with the box in her hand. 'You know where the teapot is. I won't be a minute.'

She returned in a few seconds, and we carried off our tray.

It was past one before we parted for the night. Jennie had taken care to make me comfortable. She had put fresh flowers on the dressing-table, and there, beside my bed, was the little box of biscuits she had thoughtfully provided. I munched one while I looked out of the window at the calm country sky, ruminating[4] upon Jennie's perennial merits. I have always regarded the lack of neurosis in people with awe. I am too much with brightly intelligent, highly erratic friends. In this Jennie, I decided, reposed a mystery which I and my like could not fathom.

Jennie had driven off next day to fetch the twins from a swimming-pool nearby, when Simon came home from his office.

'I'm glad Jennie's out,' he said, 'for I wanted a chance to talk to you.

'I hope you don't mind,' he said, 'but Jennie's got a horror of mice.'

'Mice?' I said.

'Yes,' said Simon, 'so don't eat biscuits in your room if you wouldn't mind. Jennie was rather upset when she saw the crumbs but of course she'd have a fit if she knew I'd told you. She'd die rather than tell you. But there it is, and I know you'll understand.'

'But Jennie put the biscuits in my room herself,' I explained. 'She packed them in a box and took them up last night.'

4. ruminating: reflecting, thinking about.

Simon looked worried. 'We've had mice before,' he said, 'and she can't bear the thought of them upstairs.'

'Jennie put the biscuits there,' I insisted, feeling all in the wrong.

'And,' I said, 'I saw Jennie pack the box. I'll ask her about it.'

'*Please,*' said Simon, 'please don't do that. She would be so hurt to think I'd spoken about it. Please,' he said, 'go on eating biscuits in your room; I shouldn't have mentioned it.'

Of course, I promised not to eat any more of the things. And Simon, with a knowing smile, said he would give me larger helpings at dinner, so that I wouldn't go hungry.

The biscuit-box had gone when I went to my room. Jennie was busy all next day preparing for a cocktail-party they were giving that night. The twins devotedly gave up their day to the cutting of sandwiches and the making of curious patterns with small pieces of anchovy on diminutive squares of toast.

Jennie wanted some provisions from the village, and I offered to fetch them. I took the car, and noticed it was almost out of petrol; I got some on the way. When I returned, these good children were eating their supper standing up in the kitchen, and without a word of protest, cleared off to bed before the guests arrived.

When Simon came home I met him in the hall. He was uneasy about the gin; he thought there might not be enough. He decided to go straight to the local and get more.

'And,' he said, 'I've just remembered. The car's almost out of petrol. I promised to drive the Rawlings' home after the party. I nearly forgot. I'll get some petrol too.'

'Oh, I got some to-day,' I said.

There were ten guests, four married couples and two unattached girls. Jennie and I did the handing round of snacks and Simon did the drinks. His specialty was a cocktail he had just discovered, called Loopamp. This Loopamp required him to make frequent excursions to the kitchen for replenishments of prune-juice and ice. Simon persuaded himself that Loopamp was in great demand among the guests. We all drank it obligingly. As he took his shakers to the kitchen for the fourth time, he called out to one of the unattached girls who was standing by the door, 'Mollie, bring that lemon-jug too, will you?'

Mollie followed him with the lemon-jug.

'Very good scholarships,' Jennie was saying to an elderly man 'Jeff came fourth among the boys, and Marjie took eleventh place in the girls. There were only fourteen scholarships, so she was lucky. If it hadn't been for the geography she'd have been near the top. Her English teacher told me.'

'Really!' said the man.

'Yes,' said Jennie. 'Mollie Thomas; you know Mollie Thomas. That's Marjie's English mistress. She's here to-night. Where's Mollie?' said Jennie, looking round.

'She's in the kitchen,' I said.

'Making Loopamp, I expect,' said Jennie. 'What a name, Loopamp!'

Simon and Jennie looked rather jaded the next morning. I put it down to the Loopamp. They had very little to say, and when Simon had left for London, I asked Jennie how she was feeling.

'Not too good,' she said. 'Not too good. I am really sorry, my dear, about the petrol. I wish you had asked me for the money. Now, here it is, and don't say another word. Simon's so touchy.'

'Touchy?'

'Well,' said Jennie; 'you know what men are like. I wish you had come to me about it. You know how scrupulous I am about debts. And so is Simon. He just didn't know you had got the petrol, and, of course, he couldn't understand why you felt hurt.'

I sent myself a wire that morning, summoning myself back to London. There wasn't a train before the 6.30, but I caught this. Simon arrived home as I was getting into the taxi, and he joined Jennie and the children on the doorstep to wave goodbye.

'Mind you come again soon,' said Jennie.

As I waved back, I noticed that the twins, who were waving to me, were not looking at me, but at their parents. There was an expression on their faces which I have only seen once before. That was at the Royal Academy, when I saw a famous portrait-painter standing bemused,[5] giving a remarkable and long look at the work of his own hands. So, with wonder, pride and bewilderment, did the twins gaze upon Jennie and Simon.

I wrote and thanked them, avoiding any reference to future meetings. By return I had a letter from Simon. 'I am sorry,' he wrote, 'that you got the impression that Mollie and I were behaving improperly in the kitchen on the night of our party. Jennie was very upset. She does not, of course doubt my fidelity, but she is distressed that you could suggest such a thing. It was very embarrassing for Jennie to hear it in front of all her friends, and I hope, for Jennie's

5. **bemused** (bī•myo͞ozd′): lost in thought.

sake, you will not mention to her that I have written you about it. Jennie would rather die than hurt your feelings. Yours ever, Simon Reeves.'

Meaning

1. Compare Jennie and Simon. Why does the narrator feel that they are such a good match?
2. What is the narrator's opinion of the twins? Why? How do you think Jennie would have reacted if she had heard "evidence" against them?
3. What aspects of their parents' characters and relationship do the twins manipulate to their own advantage?
4. What did the twins think of the narrator? How do you know?

Method

1. What mysteries about the events in the story does the author leave unsolved? Why do you think she leaves some questions unanswered?
2. What is ironic about the way the narrator describes the twins in this story?
3. Why do you think the author chose first-person narration to tell the story?
4. Explain why the author includes the letter from Simon Reeves at the end of the story. How have the tactics of the twins changed since the beginning of the story?

Language: American English Equivalents to British Expressions

In "The Twins," the author uses several British expressions which are not found in American English. For example, in referring to the airport, Muriel Spark writes the "aerodrome."

Look up each of the following words and then give its American counterpart.

Nouns

1. batman
2. petrol
3. bonnet
4. brace
5. gaff
6. sister
7. tommy
8. tram

Adjectives

1. potty	**3.** sticky	**5.** thick
2. smashing	**4.** beastly	**6.** topping

Discussion and Composition

1. Discuss whether you consider the twins' actions to be mischievous or evil. What reasons can you see for their behavior?

2. If you were the narrator in this story, would you have told Jennie and Simon the truth about their children? Why or why not? What possible problems do you see in the future for this family?

JOHN UPDIKE
(born 1932)

The stories of John Updike reveal a craftsman's attention to fine detail. His language has been compared to a newly minted coin. Every sentence is polished; his use of metaphor has been called brilliant and inventive.

Updike's fiction is usually set in small towns similar to Shillington, Pennsylvania, where he was born. He was an only child. His father was a high school teacher. Updike graduated from Harvard University summa cum laude and studied for a year in Oxford, England. After his return to America in 1955, he worked as a staff writer on *The New Yorker* magazine, which had published several of his pieces while he was still at Harvard.

Updike is no longer on *The New Yorker* staff although he still contributes his writing to the magazine, which seems to suit his ornately figurative, witty style. Since he was twenty-five, Updike has supported himself and his family with his prolific production of novels, short stories, poetry, and articles. His first book of short stories, *The Same Door,* was published in 1959. *Rabbit, Run* (1960), the story of an irresponsible husband who tries to escape from a life he finds boring, is considered his best novel. Many of Updike's stories, especially those about young people, contain elements of his own boyhood. He lives on Cape Cod in Massachusetts.

THE LUCID EYE IN SILVER TOWN

The first time I visited New York City, I was thirteen and went with my father. I went to meet my Uncle Quin and to buy a book about Vermeer.[1] The Vermeer book was my idea, and my mother's; meeting Uncle Quin was my father's. A generation ago, my uncle

1. **Vermeer** (vər•mâr′): Jan (1632–1675), a Dutch painter who gave subtle significance to ordinary subjects by his skillful use of color and light.

had vanished in the direction of Chicago and become, apparently, rich; in the last week he had come east on business and I had graduated from the eighth grade with perfect marks. My father claimed that I and his brother were the smartest people he had ever met—"go-getters," he called us, with perhaps more irony than at the time I gave him credit for—and in his visionary way he suddenly, irresistibly, felt that now was the time for us to meet. New York in those days was seven dollars away; we measured everything, distance and time, in money then. World War II was almost over but we were still living in the Depression. My father and I set off with the return tickets and a five-dollar bill in his pocket. The five dollars was for the book.

My mother, on the railway platform, suddenly exclaimed, "I *hate* the Augusts." This surprised me, because we were all Augusts—I was an August, my father was an August, Uncle Quincy was an August, and she, I had thought, was an August.

My father gazed serenely over her head and said, "You have every reason to. I wouldn't blame you if you took a gun and shot us all. Except for Quin and your son. They're the only ones of us ever had any get up and git." Nothing was more infuriating about my father than his way of agreeing.

Uncle Quin didn't meet us at Pennsylvania Station. If my father was disappointed, he didn't reveal it to me. It was after one o'clock and all we had for lunch were two candy bars. By walking what seemed to me a very long way on pavements only a little broader than those of my home town, and not so clean, we reached the hotel, which seemed to sprout somehow from Grand Central Station. The lobby smelled of perfume. After the clerk had phoned Quincy August that a man who said he was his brother was at the desk, an elevator took us to the twentieth floor. Inside the room sat three men, each in a gray or blue suit with freshly pressed pants and garters peeping from under the cuffs when they crossed their legs. The men were not quite interchangeable. One had a caterpillar-shaped mustache, one had tangled blond eyebrows like my father's, and the third had a drink in his hand—the others had drinks, too, but were not gripping them so tightly.

"Gentlemen, I'd like you to meet my brother Marty and his young son," Uncle Quin said.

"The kid's name is Jay," my father added, shaking hands with each of the two men, staring them in the eye. I imitated my father, and the mustached man, not expecting my firm handshake and stare, said, "Why, hello there, Jay!"

"Marty, would you and the boy like to freshen up? The facilities are through the door and to the left."

"Thank you, Quin. I believe we will. Excuse me, gentlemen."

"Certainly."

"Certainly."

My father and I went into the bedroom of the suite. The furniture was square and new and all the same shade of maroon. On the bed was an opened suitcase, also new. The clean, expensive smells of leather and lotion were beautiful to me. Uncle Quin's underwear looked silk and was full of fleurs-de-lis.[2] When I was through in the lavatory, I made for the living room, to rejoin Uncle Quin and his friends.

"Hold it," my father said. "Let's wait in here."

"Won't that look rude?"

"No. It's what Quin wants."

"Now Daddy, don't be ridiculous. He'll think we've died in here."

"No he won't, not my brother. He's working some deal. He doesn't want to be bothered. I know how my brother works: he got us in here so we'd stay in here."

"*Really*, Pop. You're such a schemer." But I did not want to go in there without him. I looked around the room for something to read. There was nothing, not even a newspaper, except a shiny little pamphlet about the hotel itself. I wondered when we would get a chance to look for the Vermeer book. I wondered what the men in the next room were talking about. I wondered why Uncle Quin was so short, when my father was so tall. By leaning out of the window, I could see taxicabs maneuvering like windup toys.

My father came and stood beside me. "Don't lean out too far."

I edged out inches farther and took a big bite of the high cold air, spiced by the distant street noises. "Look at the green cab cut in front of the yellow," I said. "Should they be making U-turns on that street?"

"In New York it's OK. Survival of the fittest is the only law here."

2. fleurs-de-lis (flo͝or′də·lē′): a design of three petals resembling an iris, bound together at the base; once the coat of arms of the French royal family.

"Isn't that the Chrysler Building?"

"Yes, isn't it graceful though? It always reminds me of the queen of the chessboard."

"What's the one beside it?"

"I don't know. Some big gravestone. The one deep in back, from this window, is the Woolworth Building. For years it was the tallest building in the world."

As, side by side at the window, we talked, I was surprised that my father could answer so many of my questions. As a young man, before I was born, he had traveled, looking for work; this was not *his* first trip to New York. Excited by my new respect, I longed to say something to remold that calm, beaten face.

"Do you really think he meant for us to stay out here?" I asked.

"Quin is a go-getter," he said, gazing over my head. "I admire him. Anything he wanted, from little on up, he went after it. Slam. Bang. His thinking is miles ahead of mine—just like your mother's. You can feel them pull ahead of you." He moved his hands, palms down, like two taxis, the left quickly pulling ahead of the right. "You're the same way."

"Sure, sure." My impatience was not merely embarrassment at being praised; I was irritated that he considered Uncle Quin as smart as myself. At that point in my life I was sure that only stupid people took an interest in money.

When Uncle Quin finally entered the bedroom, he said, "Martin, I hoped you and the boy would come out and join us."

"Hell, I didn't want to butt in. You and those men were talking business."

"Lucas and Roebuck and I? Now, Marty, it was nothing that my own brother couldn't hear. Just a minor matter of adjustment. Both these men are fine men. Very important in their own fields. I'm disappointed that you couldn't see more of them. Believe me, I hadn't meant for you to hide in here. Now what kind of drink would you like?"

"I don't care. I drink very little any more."

"Scotch and water, Marty?"

"Swell."

"And the boy? What about some ginger ale, young man? Or would you like milk?"

"The ginger ale," I said.

As I remember it, a waiter brought the drinks to the room, and while we were drinking them I asked if we were going to spend all afternoon in this room. Uncle Quin didn't seem to hear, but five minutes later he suggested that the boy might like to take a look around the city—Gotham, he called it. Baghdad-on-the-Subway. My father said that that would be a once-in-a-lifetime treat for the kid. He always called me "the kid" when I was sick or had lost at something or was angry—when he felt sorry for me, in short. The three of us went down in the elevator and took a taxi ride down Broadway, or up Broadway—I wasn't sure. "This is what they call the Great White Way," Uncle Quin said several times. Once he apologized, "In the daytime it's just another street." The trip didn't seem so much designed for sightseeing as for getting Uncle Quin to the Pickernut Club, a little restaurant set in a block of similar canopied places. I remember we stepped down into it and it was dark inside. A piano was playing "There's a Small Hotel."

"He shouldn't do that," Uncle Quin said. Then he waved to the man behind the piano. "How are you, Freddie? How are the kids?"

"Fine, Mr. August, fine," Freddie said, bobbing his head and smiling and not missing a note.

"That's Quin's song," my father said to me as we wriggled our way into a dark curved seat at a round table.

I didn't say anything, but Uncle Quin, overhearing some disapproval in my silence, said, "Freddie's a first-rate man. He has a boy going to Colgate[3] this autumn."

I asked, "Is that really your song?"

Uncle Quin grinned and put his warm broad hand on my shoulder; I hated, at that age, being touched. "I let them think it is," he said, oddly purring. "To me, songs are like young girls. They're all pretty."

A waiter in a red coat scurried up. "Mr. August! Back from the West? How are you, Mr. August?"

"Getting by, Jerome, getting by. Jerome, I'd like you to meet my kid brother, Martin."

"How do you do, Mr. Martin. Are you paying New York a visit? Or do you live here?"

My father quickly shook hands with Jerome, somewhat to Jerome's surprise. "I'm just up for the afternoon, thank you. I live in a hick town in Pennsylvania you never heard of."

"I see, sir. A quick visit."

3. Colgate: a university in Hamilton, New York, established in 1819.

"This is the first time in six years that I've had a chance to see my brother."

"Yes, we've seen very little of him these past years. He's a man we can never see too much of, isn't that right?"

Uncle Quin interrupted. "This is my nephew Jay."

"How do you like the big city, Jay?"

"Fine." I didn't duplicate my father's mistake of offering to shake hands.

"Why, Jerome," Uncle Quin said. "My brother and I would like to have a Scotch-on-the-rocks. The boy would like a ginger ale."

"No, wait," I said. "What kinds of ice cream do you have?"

"Vanilla and chocolate, sir."

I hesitated. I could scarcely believe it, when the cheap drugstore at home had fifteen flavors.

"I'm afraid it's not a very big selection," Jerome said.

"I guess vanilla."

"Yes, sir. One plate of vanilla."

When my ice cream came it was a golf ball in a flat silver dish; it kept spinning away as I dug at it with my spoon. Uncle Quin watched me and asked, "Is there anything especially you'd like to do?"

"The kid'd like to get into a bookstore," my father said.

"A bookstore. What sort of book, Jay?"

I said, "I'd like to look for a good book of Vermeer."

"Vermeer," Uncle Quin pronounced slowly, relishing the r's, pretending to give the matter thought. "Dutch School."

"He's Dutch, yes."

"For my own money, Jay, the French are the people to beat. We have four Degas[4] ballet dancers in our living room in Chicago, and I could sit and look at one of them for hours. I think it's wonderful, the feeling for balance the man had."

"Yeah, but don't Degas's paintings always remind you of colored drawings? For actually *looking* at things in terms of paint, for the lucid eye, I think Vermeer makes Degas look sick."

Uncle Quin said nothing, and my father, after an anxious glance across the table, said, "That's the way he and his mother talk all the time. It's all beyond me. I can't understand a thing they say."

"Your mother is encouraging you to be a painter, is she, Jay?"

4. **Degas** (də·gä′): Edgar (1834–1917), a French impressionist painter.

Uncle Quin's smile was very wide and his cheeks were pushed out as if each held a candy.

"Sure, I suppose she is."

"Your mother is a very wonderful woman, Jay," Uncle Quin said.

It was such an embarrassing remark, and so much depended upon your definition of "wonderful," that I dug at my ice cream, and my father asked Uncle Quin about his own wife, Tessie. When we left, Uncle Quin signed the check with his name and the name of some company. It was close to five o'clock.

My uncle didn't know much about the location of bookstores in New York—his last fifteen years had been spent in Chicago—but he thought that if we went to Forty-second Street and Sixth Avenue we should find something. The cab driver let us out beside a park that acted as kind of a backyard for the Public Library. It looked so inviting, so agreeably dusty, with the pigeons and the men nodding on the benches and the office girls in their taut summer dresses, that without thinking, I led the two men into it. Shimmering buildings arrowed upward and glinted through the treetops. This was New York, I felt: the silver town. Towers of ambition rose, crystalline, within me. "If you stand here," my father said, "you can see the Empire State." I went and stood beneath my father's arm and followed with my eyes the direction of it. Something sharp and hard fell into my right eye. I ducked my head and blinked; it was painful.

"What's the trouble?" Uncle Quin's voice asked.

My father said, "The poor kid's got something into his eye. He has the worst luck that way of anybody I ever knew."

The thing seemed to have life. It bit. "Ow," I said, angry enough to cry.

"If we can get him out of the wind," my father's voice said, "maybe I can see it."

"No, now, Marty, use your head. Never fool with the eyes or ears. The hotel is within two blocks. Can you walk two blocks, Jay?"

"I'm blind, not lame," I snapped.

"He has a ready wit," Uncle Quin said.

Between the two men, shielding my eye with a hand, I walked to the hotel. From time to time, one of them would take my other hand, or put one of theirs on my shoulder, but I would walk faster, and the hands would drop away. I hoped our entrance into the hotel lobby would not be too conspicuous; I took my hand from my eye and walked erect, defying the impulse to stoop. Except for the one lid being shut and possibly my face being red, I imagined I looked passably suave. However, my guardians lost no time betraying me. Not only did they walk at my heels, as if I might topple any instant, but my father told one old bum sitting in the lobby, "Poor kid got something in his eye," and Uncle Quin passing the desk called, "Send up a doctor to Twenty-eleven."

"You shouldn't have done that, Quin," my father said in the elevator. "I can get it out, now that he's out of the wind. This is happening all the time. The kid's eyes are too far front."

"Never fool with the eyes, Martin. They are your most precious tool in life."

"It'll work out," I said, though I didn't believe it would. It felt like a steel chip, deeply embedded.

Up in the room, Uncle Quin made me lie down on the bed. My father, a clean handkerchief wadded in his hand so that one corner stuck out, approached me, but it hurt so much to open the eye that I repulsed him. "Don't torment me," I said twisting my face away. "What good does it do? The doctor'll be up."

Regretfully my father put the handkerchief back into his pocket.

The doctor was a soft-handed man with little to say to anybody; he wasn't pretending to be the family doctor. He rolled my lower eyelid on a thin stick, jabbed with a Q-tip, and showed me, on the end of the Q-tip, an eyelash. He dropped three drops of yellow fluid into the eye to remove any chance of infection. The fluid stung, and I shut my eyes, leaning back into the pillow, glad it was over. When I opened them, my father was passing a bill into the doctor's hand. The doctor thanked him, winked at me, and left. Uncle Quin came out of the bathroom.

"Well, young man, how are you feeling now?" he asked.

"Fine."

"It was just an eyelash," my father said.

"*Just* an eyelash! Well I know how an eyelash can feel like a razor blade in there. But now that the young invalid is recovered, we can think of dinner."

"No, I really appreciate your kindness, Quin, but we must be getting back to the sticks. I have an eight-o'clock meeting I should be at."

"I'm extremely sorry to hear that. What sort of meeting, Marty?"

"A church council."

"So you're still doing church work. Well, God bless you for it."

"Grace wanted me to ask you if you couldn't possibly come over some day. We'll put you up overnight. It would be a real treat for her to see you again."

Uncle Quin reached up and put his arm around his younger brother's shoulders. "Martin, I'd like that better than anything in the world. But I am solid with appointments, and I must head west this Thursday. They don't let me have a minute's repose. Nothing would please my heart better than to share a quiet day with you and Grace in your home. Please give her my love, and tell her what a wonderful boy she is raising. The two of you are raising."

My father promised, "I'll do that." And, after a little more fuss, we left.

"The child better?" the old man in the lobby called to us on the way out.

"It was just an eyelash, thank you, sir," my father said.

When we got outside, I wondered if there were any bookstores still open.

"We have no money."

"None at all?"

"The doctor charged five dollars. That's how much it costs in New York to get something in your eye."

"I didn't do it on purpose. Do you think I pulled out the eyelash and stuck it in there myself? I didn't tell you to call the doctor."

"I know that."

"Couldn't we just go into a bookstore and look a minute?"

"We haven't time, Jay."

But when we reached Pennsylvania Station, it was over thirty minutes until the next train left. As we sat on a bench, my father smiled reminiscently. "Boy, he's smart, isn't he? His thinking is sixty light-years ahead of mine."

"Whose?"

"My brother. Notice the way he hid in the bathroom until the doctor was gone? That's how to make money. The rich man collects dollar bills like the stamp collector collects stamps. I knew he'd do it. I knew it when he told the clerk to send up a doctor that I'd have to pay for it."

"Well, why *should* he pay for it? *You* were the person to pay for it."

"That's right. Why should he?" My father settled back, his eyes forward, his hands crossed and limp in his lap. The skin beneath his chin was loose; his temples seemed concave. The liquor was probably disagreeing with him. "That's why he's where he is now, and that's why I am where I am."

The seed of my anger seemed to be a desire to recall him to himself, to scold him out of being old and tired. "Well, why'd you bring along only five dollars? You might have known something would happen."

"You're right, Jay. I should have brought more."

"Look. Right over there is an open bookstore. Now if you had brought *ten* dollars–"

"Is it open? I don't think so. They just left the lights in the window on."

"What if it isn't? What does it matter to us? Anyway, what kind of art book can you get for five dollars? Color plates cost money. How much do you think a decent book of Vermeer costs? It'd be cheap at fifteen dollars, even secondhand, with the pages all crummy and full of spilled coffee." I kept on, shrilly flailing the passive and infuriating figure of my father, until we left the city. Once we were on the homeward train, my tantrum ended; it had been a kind of ritual, for both of us, and he had endured my screams complacently, nodding assent, like a midwife assisting at the birth of family pride. Years passed before I needed to go to New York again.

Meaning

1. What do you learn about each of Jay's parents in the first two paragraphs of this story? What sort of boy is Jay?
2. In what way does Uncle Quin fit the image of a successful man? Where is there evidence that, in spite of success, Uncle Quin lacks character?
3. One minute Jay says that he didn't duplicate his father's mistake of offering to shake hands with Jerome. The next minute he is astounded that the Pickernut Club has only two flavors of ice cream, when the cheap drugstore at home has fifteen flavors. What does each reaction tell you about the boy?
4. What thoughts were running through Jay's mind just before he became temporarily blinded? What meaning would you attach to this incident? Give specific reasons for your answer.

Method

1. Explain the significance of the title. Who actually possesses the "lucid eye in silver town" at the time these three people meet?
2. How is the character of the father developed in the story? Does your opinion of the father change or remain the same?
3. What are the conflicts in the story?

Language: The Use of Allusions

An *allusion* is a reference to some person, place, or thing, usually from history or literature, that will give new meaning to a present topic. For example, if someone calls you Scrooge, you had better check your attitude toward money. If someone alludes to you as Cleopatra, it probably means that you are attractive.

In "The Lucid Eye in Silver Town," Uncle Quin calls New York "Gotham" and "Baghdad-on-the-Subway." Gotham was the name of an English village noted in legend for the "foolish" behavior of its inhabitants. In order to keep King John from building a castle there with its high cost to them, they deliberately pretended to be stupid when the royal messengers arrived. As used to designate New York, the word has come to mean "a place of fools."

Baghdad was O. Henry's synonym for Manhattan. Often in his stories he compared New York to the fabulous city of Baghdad, made famous in the tales of *The Arabian Nights.*

Use each of the following in a sentence that will show that you know its meaning:

1. Lot's wife
2. Hercules
3. Helen of Troy
4. Rip Van Winkle
5. Nero
6. Einstein

Discussion and Composition

1. The endings of "The Return of Corporal Greene" and "The Lucid Eye in Silver town" are similar. In the former, Ben Greene shocks his parents by shouting accusations at them; in the latter, Jay August throws a tantrum in his father's presence. Write a composition in which you compare **a.** the immediate cause of the outburst at the end of each story, **b.** the underlying reasons, and **c.** each boy's assessment of his conduct.

2. Both "My Oedipus Complex" and "The Lucid Eye in Silver Town" are narrated in the first person, from the point of view of a young boy. Compare and contrast the impression that each boy had of his father. What traits does each boy feel his father lacks? When, if at all, does each boy come to understand his father? Base your analysis on specific incidents from the story. Begin your composition with a characterization of each father.

3. What is your idea of a successful adult? Discuss the personal qualities and achievements that would mean success to you as an adult in our society.

KURT VONNEGUT
(born 1922)

His protests of war, environmental pollution, and dehumanizing occupations have made Kurt Vonnegut one of the most provocative writers of the twentieth century. Vonnegut was born in Indianapolis, Indiana, the son of an architect who lost most of his wealth during the Depression. Urged by his father to study "something useful," Vonnegut majored in chemistry and biology at Cornell University. In 1943, he enlisted in the army and was captured a year later at the Battle of the Bulge. Imprisoned in Dresden, he was one of the few who survived the Allied fire-bombing.

Returning to the United States in 1945, Vonnegut studied anthropology at the University of Chicago. In the late 1940s he did public relations work at a large corporation in New York. In 1950, his first story, "Report on the Barnhouse Effect," was published. The following year he moved to Cape Cod, Massachusetts, where he taught English, wrote advertising, and sold cars to support his family until he was able to make enough money to spend all of his time writing.

Vonnegut's first novel, *Player Piano* (1952), satirizes automation. His most innovative and best known work is *Slaughterhouse Five,* which is based on his experiences in Dresden.

In addition to novels and short stories, Vonnegut has written several plays and many articles. His work often contains elements of fantasy, especially science fiction. Unlike much of Vonnegut's work, "Tom Edison's Shaggy Dog" is not a pessimistic satire, but an example of the author's lighter, more humorous stories.

TOM EDISON'S SHAGGY DOG

Two old men sat on a park bench one morning in the sunshine of Tampa, Florida—one trying doggedly to read a book he was plainly enjoying while the other, Harold K. Bullard, told him the story of his life in the full, round, head tones of a public address system. At their feet lay Bullard's Labrador retriever, who further tormented the aged listener by probing his ankles with a large, wet nose.

Bullard, who had been, before he retired, successful in many fields, enjoyed reviewing his important past. But he faced the problem that complicates the lives of cannibals—namely: that a single victim cannot be used over and over. Anyone who had passed the time of day with him and his dog refused to share a bench with them again.

So Bullard and his dog set out through the park each day in quest of new faces. They had had good luck this morning, for they had found this stranger right away, clearly a new arrival in Florida, still buttoned up tight in heavy serge, stiff collar and necktie, and with nothing better to do than read.

"Yes," said Bullard, rounding out the first hour of his lecture, "made and lost five fortunes in my time."

"So you said," said the stranger, whose name Bullard had neglected to ask. "Easy, boy. No, no, no, boy," he said to the dog, who was growing more aggressive toward his ankles.

"Oh? Already told you that, did I?" said Bullard.

"Twice."

"Two in real estate, one in scrap iron, and one in oil and one in trucking."

"So you said."

"I did? Yes, guess I did. Two in real estate, one in scrap iron, one in oil, and one in trucking. Wouldn't take back a day of it."

"No, I suppose not," said the stranger. "Pardon me, but do you suppose you could move your dog somewhere else? He keeps—"

"Him?" said Bullard, heartily. "Friendliest dog in the world. Don't need to be afraid of him."

"I'm not afraid of him. It's just that he drives me crazy, sniffing at my ankles."

"Plastic," said Bullard, chuckling.

"What?"

"Plastic. Must be something plastic on your garters. By golly, I'll bet it's those little buttons. Sure as we're sitting here, those buttons must be plastic. That dog is nuts about plastic. Don't know why that is, but he'll sniff it out and find it if there's a speck around. Must be a deficiency in his diet, though, by gosh, he eats better than I do. Once he chewed up a whole plastic humidor.[1] Can you beat it? *That's* the

1. **humidor** (hū′mə•dôr): a box for keeping tobacco moist.

business I'd go into now, by glory, if the pill rollers hadn't told me to let up, to give the old ticker a rest."

"You could tie the dog to that tree over there," said the stranger.

"I get so darn' sore at all the youngsters these days!" said Bullard. "All of 'em mooning around about no frontiers any more. There never have been so many frontiers as there are today. You know what Horace Greeley[2] would say today?"

"His nose is wet," said the stranger, and he pulled his ankles away, but the dog humped forward in patient pursuit. "Stop it, boy!"

"His wet nose shows he's healthy," said Bullard. " 'Go plastic, young man!' That's what Greeley'd say. 'Go atom, young man!' "

The dog had definitely located the plastic buttons on the stranger's garters and was cocking his head one way and another, thinking out ways of bringing his teeth to bear on those delicacies.

"Scat!" said the stranger.

" 'Go electronic, young man!' " said Bullard. "Don't talk to me about no opportunity any more. Opportunity's knocking down every door in the country, trying to get in. When I was young, a man had to go out and find opportunity and drag it home by the ears. Nowadays–"

"Sorry," said the stranger, evenly. He slammed his book shut, stood and jerked his ankle away from the dog. "I've got to be on my way. So good day, sir."

He stalked across the park, found another bench, sat down with a sigh and began to read. His respiration had just returned to normal, when he felt the wet sponge of the dog's nose on his ankles again.

"Oh–it's you!" said Bullard, sitting down beside him. "He was tracking you. He was on the scent of something, and I just let him have his head. What'd I tell you about plastic?" He looked about contentedly. "Don't blame you for moving on. It was stuffy back there. No shade to speak of and not a sign of a breeze."

"Would the dog go away if I bought him a humidor?" said the stranger.

"Pretty good joke, pretty good joke," said Bullard, amiably. Suddenly he clapped the stranger on his knee. "Sa-ay, you aren't in plastics are you? Here I've been blowing off about plastics, and for all I know that's your line."

2. **Horace Greeley:** American newspaper editor (1811–1872) whose advice was "Go West, young man."

"My line?" said the stranger crisply, laying down his book. "Sorry—I've never had a line. I've been a drifter since the age of nine, since Edison set up his laboratory next to my home, and showed me the intelligence analyzer."

"Edison?" said Bullard. "Thomas Edison, the inventor?"

"If you want to call him that, go ahead," said the stranger.

"If I *want* to call him that?"—Bullard guffawed—"I guess I just will! Father of the light bulb and I don't know what all."

"If you want to think he invented the light bulb, go ahead. No harm in it." The stranger resumed his reading.

"Say, what is this?" said Bullard, suspiciously. "You pulling my leg? What's this about an intelligence analyzer? I never heard of that."

"Of course you haven't," said the stranger. "Mr. Edison and I promised to keep it a secret. I've never told anyone. Mr. Edison broke his promise and told Henry Ford, but Ford made him promise not to tell anybody else—for the good of humanity."

Bullard was entranced. "Uh, this intelligence analyzer," he said, "it analyzed intelligence, did it?"

"It was an electric butter churn," said the stranger.

"Seriously now," Bullard coaxed.

"Maybe it *would* be better to talk it over with someone," said the stranger. "It's a terrible thing to keep bottled up inside me, year in and year out. But how can I be sure that it won't go any further?"

"My word as a gentleman," Bullard assured him.

"I don't suppose I could find a stronger guarantee than that, could I?" said the stranger, judiciously.

"There is no stronger guarantee," said Bullard, proudly. "Cross my heart and hope to die!"

"Very well." The stranger leaned back and closed his eyes, seeming to travel backward through time. He was silent for a full minute, during which Bullard watched with respect.

"It was back in the fall of eighteen seventy-nine," said the stranger at last, softly. "Back in the village of Menlo Park, New Jersey. I was a boy of nine. A young man we all thought was a wizard had set up a laboratory next door to my home, and there were flashes and crashes inside, and all sorts of scary goings on. The neighborhood children were warned to keep away, not to make any noise that would bother the wizard.

"I didn't get to know Edison right off, but his dog Sparky and I got to be steady pals. A dog a whole lot like yours, Sparky was, and we used to wrestle all over the neighborhood. Yes, sir, your dog is the image of Sparky."

"Is that so?" said Bullard, flattered.

"Gospel," replied the stranger. "Well, one day Sparky and I were wrestling around, and we wrestled right up to the door of Edison's laboratory. The next thing I knew, Sparky had pushed me in through the door, and bam! I was sitting on the laboratory floor, looking up at Mr. Edison himself."

"Bet he was sore," said Bullard, delighted.

"You can bet I was scared," said the stranger. "I thought I was face to face with Satan himself. Edison had wires hooked to his ears and running down to a little black box in his lap! I started to scoot, but he caught me by my collar and made me sit down.

" 'Boy,' said Edison, 'it's always darkest before the dawn. I want you to remember that.'

" 'Yes, sir,' I said.

" 'For over a year, my boy,' Edison said to me, 'I've been trying to find a filament that will last in an incandescent lamp. Hair, string, splinters—nothing works. So while I was trying to think of something else to try, I started tinkering with another idea of mine, just letting off steam. I put this together,' he said, showing me the little black box. 'I thought maybe intelligence was just a certain kind of electricity, so I made this intelligence analyzer here. It works! You're the first one to know about it, my boy. But I don't know why you shouldn't be. It will be your generation that will grow up in the glorious new era when people will be as easily graded as oranges.' "

"I don't believe it!" said Bullard.

"May I be struck by lightning this very instant!" said the stranger. "And it did work, too. Edison had tried out the analyzer on the men in his shop, without telling them what he was up to. The smarter a man was, by gosh, the farther the needle on the indicator in the little black box swung to the right. I let him try it on me, and the needle just lay where it was and trembled. But dumb as I was, then is when I made my one and only contribution to the world. As I say, I haven't lifted a finger since."

"Whadja do?" said Bullard, eagerly.

"I said, 'Mr. Edison, sir, let's try it on the dog.' And I wish you could have seen the show that dog put on when I said it! Old Sparky barked and howled and scratched to get out. When he saw we meant business, that he wasn't going to get out, he made a beeline right for the intelligence analyzer and knocked it out of Edison's hands. But we cornered him, and Edison held him down while I touched the wires to his ears. And would you believe it, that needle sailed clear across the dial, way past a little red pencil mark on the dial face!"

"The dog busted it," said Bullard.

" 'Mr. Edison, sir,' I said, 'what's that red mark mean?'

" 'My boy,' said Edison, 'it means that the instrument is broken, because that red mark is me.' "

"I'll say it was broken" said Bullard.

The stranger said gravely. "But it wasn't broken. No, sir. Edison checked the whole thing, and it was in apple-pie order. When Edison told me that, it was then that Sparky, crazy to get out, gave himself away."

"How?" said Bullard, suspiciously.

"We really had him locked in, see? There were three locks on the door—a hook and eye, a bolt, and a regular knob and latch. That dog stood up, unhooked the hook, pushed the bolt back and had the knob in his teeth when Edison stopped him."

"No!" said Bullard.

"Yes!" said the stranger, his eyes shining. "And then is when Edison showed me what a great scientist he was. He was willing to face the truth, no matter how unpleasant it might be.

" 'So!' said Edison to Sparky, 'Man's best friend, huh? Dumb animal, huh?'

"That Sparky was a caution. He pretended not to hear. He scratched himself and bit fleas and went growling at ratholes—anything to get out of looking Edison in the eye.

" 'Pretty soft, isn't it, Sparky?" said Edison. 'Let somebody else worry about getting food, building shelters and keeping warm, while you sleep in front of a fire or go chasing after the girls or raise hell with the boys. No mortgages, no politics, no war, no work, no worry. Just wag the old tail or lick a hand, and you're all taken care of.'

" 'Mr. Edison,' I said, 'do you mean to tell me that dogs are smarter than people?'

" 'Smarter?' said Edison. 'I'll tell the world! And what have I been doing for the past year? Slaving to work out a light bulb so dogs can play at night!'

" 'Look, Mr. Edison,' said Sparky, 'why not—' "

"Hold on!" roared Bullard.

"Silence!" shouted the stranger, triumphantly. " 'Look, Mr.

Edison,' said Sparky, 'why not keep quiet about this? It's been working out to everybody's satisfaction for hundreds of thousands of years. Let sleeping dogs lie. You forget all about it, destroy the intelligence analyzer, and I'll tell you what to use for a lamp filament.' "

"Hogwash!" said Bullard, his face purple.

The stranger stood. "You have my solemn word as a gentleman. That dog rewarded *me* for my silence with a stock-market tip that made me independently wealthy for the rest of my days. And the last words that Sparky ever spoke were to Thomas Edison. 'Try a piece of carbonized cotton thread,' he said. Later, he was torn to bits by a pack of dogs that had gathered outside the door, listening."

The stranger removed his garters and handed them to Bullard's dog. "A small token of esteem, sir, for an ancestor of yours who talked himself to death. Good day." He tucked his book under his arm and walked away.

Meaning

1. A *shaggy dog story* is an anecdote that has a surprise ending (not always involving a dog) and containing humorously unreal behavior. How does "Tom Edison's Shaggy Dog" fit this definition?
2. Do you think the story is humorous? Why or why not?
3. What happened to Sparky? What was the source of the stranger's wealth?
4. Why does the stranger tell the story? How is the point of the story related to the conflict between Bullard and the stranger?

Method

1. At what point in the story does Bullard realize that he is being fooled? At what point do you realize that the stranger has made up the story to get even with Bullard?
2. "Tom Edison's Shaggy Dog" tells of two meetings between Bullard and a newcomer to Florida. How does the author convey the impression that Bullard is in control of the situation during the first encounter? How do you know that the roles of tormentor and victim have been reversed in the second encounter?
3. Point out some examples of ironic dialogue in the story.
4. Why are you told so little about the stranger, not even his name? Describe his character as it is revealed in the story.

Language: Repetition for Effect

Although repetition is more common in poetry than it is in prose, a short story writer may repeat words and phrases to achieve a particular effect. In "Tom Edison's Shaggy Dog," repetition is used to characterize Bullard. In the first conversation between Bullard and the stranger, notice that Bullard repeats, sometimes with slight variation, almost everything he says. Find the places in the story where Bullard repeats the following words and phrases:

"plastic"
"go"
"opportunity"
"Two in real estate, one in scrap iron, one in oil, and one in trucking"

How do these words help to characterize him? What is ironic about his repetition of the words *go* and *opportunity*?

Later, as the stranger tells his story to Bullard, the phrase "My word as a gentleman" is repeated. Why is this ironic?

Discussion and Composition

1. Write a composition in which you tell how your idea of what is humorous has changed since you were a young child. If you have forgotten, ask children who are approximately five, eight, and twelve what they consider to be funny.

2. Write an essay on the subject of humor in "Tom Edison's Shaggy Dog." Begin by defining humor. Then give examples from the story that support your definition.

3. Write a story about a funny incident that has happened to you. Use dialogue to help your readers know the characters in your story.

4. Compare and contrast the characterization of Bullard and the stranger.

LUIGI PIRANDELLO
(1867–1936)

His innovative ideas as a writer of plays brought fame to Luigi Pirandello when he was in his mid-fifties. His unique use of the "play within a play" allowed an unusual dialogue of ideas between characters and playwright, fiction and reality, which had a major influence on modern drama. Until his play *Six Characters in Search of an Author* was performed in the 1920s, Pirandello was known in Italy primarily as a realistic storyteller.

The son of a wealthy merchant, Pirandello was born in Sicily. He studied at the University of Rome and received a doctorate in linguistics in 1891 from the University of Bonn in Germany. Although he published some poetry and short stories in the 1890s, Pirandello did not have to support himself until 1903, when a landslide closed the mine that had been the source of his family's wealth. To supplement his writing income, Pirandello taught Italian at a college in Rome, and did translations. His wife, despairing over their financial problems, became insane. The stories and novels that he wrote during the next fourteen years, when he cared for his wife at home, explore the human personality, especially the subconscious forces that influence behavior.

After he began to achieve recognition as a dramatist, Pirandello opened his own theater in Rome and toured Europe with his acting company.

Pirandello believed that life is "a very sad piece of buffoonery." He pitied people who fool themselves by basing their lives on illusions. Yet he realized that each person creates his or her own reality.

WAR

The passengers who had left Rome by the night express had had to stop until dawn at the small station of Fabriano in order to continue their journey by the small old-fashioned local joining the main line with Sulmona.

At dawn, in a stuffy and smoky second-class carriage,[1] in which five people had already spent the night, a bulky woman in deep mourning was hoisted in—almost like a shapeless bundle. Behind her, puffing and moaning, followed her husband—a tiny man, thin and weakly, his face death-white, his eyes small and bright—looking shy and uneasy.

Having at last taken a seat, he politely thanked the passengers who had helped his wife and who had made room for her; then he turned around to the woman trying to pull down the collar of her coat, and politely inquired:

"Are you all right, dear?"

The wife, instead of answering, pulled up her collar again to her eyes, so as to hide her face.

"Nasty world," muttered the husband with a sad smile.

And he felt it his duty to explain to his traveling companions that the poor woman was to be pitied, for the war was taking away from her her only son, a boy of twenty, to whom both had devoted their entire life, even breaking up their home at Sulmona to follow him to Rome, where he had to go as a student, then allowing him to volunteer for war with an assurance, however, that at least for six months he would not be sent to the front, and now all of a sudden receiving a wire saying that he was due to leave in three days' time and asking them to go and see him off.

The woman under the big coat was twisting and wriggling, at times growling like a wild animal, feeling certain that all those explanations would not have aroused even a shadow of sympathy from those people who—most likely—were in the same plight as herself. One of them, who had been listening with particular attention, said:

"You should thank God that your son is only leaving now for the front. Mine was sent there the first day of the war. He has already come back twice wounded and been sent back again to the front."

"What about me? I have two sons and three nephews at the front," said another passenger.

"Maybe, but in our case it is our *only* son," ventured the husband.

"What difference can that make? You may spoil your only son with excessive attention, but you cannot love him more than you would all your other children if you had any. Paternal love is not like

1. **second-class carriage:** a coach-car, moderately priced. It is divided into separate compartments each containing two long, facing seats.

bread that can be broken into pieces and split among the children in equal shares. A father gives *all* his love to each of his children without discrimination, whether it be one or ten, and if I am suffering now for my two sons, I am not suffering half for each of them but double."

"True . . . true . . ." sighed the embarrassed husband, "but suppose (of course we all hope it will never be your case) a father has two sons at the front and he loses one of them, there is still one left to console him . . . while. . . ."

"Yes," answered the other, getting cross, "a son left to console him but also a son left for whom he must survive, while in the case of the father of an only son if the son dies the father can die too and put and end to his distress. Which of the two positions is the worse? Don't you see how my case would be worse than yours?"

"Nonsense," interrupted another traveler, a fat, red-faced man with bloodshot eyes of the palest gray.

He was panting. From his bulging eyes seemed to spurt inner violence of an uncontrolled vitality which his weakened body could hardly contain.

"Nonsense," he repeated, trying to cover his mouth with his hand so as to hide the two missing front teeth. "Nonsense. Do we give life to our children for our own benefit?"

"The other travelers stared at him in distress. The one who had had his son at the front since the first day of war sighed: "You are right. Our children do not belong to us; they belong to the Country. . . ."

"Bosh," retorted the fat traveler. "Do we think of the Country when we give life to our children? Our sons are born because . . . well, because they must be born, and when they come to life they take our own life with them. This is the truth. We belong to them but they never belong to us. And when they reach twenty they are exactly what we were at their age. We too had a father and mother, but there were so many other things as well . . . girls, cigarettes, illusions, new ties . . . and the Country, of course, whose call we would have answered—when we were twenty—even if father and mother had said no. Now at our age, the love of our Country is still great, of course, but stronger than it is the love of our children. Is there any one of us here who wouldn't gladly take his son's place at the front if he could?"

There was a silence all around, everybody nodding as to approve.

"Why then," continued the fat man, "shouldn't we consider the feelings of our children when they are twenty? Isn't it natural that at their age they should consider the love for their Country (I am speaking of decent boys, of course) even greater than the love for us? Isn't it natural that it should be so, as after all they must look upon us as upon old boys who cannot move any more and must stay at home? If Country exists, if Country is a natural necessity, like bread, of which each of us must eat in order not to die of hunger, somebody must go to defend it. And our sons go, when they are twenty, and they don't want tears, because if they die, they die inflamed and happy (I am speaking, of course, of decent boys). Now, if one dies young and happy, without having seen the ugly side of life, the boredom of it, the pettiness, the bitterness of disillusion . . . what more can we ask for him? Everyone should stop crying; everyone should laugh, as I do . . . or at least thank God—as I do—because my son, before dying, sent me a message saying that he was dying satisfied at having ended his life in the best way he could have wished. That's why, as you see, I do not even wear mourning."

He shook his light fawn[2] coat so as to show it; his livid lip over his missing teeth was trembling, his eyes were watery and motionless, and soon after he ended with a shrill laugh which might well have been a sob.

"Quite so . . . quite so . . ." agreed the others.

The woman who, bundled in a corner under her coat, had been sitting and listening, had for the last three months tried to find in the words of her husband and her friends something to console her in her deep sorrow, something that might show her how a mother should resign herself to send her son not even to death but to a probably dangerous life. Yet not a word had she found among the many which had been said . . . and her grief had been greater in seeing that nobody—as she thought—could share her feelings.

But now the words of the traveler amazed and almost stunned her. She suddenly realized that it wasn't the others who were wrong and could not understand her but herself who could not rise up to the same height as those fathers and mothers willing to resign themselves, without crying, not only to the departure of their sons but even to their death.

She lifted her head, she bent over from her corner trying to listen with great attention to the details which the fat man was giving

2. **fawn:** light grayish-brown.

to his companions about the way his son had fallen as a hero, for his King and his Country, happy and without regrets. It seemed to her that she had stumbled into a world she had never dreamed of, a world so far unknown to her, and she was so pleased to hear everyone joining in congratulating that brave father who could so stoically[3] speak of his child's death.

Then suddenly, just as if she had heard nothing of what had been said and almost as if waking up from a dream, she turned to the old man, asking him:

"Then ... is your son really dead?"

Everybody stared at her. The old man, too, turned to look at her, fixing his great, bulging, horribly watery light-gray eyes deep in her face. For some little time he tried to answer, but words failed him. He looked and looked at her, almost as if only then—at that silly, incogruous question—he had suddenly realized at last that his son was really dead ... gone forever ... forever. His face contracted, became horribly distorted, then he snatched in haste a handkerchief from his pocket, and to the amazement of everyone broke into harrowing, heart-rendering, uncontrollable sobs.

3. **stoically** (stō′ĭk•ə•lē): apparently unmoved by pain.

Meaning

1. As the fat woman listens to the explanations of the fat, red-faced man, what aspects of the man's arguments appeal to her? Is her question really silly and incongruous?
2. An *allegory* is a story in which the characters are personifications of ideas or abstract values. Let us assume that the fat woman represents emotion; the fat, red-eyed man, reason and duty. Ironically, the simple question of the woman, who was almost persuaded by the man's arguments, reduced the "stoical" man to tears. What is the theme of the story?
3. What is the climax of the story? What is the dénouement? What hints of the fat man's true state of mind does Pirandello give early in the story?

Method

1. Explain why the author does not give names to his characters.
2. There is very little physical action in this story, but there is movement on the part of the characters. How do the movements of the fat woman and the man with the fawn-colored coat reflect their feelings and attitudes?
3. The setting of the story is World War I, when Italy and the Allies were fighting against Germany and Austria. Is this why Pirandello entitled his story "War"? Is there anything else in conflict or at war in the story?
4. Why did the author make his characters so physically unattractive?

Language: Using Adjectives

Pirandello at times uses several adjectives that complement one another. Each adjective has a special meaning that provides an effect of mounting ugliness, horror, and despair.

Notice how the adjectives in each of the following descriptions have been carefully chosen to heighten the impression he wants to convey.

1. ". . . a tiny man, thin and weakly, his face death-white, his eyes small and bright–looking shy and uneasy."
2. ". . . a fat, red-faced man with bloodshot eyes of the palest gray."
3. ". . . harrowing, heart-rendering, uncontrollable sobs."

Discussion and Composition

1. "We belong to them [our sons] but they never belong to us." In an essay, explain how "Escape to the City" and "War" illustrate this quotation.

2. "It's better to die young and happy than to see the ugly side of life." Write an essay in which you agree or disagree with this statement.

3. Write an essay in which you describe your feelings about war. How has war become more terrible in modern times?

EUGENIA COLLIER
(born 1928)

As an educator and writer, Eugenia Collier has used her considerable talents to further the cause of black people in America. In fact, she has said that her blackness has been the source of her creativeness.

Educated at Howard University, Columbia, and the University of Maryland, she has taught at Howard, the University of Maryland, Community College of Baltimore, Morgan State University, and Atlanta University, among others. For ten years she functioned as a case worker for the Baltimore Department of Public Welfare. She lectured on a television series called "The Negro in History" and was executive producer for another series on black American folklore.

"Marigolds," which won the Gwendolyn Brooks Award for fiction in 1969, presents a vivid portrait of growing up black and female in twentieth-century America.

MARIGOLDS

When I think of the home town of my youth, all that I seem to remember is dust—the brown, crumbly dust of late summer—arid, sterile dust that gets into the eyes and makes them water, gets into the throat and between the toes of bare brown feet. I don't know why I should remember only the dust. Surely there must have been lush green lawns and paved streets under leafy shade trees somewhere in town; but memory is an abstract painting—it does not present things as they are, but rather as they *feel.* And so, when I think of that time and that place, I remember only the dry September of the dirt roads and grassless yards of the shantytown where I lived. And one other thing I remember, another incongruency of memory—a brilliant splash of sunny yellow against the dust—Miss Lottie's marigolds.

Whenever the memory of those marigolds flashes across my mind, a strange nostalgia comes with it and remains long after the picture has faded. I feel again the chaotic emotions of adolescence, illusive as smoke, yet as real as the potted geranium before me now. Joy and rage and wild animal gladness and shame become tangled together in the multicolored skein of 14-going-on-15 as I recall that devastating moment when I was suddenly more woman than child, years ago in Miss Lottie's yard. I think of those marigolds at the strangest times; I remember them vividly now as I desperately pass away the time waiting for you, who will not come.

I suppose that futile waiting was the sorrowful background music of our impoverished little community when I was young. The Depression that gripped the nation was no new thing to us, for the black workers of rural Maryland had always been depressed. I don't know what it was that we were waiting for; certainly not for the prosperity that was "just around the corner," for those were white folks' words, which we never believed. Nor did we wait for hard work and thrift to pay off in shining success as the American Dream promised, for we knew better than that, too. Perhaps we waited for a miracle, amorphous in concept but necessary if one were to have the grit to rise before dawn each day and labor in the white man's vineyard until after dark, or to wander about in the September dust offering one's sweat in return for some meager share of bread. But God was chary with miracles in those days, and so we waited—and waited.

We children, of course, were only vaguely aware of the extent of our poverty. Having no radios, few newspapers, and no magazines, we were somewhat unaware of the world outside our community. Nowadays we would be called "culturally deprived" and people would write books and hold conferences about us. In those days everybody we knew was just as hungry and ill-clad as we were. Poverty was the cage in which we all were trapped, and our hatred of it was still the vague, undirected restlessness of the zoo-bred flamingo who knows that nature created him to fly free.

As I think of those days I feel most poignantly the tag-end of summer, the bright dry times when we began to have a sense of shortening days and the imminence of the cold.

By the time I was 14 my brother Joey and I were the only children left at our house, the older ones having left home for early marriage or the lure of the city, and the two babies having been sent to relatives who might care for them better than we. Joey was three years younger than I, and a boy, and therefore vastly inferior. Each morning our mother and father trudged wearily down the dirt road and around the bend, she to her domestic job, he to his daily unsuccessful quest for work. After our few chores around the tumble-down shanty, Joey and I were free to run wild in the sun with other children similarly situated.

For the most part, those days are ill-defined in my memory, running together and combining like a fresh water-color painting left out in the rain. I remember squatting in the road drawing a picture in the dust, a picture which Joey gleefully erased with one sweep of his dirty foot. I remember fishing for minnows in a muddy creek and watching sadly as they eluded my cupped hands, while Joey laughed uproariously. And I remember, that year, a strange restlessness of body and of spirit, a feeling that something old and familiar was ending, and something unknown and therefore terrifying was beginning.

One day returns to me with special clarity for some reason, perhaps because it was the beginning of the experience that in some inexplicable way marked the end of innocence. I was loafing under the great oak tree in our yard, deep in some reverie which I have now forgotten except that it involved some secret, secret thoughts of one of the Harris boys across the yard. Joey and a bunch of kids were bored now with the old tire suspended from an oak limb which had kept them entertained for awhile.

"Hey, Lizabeth," Joey yelled. He never talked when he could yell. "Hey, Lizabeth, let's us go somewhere."

I came reluctantly from my private world. "Where at, Joey?"

The truth was that we were becoming tired of the formlessness of our summer days. The idleness whose prospect had seemed so beautiful during the busy days of spring now had degenerated to an almost desperate effort to fill up the empty midday hours.

"Let's go see can we find us some locusts on the hill," someone suggested.

Joey was scornful. "Ain't no more locusts there. Y'all got 'em all while they was still green."

The argument that followed was brief and not really worth the effort. Hunting locust trees wasn't fun any more by now.

"Tell you what," said Joey finally, his eyes sparkling. "Let's us go over to Miss Lottie's."

The idea caught on at once, for annoying Miss Lottie was always fun. I was still child enough to scamper along with the group over rickety fences and through bushes that tore our already raggedy clothes, back to where Miss Lottie lived. I think now that we must have made a tragicomic spectacle, five or six kids of different ages, each of us clad in only one garment—the girls in faded dresses that were too long or too short, the boys in patchy pants, their sweaty brown chests gleaming in the hot sun. A little cloud of dust followed our thin legs and bare feet as we tramped over the barren land.

When Miss Lottie's house came into view we stopped, ostensibly to plan our strategy, but actually to reinforce our courage. Miss Lottie's house was the most ramshackle of all our ramshackle homes. The sun and rain had long since faded its rickety frame siding from white to a sullen gray. The boards themselves seemed to remain upright not from being nailed together but rather from leaning together like a house that a child might have constructed from cards. A brisk wind might have blown it down, and the fact that it was still standing implied a kind of enchantment that was stronger than the elements. There it stood, and as far as I know is standing yet—a gray rotting thing with no porch, no shutters, no steps, set on a cramped lot with no grass, not even any weeds—a monument to decay.

In front of the house in a squeaky rocking chair sat Miss Lottie's son, John Burke, completing the impression of decay. John Burke was what was known as "queer-headed." Black and ageless, he sat, rocking day in and day out in a mindless stupor, lulled by the monotonous squeak-squawk of the chair. A battered hat atop his shaggy head shaded him from the sun. Usually John Burke was totally unaware of everything outside his quiet dream world. But if you disturbed him, if you intruded upon his fantasies, he would become enraged, strike out at you, and curse at you in some strange enchanted language which only he could understand. We children made a game of thinking of ways to disturb John Burke and then to elude his violent retribution.

But our real fun and our real fear lay in Miss Lottie herself. Miss Lottie seemed to be at least a hundred years old. Her big frame still held traces of the tall, powerful woman she must have been in youth, although it was now bent and drawn. Her smooth skin was a dark reddish-brown, and her face had Indian-like features and the stern stoicism that one associates with Indian faces. Miss Lottie didn't like intruders either, especially children. She never left her yard, and nobody ever visited her. We never knew how she managed those necessities which depend on human interaction—how she ate, for example, or even whether she ate. When we were tiny children, we thought Miss Lottie was a witch and we made up tales, that we half believed ourselves, about her exploits. We were far too sophisticated now, of course, to believe the witch-nonsense. But old fears have a way of clinging like cobwebs, and so when we sighted the tumble-down shack, we had to stop to reinforce our nerves.

"Look, there she is," I whispered, forgetting that Miss Lottie could not possibly have heard me from that distance. "She's fooling with them crazy flowers."

"Yeh, look at 'er."

Miss Lottie's marigolds were perhaps the strangest part of the picture. Certainly they did not fit in with the crumbling decay of the rest of her yard. Beyond the dusty brown yard, in front of the sorry gray house, rose suddenly and shockingly a dazzling strip of bright blossoms, clumped together in enormous mounds, warm and passionate and sun-golden. The old black witch-woman worked on them all summer, every summer, down on her creaky knees, weeding and cultivating and arranging, while the house crumbled and John Burke rocked. For some perverse reason, we children hated those marigolds. They interfered with the perfect ugliness of the place; they were too beautiful; they said too much that we could not understand, they did not make sense. There was something in the vigor with which the old woman destroyed the weeds that intimidated us. It should have been a comical sight—the old woman with the man's hat on her cropped white head, leaning over the bright mounds, her big backside in the air—but it wasn't comical, it was something we could not name. We had to annoy her by whizzing a pebble into her flowers or by yelling a dirty word, then dancing away from her rage, revelling in our youth and mocking her age. Actually, I think it was the flowers we wanted to destroy, but nobody had the nerve to try it, not even Joey, who was usually fool enough to try anything.

"Y'all git some stones," commanded Joey now, and was met with instant giggling obedience as everyone except me began to gather pebbles from the dusty ground. "Come on, Lizabeth."

I just stood there peering through the bushes, torn between wanting to join the fun and feeling that it was all a bit silly.

"You scared, Lizabeth?"

I cursed and spat on the ground—my favorite gesture of phony bravado. "Y'all children get the stones, I'll show you how to use 'em."

I said before that we children were not consciously aware of how thick were the bars of our cage. I wonder now, though, whether we were not more aware of it than I thought. Perhaps we had some dim notion of what we were, and how little chance we had of being anything else. Otherwise, why would we have been so preoccupied with destruction? Anyway, the pebbles were collected quickly, and everybody looked at me to begin the fun.

"Come on, y'all."

We crept to the edge of the bushes that bordered the narrow road in front of Miss Lottie's place. She was working placidly, kneeling over the flowers, her dark hand plunged into the golden mound. Suddenly "zing"—an expertly-aimed stone cut the head off one of the blossoms.

"Who out there?" Miss Lottie's backside came down and her head came up as her sharp eyes searched the bushes. "You better git!"

We had crouched down out of sight in the bushes, where we stifled the giggles that insisted on coming. Miss Lottie gazed warily across the road for a moment, then cautiously returned to her weeding. "Zing"—Joey sent a pebble into the blooms, and another marigold was beheaded.

Miss Lottie was enraged now. She began struggling to her feet, leaning on a rickety cane and shouting, "Y'all git! Go on home!" Then the rest of the kids let loose with their pebbles, storming the flowers and laughing wildly and senselessly at Miss Lottie's impotent rage. She shook her stick at us and started shakily toward the road crying, "Git 'long! John Burke! John Burke, come help!"

Then I lost my head entirely, mad with the power of inciting such rage, and ran out of the bushes in the storm of pebbles, straight toward Miss Lottie chanting madly, "Old witch, fell in a ditch, picked up a penny and thought she was rich!" The children screamed with delight, dropped their pebbles and joined the crazy dance, swarming around Miss Lottie like bees and chanting, "Old lady witch!" while she screamed curses at us. The madness lasted only a moment, for John Burke, startled at last, lurched out of his chair, and we dashed for the bushes just as Miss Lottie's cane went whizzing at my head.

I did not join the merriment when the kids gathered again under the oak in our bare yard. Suddenly I was ashamed, and I did not like being ashamed. The child in me sulked and said it was all in fun, but the woman in me flinched at the thought of the malicious attack that I had led. The mood lasted all afternoon. When we ate the beans and rice that was supper that night, I did not notice my father's silence, for he was always silent these days, nor did I notice my mother's absence, for she always worked until well into evening. Joey and I had a particularly bitter argument after supper; his exuberance got on my nerves. Finally I stretched out upon the palette in the room we shared and fell into a fitful doze.

When I awoke, somewhere in the middle of the night, my mother had returned, and I vaguely listened to the conversation that was audible through the thin walls that separated our rooms. At first I heard no words, only voices. My mother's voice was like a cool, dark room in summer—peaceful, soothing, quiet. I loved to listen to it; it made things seem alright somehow. But my father's voice cut through hers, shattering the peace.

"Twenty-two years, Maybelle, 22 years," he was saying, "and I got nothing for you, nothing, nothing."

"It's all right, honey, you'll get something. Everybody out of work now, you know that."

"It ain't right. Ain't no man ought to eat his woman's food year in and year out, and see his children running wild. Ain't nothing right about that."

"Honey, you took good care of us when you had it. Ain't nobody got nothing nowadays."

"I ain't talking about nobody else, I'm talking about *me*. God knows I try." My mother said something I could not hear, and my father cried out louder, "What must a man do, tell me that?"

"Look, we ain't starving. I git paid every week, and Mrs. Ellis is real nice about giving me things. She gonna let me have Mr. Ellis' old coat for you this winter—"

"Damn Mr. Ellis' coat! And damn his money! You think I want white folks' leavings? Damn, Maybelle"—and suddenly he sobbed, loudly and painfully, and cried helplessly and hopelessly in the dark night. I had never heard a man cry before. I did not know men ever cried. I covered my ears with my hands but could not cut off the sound of my father's harsh, painful, despairing sobs. My father was a strong man who would whisk a child upon his shoulders and go singing through the house. My father whittled toys for us and laughed so loud that the great oak seemed to laugh with him, and taught us how to fish and hunt rabbits. How could it be that my father was crying? But the sobs went on, unstifled, finally quieting until I could hear my mother's voice, deep and rich, humming softly as she used to hum to a frightened child.

The world had lost its boundary lines. My mother, who was small and soft, was now the strength of the family; my father, who was the rock on which the family had been built, was sobbing like the tiniest child. Everything was suddenly out of tune, like a broken accordion. Where did I fit into this crazy picture? I do not now remember my thoughts, only a feeling of great bewilderment and fear.

Long after the sobbing and the humming had stopped, I lay on the palette, still as stone with my hands over my ears, wishing that I too could cry and be comforted. The night was silent now except for the sound of the crickets and of Joey's soft breathing. But the room was too crowded with fear to allow me to sleep, and finally, feeling the terrible aloneness of 4 A.M., I decided to awaken Joey.

"Ouch! What's the matter with you? What you want?" he demanded disagreeably when I had pinched and slapped him awake.

"Come on, wake up."

"What for? Go 'way."

I was lost for a reasonable reply. I could not say, "I'm scared and I don't want to be alone," so I merely said, "I'm going out. If you want to come, come on."

The promise of adventure awoke him. "Going out now? Where at, Lizabeth? What you going to do?"

I was pulling my dress over my head. Until now I had not thought of going out. "Just come on," I replied tersely.

I was out the window and halfway down the road before Joey caught up with me.

"Wait, Lizabeth, where you going?"

I was running as if the furies were after me, as perhaps they were—running silently and furiously until I came to where I had half-known I was headed: to Miss Lottie's yard.

The half-dawn light was more eerie than complete darkness, and in it the old house was like the ruin that my world had become—foul and crumbling, a grotesque caricature. It looked haunted, but I was not afraid because I was haunted too.

"Lizabeth, you lost your mind?" panted Joey.

I had indeed lost my mind, for all the smoldering emotions of that summer swelled in me and burst—the great need for my mother who was never there, the hopelessness of our poverty and degradation, the bewilderment of being neither child nor woman and yet both at once, the fear unleashed by my father's tears. And these feelings combined in one great impulse toward destruction.

"Lizabeth!"

I leaped furiously into the mounds of marigolds and pulled madly, trampling and pulling and destroying the perfect yellow blooms. The fresh smell of early morning and of dew-soaked marigolds spurred me on as I went tearing and mangling and sobbing while Joey tugged my dress or my waist crying, "Lizabeth, stop, please stop!"

And then I was sitting in the ruined little garden among the uprooted and ruined flowers, crying and crying, and it was too late to undo what I had done. Joey was sitting beside me, silent and frightened not knowing what to say. Then "Lizabeth, look."

I opened my swollen eyes and saw in front of me a pair of large calloused feet; my gaze lifted to the swollen legs, the age-distorted body clad in a tight cotton night dress, and then the shadowed Indian face surrounded by stubby white hair. And there was no rage in the face now, now that the garden was destroyed and there was nothing any longer to be protected.

"M-miss Lottie!" I scrambled to my feet and just stood there and stared at her, and that was the moment when childhood faded and womanhood began. That violent, crazy act was the last act of childhood. For as I gazed at the immobile face with the sad, weary eyes, I gazed upon a kind of reality which is hidden to childhood. The witch was no longer a witch but only a broken old woman who had dared to create beauty in the midst of ugliness and sterility. She had been born in squalor and lived in it all her life. Now at the end of that life she had nothing except a falling-down hut, a wrecked body, and John Burke, the mindless son of her passion. Whatever verve there was left in her, whatever was of love and beauty and joy that had not been squeezed out by life, had been there in the marigolds she had so tenderly cared for.

Of course I could not express the things that I knew about Miss Lottie as I stood there awkward and ashamed. The years have put words to the things I knew in that moment, and as I look back upon it, I know that the moment marked the end of innocence. Innocence involves an unseeing acceptance of things at face value, an ignorance of the area below the surface. In that humiliating moment I looked beyond myself and into the depths of another person. This was the beginning of compassion, and one cannot have both compassion and innocence.

The years have taken me worlds away from that time and that place, from the dust and squalor of our lives and from the bright thing that I destroyed in a blind childish striking out at God-knows-what. Miss Lottie died long ago and many years have passed since I last saw her hut, completely barren at last, for despite my wild contrition she never planted marigolds again. Yet, there are times when the image of those passionate yellow mounds returns with a painful poignancy. For one does not have to be ignorant and poor to find that his life is barren as the dusty yards of our town. And I too have planted marigolds.

Meaning and Method

1. Why does Lizabeth's anger focus on Miss Lottie's marigolds? What is the flower a symbol of?
2. What is Lizabeth's mood when she mounts her second assault on the garden?
3. How does Lizabeth's attitude differ from that of the children she is leading?
4. Why do you suppose Miss Lottie's reaction to the second attack is different from the first?
5. Writers occasionally state their theme quite explicitly. How do the last two sentences of the story state the theme? How is the theme anticipated in the opening paragraph?

Language: Forming Adjectives from Nouns

Lizabeth describes her behavior as "childish." The word *childish* is an example of an adjective that is formed from a noun by the addition of a suffix. The suffix *-ish* means "tending towards or interested in." Examples are *Scottish, Turkish, bookish.* Notice that the *t* in Scot is doubled when the suffix is added.

The suffixes *-ian,* meaning "belonging to a class or order," and *-esque,* meaning "resembling or having the style of," are often added to nouns to form adjectives. When added to the proper noun *Arab,* for example, they form the adjectives *Arabian* and *arabesque.* (The latter originally meant "after the manner or style of the Arabs.") The horror stories of Edgar Allan Poe are referred to as tales of the grotesque and arabesque. How would you interpret the adjective *arabesque* as used here?

The addition of the suffix *-ian* often calls for a change in the accent or stress of a word; Arab (ăr′əb) becomes Arabian (ə•rā′bē•ən).

The suffix *-al,* meaning "pertaining to," is another addition, providing adjectives such as *musical, electrical,* and *adjectival.*

Make adjectives from each of the following nouns by adding the suffix *-al, -esque, -ian,* or *-ish.* Check your dictionary to see that you spell and pronounce the adjectives correctly.

1. anecdote
2. Dane
3. Dickens
4. Finn
5. picture
6. Roman
7. folklore
8. grammar
9. autumn

Discussion and Composition

1. The narrator in "Marigolds" says, "One cannot have both innocence and compassion." Discuss.

2. Using the description of Miss Lottie in this story as a model, write a character sketch of a person you remember.

3. Write a composition on the conflict going on in the mind and heart of the narrator of "Marigolds." Include an evaluation of her success or failure in resolving the conflict.

4. Compare and contrast the living conditions of the characters in "Marigolds" with those in "A Visit to Grandmother."

A GLOSSARY OF LITERARY TERMS

Abstract and Concrete Terms: *abstract terms* are words and phrases that refer to intangible qualities, ideas, or general classes; abstractions have no specific physical reality that is readily apparent to any of the senses. Examples of abstract terms are *justice, peace,* and *hope. Concrete terms* stand for objects that can be perceived by the senses. *Brick, box,* and *typewriter* are examples of concrete terms.

Allegory: a narrative in verse or prose in which objects, characters, or actions stand for abstract ideas or moral qualities. An allegory has both literal, or real, and symbolic levels of meaning.

Alliteration: the repetition of the same consonant sound, usually at the beginnings of words. Alliteration may sometimes be used in prose, though it is mainly a poetic device. For example:

"But that beard! that bristly, thick, square beard of a stranger!"

Allusion: a reference to a person, place, event, or artistic work that the author expects the reader to recognize. An allusion may be drawn from literature, history, geography, scripture, or mythology. A statement is enriched by an allusion because in a few words an author can evoke a particular atmosphere, story, or historical place.

Ambiguity: double meaning. In literature, an author may deliberately use ambiguity to produce subtle or multiple variations in meaning.

Analogy: a form of comparison which points out the likenesses between two dissimilar objects; it attempts to use a familiar object or idea to illustrate or to introduce a subject that is unfamiliar or complex.

Anecdote: a brief account, sometimes biographical, or an interesting or entertaining incident. In writing an essay, a writer may use an anecdote to introduce or illustrate a topic.

Antagonist: the force or character opposing the main character or Protagonist.

Antonym: a word opposite in meaning to another word. For the word *happy,* for example, the following nouns are antonyms: *sad, depressed,* and *melancholy.*

Argumentation: a type of writing that attempts to convince the reader of the logic and the merits of a particular viewpoint (especially by giving specific reasons and examples), or that attempts to persuade the reader to accept a particular belief or opinion.

Assonance: repetition of the same or similar vowel sounds in words close together.

"Some distant lamp of lighted window gleamed below me."

Atmosphere: the prevailing mental and emotional climate of a story; something the reader senses or feels. Setting and Mood help to create and heighten atmosphere. Edgar Allan Poe is noted for creating stories of atmosphere. In "The Cask of Amontillado" for example, an atmosphere of terror prevails.

Autobiography and Biography: both types of literature attempt to present an account of a person's life, usually in chronological order, using whatever facts, events, and other evidence are available. The *autobiography* is an account written by persons about themselves; the *biography* is written by another person.

Character: a person (sometimes a group of people, an animal, or a physical force) invented by an author.

Character foil: a character who serves by contrast to emphasize the qualities of another character. For example, the appearance of a particularly lazy, shiftless, and unenterprising character will strengthen the reader's impression of an active, ambitious, and aggressive character.

Characterization: the techniques an author uses to develop the personality of fictional characters so that they seem believable, act consistently, and speak naturally. These methods include characterization through:

a. direct analysis by the author of a character's thoughts, feelings, and actions;
b. physical description of a character's appearance;
c. description of a character's surroundings, such as the room in which he or she lives or works;
d. the speech or conversations of a character;
e. the behavior or actions of a character;
f. a character's reactions to events, situations, and other people;
g. the responses or reactions of other people in the story to a character's behavior, and in some cases, their remarks and conversations about the character;
h. the presentation of a character's thoughts through a stream of consciousness; that is, the author attempts to produce the uninterrupted flow (stream) of thoughts, feelings, associations, and memories that might take place in a character's mind (consciousness) at any given moment;
i. a combination of two or more of these methods.

Cliché: any trite or commonplace expression that is no longer fresh or effective because it has been used too often. *Fair and square, the finishing touch, fit for a king, bundle of nerves,* and *clear as a bell* are examples of worn-out expressions.

Climax: the high point or turning point of a story. The author builds up to the climax through a series of increasingly more complex incidents.

Coherence: the logical and clear relationship of one sentence to another within a paragraph and of one paragraph to another within a composition. Coherence is the quality in writing that links and binds the related parts of the composition into a unified whole. It is achieved through the use of transitional words and phrases (*accordingly, on the contrary, first, finally, however, nevertheless*); linking expressions (*this, these, they, it, that, he or she*), the repetition of key terms, and synonyms. **Unity** and **Emphasis** are also necessary for effective writing.

Commercial or Craft Story: a "formula" story written according to a set pattern. The plot is contrived, filled with coincidence, and has strong suspense. The characters are *stereotyped* and the theme is usually a conventional one (see **Theme**). Such stories often have an overflow of emotion and a romantic tone. There is little originality of character or theme, in contrast to the *quality* or *literary* story.

Comparison and Contrast: in writing, a method used to clarify and illustrate a subject. *Comparison* shows the similarities between two things, and *contrast* details the differences between things. They are often used together, but can be used separately. (See **Contrast.**)

Complication: rising action of incidents in a plot, building to the climax of a story or play.

Concrete Terms: (see **Abstract and Concrete Terms.**)

Conflict: the clash between opposing forces, people, or ideas in a story or play.

Connotation: the associated or suggested meaning(s) of a word, in addition to its literal meaning (see **Denotation**). The word *snowstorm,* for example, implies additional meanings beyond its literal meaning as "a storm with a fall of snow."

Context: for a word, the other words and phrases so closely surrounding it that they affect its meaning or use. Context often determines a word's meaning, as in the case of "rich" in the following examples:

> "South Africa is *rich* in mineral resources."
> "Strawberry shortcake is too *rich* for me."

For an event or incident, *context* includes the situation and circumstances that surround the event; we often speak of a specific event in its historical context.

Contrast: a striking difference between two things. In literature, to heighten or clarify a situation, an author may contrast ideas, personalities, or images. (See also **Comparison and Contrast.**)

Denotation: the literal or "dictionary" meaning of a word. (See also **Connotation.**)

Dénouement (dā•nōō•män): that part of the plot where the outcome or solution (permanent or temporary) of the main character's major problem is made known.

Description: the purpose of description is to make the reader share as intensely as possible in the sensory experiences of the writer; that is, the writer wants his or her audience to see, hear, smell, taste, or touch, in imagination, those things which the writer describes.

Dialect: the speech that is characteristic of a particular group or of the inhabitants of a specific geographical region. In literature, dialect may be used as part of a characterization.

Dialogue: the conversation carried on by two or more characters in a story.

Diction: An author's choice, arrangement, and use of words.

Dramatic Monologue: speech or narrative by a person who reveals his or her own character while speaking or telling the story.

Emphasis: in writing, stressing what is important in the right places. It is achieved through the effective arrangement of words, sentences, paragraphs, and sections of a composition. **Unity** (sticking to the topic) and **Coherence** (logically relating all parts of a composition) are also essential for effective writing. See entries for each.

Epiphany: insight into life, or a moment of self-discovery, usually during a time of emotional or mental crisis.

Episode: one of a progressive series of occurrences or significant events in the plot of a story.

Exposition: in fiction, that part of a story or play where the author provides background material about the past life of characters and about events that have taken place before the story opens. The reader must know this information in order to understand the problem to be solved, and to believe in the main action of the story.

As a form of discourse, exposition is writing intended to give information, explain something, or develop an idea.

Fable: a brief narrative in prose or verse intended to teach a moral lesson. Many fables, such as those of the Greek writer Aesop, are beast fables, in which animals speak and act as if they were human.

Fantasy: a work that deliberately employs unrealistic, highly imaginative, unbelievable elements; or a departure from reality. A fantasy might take place in a dreamlike world, present unreal characters, or project scientific principles into the future (as in science-fiction stories such as Arthur Clarke's "History Lesson." A fantasy can be a whimsical form of entertainment, or can offer a serious comment on reality. It usually has more than one level of meaning.

Figurative Language: language that gives new shape or form to the standard or literal manner of expression by means of imaginative comparisons called *figures of speech.* **Simile, metaphor,** and **personification** are among the most common figures of speech (see entries for each).

Flashback: a device by which an author interrupts the logical time sequence of a story or play to relate an episode that occurred prior to the opening situation.

Foreshadowing: hints or clues; a shadow of things to come. The use of foreshadowing stimulates interest and suspense and helps prepare the reader for the outcome.

Form and Content: in literature, *form* is the structure, pattern, or organization of a work of art that gives it a particular appearance or aspect. The short story is one form of fiction; the sonnet is one form of poetry. *Content* refers to the subject matter, ideas, or impressions shaped or governed by the form of the work.

For purposes of discussion, content (what is said) may be distinguished from form (how it is said), but the overall meaning and effect of a work of art stems from the successful fusion of both form and content.

Frame story: a story which is placed within the framework of another story; a story within a story. The outer story embodies the reason for the inner story, which is usually the more significant of the two.

Homonym: a word that is distinct from, but has the same spelling and pronunciation as, another word. *Hail* meaning "to call loudly" and *hail* meaning "small lumps of ice" are true homonyms. They are the same in spelling and pronunciation, but different in meaning, function, and origin. *Hail* and *hale,* however, are not true homonyms. They are homophones, being alike only in pronunciation.

Hyperbole (hī·pûr′bə·lē): a deliberate exaggeration for the purpose of emphasis or humor; overstatement. "I'm dying to hear what happened," is an example of hyperbole.

Idiom: an expression that could not be understood if analyzed logically word by word, but is nevertheless used naturally. *To turn the corner, to carry out,* and *seldom if ever* are examples of idioms. When the term is used in reference to an overall manner of expression, it denotes language natural to native speakers of a language.

Imagery: the *images,* or pictures and impressions, made in the reader's mind by the author's words. Although most imagery creates visual pictures, some appeals to the senses of touch, taste, smell, and hearing as well. Imagery results from the use of figurative language and vivid description.

Immediacy: the quality in writing which makes the reader feel directly involved in the action of a story, not just reading about it. Immediacy is closely related to atmosphere and setting. For example, the reader will be more able to sense the fear and danger that a heroine faces when the author places her in a dark, dingy, locked room.

Irony: a way of speaking or writing in which the author's words mean the opposite of what they seem to say. For example, a writer might say of a character who has just taken several clumsy falls on the ice, "What a fine skater he turned out to be!"

It is not necessary for irony to be in a story but it is usually present to some degree. Setting, for example, may be used to establish irony. A beautiful spring day may be the background for a story of disappointment and unhappiness. A situation may be ironic when an event takes place that turns out to be the opposite of what the reader expected.

Jargon: (sometimes called argot, parlance, shoptalk, and vernacular) the special vocabulary of an identifiable group, occupation, art, science, trade, sect, or sport, such as *football* jargon. *Jargon* can also refer to language full of long words and circumlocutions serving little purpose other than to impress and bewilder the average person.

Legend: a story about a national hero, folk hero, saint, tribe, people, or historical event that has been handed down from the past, usually by word of mouth. Although they are popularly regarded as historical, legends contain facts that have been exaggerated or changed to suit each storyteller's purpose. King Arthur and his Knights are legendary heroes of England. In America, facts about such historical figures as Dan'l Webster and Abe Lincoln have been the basis for romantic and imaginary tales.

Local Color: details of dress, speech, locale, customs, and traditions which give an impression of the local "atmosphere" of a particular place.

Stories of "local color" flourished in American literature in the years following the War Between the States. Authors wrote about specific regions of the United States, as Bret Harte, the West; Mark Twain, California and the Mississippi region; and Sarah Orne Jewett, the Maine coast. An attempt was made to copy local dialects and to depict the characteristic appearance, mannerisms, and customs of the people and the period.

Melodrama: (from Greek *melos,* "song," plus *drama,* "drama") any play or drama with **a.** a sensational plot, **b.** characters who make extravagant displays of deep emotion, and **c.** an atmosphere of heavy sentimentality.

Metaphor: a likeness expressed in figurative language in which one thing is compared to another without using *like* or *as.* For example:

"Shimmering buildings arrowed upward. . . ."

Mood: the predominating emotional atmosphere or feeling created in a literary work by its tone or tones. (See also **Atmosphere, Setting,** and **Tone.**)

Motif: an image or phrase that recurs, and thus provides a pattern within a work of literature.

Motivation: the force which drives a character to some action. Outside events and environmental influences may cause a character to act, or action may stem from a need, an inclination, a goal, or an inner fear.

Myth: a tale or story, related to *legend,* usually focusing on the deeds of gods or superhuman heroes. Myths played an important role in ancient cultures by helping to explain or justify the mysteries of nature and the universe. Bulfinch's *Mythology* is a well-known collection of the myths of ancient Greece and Rome. As a loose term, *myth* can denote any invented or grossly exaggerated story.

Narrative: the telling of an event or series of incidents that together make up a meaningful action; a story.

Narrator: one who narrates, or tells, a true or fictional story. The narrator may be a major or minor participant in the action of the narrative, or simply an observer of the action.

Novella: an extended short story that goes beyond the average short story length of two to three thousand words. A long short story is also sometimes called a *novelette.*

Objectivity: the quality in writing that is free from the expression of the author's personal sentiments, and opinions.

Onomatopoeia (on′ə•mat′ə•pē′ə)**:** the use of words that imitate the sound, action, or idea they represent. Sometimes a single word sounds like the thing it describes, as *cuckoo* or *twitter.* Sometimes several words are grouped together to imitate a sound, as "murmuring of innumerable bees."

Paragraph Development, Methods of: there are several ways of developing a paragraph after introducing the main subject or idea in a topic sentence. The methods include **a.** giving many details and particulars, **b.** giving specific examples and illustrations, **c.** telling an incident or anecdote, **d.** offering reasons, and **e.** using comparison and/or contrast.

Paraphrase: the restatement of a line, passage, or entire work, giving the meaning in another form, usually to clarify or amplify the original.

Pathos: the quality in writing that prompts the reader's feelings of sympathy or pity for a character. The term is from the Greek *pathein,* "to suffer."

Personification: a figure of speech in which a nonhuman or inanimate object, quality, or idea is given human characteristics or powers. For example:

"... snow falling so fast it weaves a web...."

Plot: the arrangement of incidents, details, and elements of conflict in a story. Plot is usually divided into the following stages:

a. the *situation,* or problem, in which a narrative begins;

b. the *complications,* or entanglements, produced by new or complex events and involvements;

c. the *rising action,* or advancing movement, toward an event or moment when something decisive has to happen;

d. the *climax,* or most intense moment or event, usually occurring near a narrative's major *turning point* or *crisis,* the moment when the main character turns toward a (good or bad) solution of the problem;

e. the *denouement,* unraveling, or ending of the problem with which the story began.

Point of View: the outlook from which the story is told. Each viewpoint allows the author a particular range or scope. There are two basic points of view:

a. first-person narrator (author participant). The narrative is told by a major or minor character in his or her own words. The author, through this "I" narrator, is limited to his or her scope of knowledge, degree of involvement, and powers of observation and expression. Ernest Hemingway's "In Another Country" is an example of first-person narration.

b. third-person narrator (author omniscient). The author serves as an unrestricted, all-knowing observer who describes and comments upon the characters and action in a narrative. The omniscient author knows everything there is to know about the characters—their thoughts, motives, actions, and reactions.

To maintain more of an illusion of reality, many modern short-story writers adopt a *limited omniscient point of view.* An author using this device tells the inner thoughts and feelings of one character only, usually the main character. We are never told what other characters are thinking; we must infer this from their external acts. Shirley Jackson uses the limited omniscient point of view in "Trial by Combat."

Sometimes an author narrating in the third person attempts to keep his or her personal feelings *objective,* or impartial and detached. In contrast, when the author's opinions about the characters or events in the story are obvious, the writing is called *subjective.*

Protagonist: the main character, hero or heroine, in a story or drama. (The word, which comes from the Greek *prōtos* meaning "first" and *agōnistēs* meaning "contestant, actor," was originally used to designate the actor who played the chief role in a Greek drama.) See also **Antagonist.**

Quality or Literary Story: a story that reveals the author's originality and imagination in creating natural and interesting characters, realistic situations, and meaningful, often unconventional themes. It is usually written for those who appreciate "serious" literature. There is no set formula to be followed in writing the quality story as there is for the **commercial** or **craft** story.

Realism: the attempt to present life as it actually is without distortion or idealization. Realism often depicts the everyday life and speech of ordinary people.

A literary movement called realism began in America in the late nineteenth century with the works of the American critic and novelist William Dean Howells. The movement reflected the increased interest in the methods of science and registered a protest against the extravagance of feeling and emotion found in romanticism.

Repetition: the use of the same word, phrase, sentence, idea (or some slight variation of these) to achieve emphasis. Some repetition is found in prose, but it is most often used in poetry.

Rhythm: in poetry, the regular rise and fall of strong and weak syllables. (As the accent becomes more fixed and systematized, it approaches *meter.*) In prose, although rhythm is often present, it is irregular and approximate; prose rhythm is the effective and pleasing arrangement of meaningful sounds in a sentence.

Rising Action: that part of the plot where the action moves or rises toward a climactic event or moment where something is going to happen that will affect the fortunes (good or bad) of the main character.

Romanticism: the attempt to present life as the writer would like it to be; it pictures life in a picturesque, fanciful, exotic, emotional, or imaginative manner, and often reflects the writer's strong interest in nature and love of the strange and the supernatural. It is the opposite of realism, which deals with the ordinary events of everyday life in an unsentimental and factual manner.

A literary movement called romanticism flourished in English literature in the early nineteenth century with the works of such writers as Wordsworth, Coleridge, Byron, Shelley, and Keats, and in American literature in the mid-nineteenth century with the works of such authors as Longfellow, Hawthorne, and Melville.

Satire: the use of ridicule, sarcasm, wit, or irony in order to expose, set right, or destroy a vice, folly, breach of good taste, or social evil. Satire may range from gentle ridicule to bitter attack.

Science fiction: a type of *fantasy* that combines real knowledge of scientific facts and principles with imaginative speculations as to what life will be like in the future, or on another planet.

Sentiment and Sentimentality: *sentiment* is honest emotion. *Sentimentality* means having more sentiment or feeling than the situation calls for; artificial emotion.

Setting: the time and place of the events in a story; the physical background. The importance of setting as a story element depends on the extent of its contribution to characterization, plot, theme, and atmosphere. For example, a landscape that is uninviting, dull, and barren may be the backdrop for a story of loneliness and despair.

Setting is most often stressed in stories of *local color* where the author wishes to recreate the flavor and characteristics of a particular region or community. It also plays an important role in *science-fiction* stories where the author must have readers believe in the world of the future. In some cases, setting can play a central role. (See **Atmosphere.**)

Simile: a stated comparison or likeness expressed in figurative language and introduced by terms such as *like, as, so, as if,* and *as though.* For example:

> "The dark sand of the desert . . . glittered like steel struck with a bright light."

Sketch: a short, simply constructed work, usually about a single character, place, or incident. A *character sketch,* for example, may be a brief study of a person's characteristics and personality. As in art, a sketch may also be a "rough" or preliminary draft for a longer, more complex work.

Soliloquy: in drama, a speech delivered by a character alone on the stage or apart from the other characters. As a literary device, it is used to reveal character or give information to the reader or the audience.

Stereotype (Stock Character): an artificially conventional type of fictional character rather than an authentic human being. A stock character either possesses traits supposed to be characteristic of a particular class, or reminds the reader of characters often read about or seen on T.V. Examples are the heavy-drinking newspaper reporter who always types with two fingers, the designing woman, the dumb blonde, and the gangster with a rough exterior and a heart of gold. Such characters always act the same way and reveal the same traits of character. Authors who wish to have the reader believe in a character do not use such oversimplified people in their stories. (See **Characterization.**)

Stream of Consciousness: in fiction, a literary technique by which characters and actions are presented through the flow of inner thoughts, feelings, reflections, memories, and mental images of one or more characters.

Style: a writer's distinctive or characteristic form of expression. Style is determined by the choice and arrangement of words, sentence structure, the use of figurative language, rhythm, and tone.

Subjectivity: the quality of writing in which the author's opinions, sympathies, personal beliefs, or tastes are obvious and sometimes even dominate the work. An autobiography, for example, is usually subjective. The author of a biography, however, generally strives for *objectivity.*

Surprise Ending: in fiction, an unexpected twist of plot at the conclusion of a story; a trick ending. It should be carefully foreshadowed to produce its striking effect. O. Henry often wrote stories with surprise endings.

Suspense: the uncertainty, expectancy, or tension that builds up as the climax of a narrative approaches; curiosity regarding the outcome of a narrative.

Symbol: a person, place, event, or object that is real in itself and also represents or suggests a relationship or association. For example, a heart symbolizes affection and love; a horseshoe, good luck; a lily, purity; a skull, mortality; and a torch, immortality. In fiction, some symbols have *universal* meaning, such as the association of spring with youth and winter with old age.

Some symbols are *personal,* that is, they have a special meaning within the context of a story. A character's name, for instance, may suggest her personality. "Candide" may be a name associated with a frank, outspoken, and "candid" character. The action of a story may also be symbolic. A long sea voyage might, during the course of a story, come to signify a person's journey through life.

The first time we read a story we might take the character's name, the objects that surround him or her, the setting, or the plot *literally.* On a second reading we may realize that one (or more) of these elements has a significance or meaning beyond itself.

Synonym: a word having the same meaning or meanings as another word or words in the same language, or having the same approximate meaning as another word. Most synonyms are interchangeable but at the same time vary widely in connotation. A standard dictionary of synonyms is Roget's *Thesaurus.* For the word *quarrel,* for example, Roget's lists the following nouns as synonyms: dispute, controversy, altercation, fight, squabble, contention, strife, set-to [colloquial], run-in [slang, U.S.], bicker, *démêlé* [French], feud, and vendetta.

Theme: the main idea of a literary work; the general truth behind the story of a particular individual in a particular situation. The theme of most short stories is usually implied rather than stated.

A *conventional* or traditional theme is one that conforms to our established moral standards and codes of behavior. Some familiar themes are that love conquers all, crime doesn't pay, or good triumphs over evil. Such oversimplified views of life are most often found in the commercial or craft story.

An *unconventional* theme is often critical of fashionable and established customs and ideas. The story of a young man who is unable to rise above the poverty into which he is born unless he resorts to dishonest dealings may suggest the theme that it is impossible to achieve success and remain honest. Another story may show that in some cases self-sacrifice can create more unhappiness than happiness. Such themes are usually found in a literary or quality story.

You should be able to state the theme of a story in one or two sentences. It is not a summary or an account of the plot. It is simply a general statement of the concept about life that the author had in mind, and embodied in the story.

Theme Statement (Statement of Theme)**:** in an essay, the theme is the main idea, point, or topic to be discussed. A statement of theme usually appears near the beginning of a discussion. It is often accompanied by a statement of the author's purpose.

Tone: the attitude of the writer toward his or her subject, characters, and readers. An author may be sympathetic and sorrowful, may wish to provoke, shock, or anger, or may write in a humorous way and intend simply to entertain. To misjudge the tone of a work is to miss its full meaning.

Topic Sentence: A clear, brief statement of what will be discussed in the paragraph; it is usually placed at the beginning of the paragraph. (See also **Paragraph Development, Methods of.**)

Understatement: the representation of something as less than it really is for the purpose of emphasis or humor. For example, in agreeing with a friend's praise of a new sports car, the owner might say, "It is rather nice, isn't it."

Unity: in writing, the organizing principle that links together all the parts of a work. In essay writing, this means the singleness of purpose, theme, or topic (or all three) that links all the subordinate parts of a composition into a whole. See also **Coherence** and **Emphasis.** In fiction writing, unity means that all the elements of a narrative relate to a single controlling idea.

The very nature of the short story gives to it a greater unity than that found in other fictional forms, such as the *novel.* A short story is usually limited to one main conflict, focuses on one significant episode, presents one main theme, is told from one point of view, and attempts to create a single, unified effect. A novel, on the other hand, may become long and involved, relate numerous key events in the life of its main characters, and analyze several aspects of personality. It is not concentrated or confined. The short story, because it must give exactly enough information to create its desired effect, is more intense.

Vignette: a brief, yet significant sketch of a person or event. The meaning of a vignette is usually subtly implied rather than stated. It often forms part of a longer work.

THE LANGUAGE ARTS PROGRAM LIST OF SKILLS

Throughout the text, language arts have been integrated with the presentation of literature. The majority of language-arts activities appear in the end-of-selection questions and assignments under the headings **Meaning, Method, Language, Composition,** and **Composition and Discussion.** Others are introduced and discussed in the general introductions, and still others, especially those concerning word origins and derivations, are covered in text footnotes.

The following indexes are intended to serve as guidelines to specific aspects of the language-arts program in *A Book of Short Stories—2*

LITERARY TERMS AND TYPES

VOCABULARY DEVELOPMENT

COMPOSITION

Narration:

Description:

Exposition:

Argumentation:

C 4
D 5
E 6
F 7
G 8
H 9
I 0
J 1